World Englishes

Edinburgh Textbooks on the English Language – Advanced

General Editor
Heinz Giegerich, Professor Emeritus of English Linguistics, University of Edinburgh

Editorial Board
Heinz Giegerich, University of Edinburgh – General Editor
Laurie Bauer (University of Wellington)
Olga Fischer (University of Amsterdam)
Willem Hollmann (Lancaster University)
Marianne Hundt (University of Zurich)
Rochelle Lieber (University of New Hampshire)
Bettelou Los (University of Edinburgh)
Robert McColl Millar (University of Aberdeen)
Donka Minkova (UCLA)
Edgar Schneider (University of Regensburg)
Graeme Trousdale (University of Edinburgh)

Titles in the series include:

The Pragmatics of Fiction: Literature, Stage and Screen Discourse
Miriam A. Locher and Andreas H. Jucker

English Syntax: A Minimalist Account of Structure and Variation
Elspeth Edelstein

Construction Grammar and its Application to English, 2nd edition
Martin Hilpert

Pragmatics
Chris Cummins

Corpus Linguistics and the Description of English, 2nd edition
Hans Lindquist and Magnus Levin

Modern Scots: An Analytical Survey
Robert McColl Millar

Contemporary Stylistics: Language, Cognition, Interpretation
Alison Gibbons and Sara Whiteley

A Critical Account of English Syntax: Grammar, Meaning, Text
Keith Brown and Jim Miller

English Historical Semantics
Christian Kay and Kathryn Allan

A Historical Syntax of English
Bettelou Los

Morphological Theory and the Morphology of English
Jan Don

A Historical Phonology of English
Donka Minkova

English Historical Pragmatics
Andreas Jucker and Irma Taavitsainen

English Historical Sociolinguistics
Robert McColl Millar

A Historical Morphology of English
Don Ringe

World Englishes: The Local Lives of a Global Language
Bertus van Rooy

Visit the Edinburgh Textbooks in the English Language website at
https://edinburghuniversitypress.com/series-edinburgh-textbooks-on-the-english-language-advanced.html

World Englishes

The Local Lives of a Global Language

Bertus van Rooy

EDINBURGH
University Press

Edinburgh University Press is one of the leading university presses in the UK. We publish academic books and journals in our selected subject areas across the humanities and social sciences, combining cutting-edge scholarship with high editorial and production values to produce academic works of lasting importance. For more information visit our website: edinburghuniversitypress.com

© Bertus van Rooy, 2024

Edinburgh University Press Ltd
The Tun – Holyrood Road
12(2f) Jackson's Entry
Edinburgh EH8 8PJ

Typeset in Janson MT
by Cheshire Typesetting Ltd, Cuddington, Cheshire

A CIP record for this book is available from the British Library

ISBN 978 1 4744 8629 3 (hardback)
ISBN 978 1 4744 8630 9 (paperback)
ISBN 978 1 4744 8631 6 (webready PDF)
ISBN 978 1 4744 8632 3 (epub)

The right of Bertus van Rooy to be identified as the author of this work has been asserted in accordance with the Copyright, Designs and Patents Act 1988, and the Copyright and Related Rights Regulations 2003 (SI No. 2498).

Contents

Preface vi

Part 1 Perspectives

1 English going global 3
2 Using English 23
3 Reshaping English 43

Part 2 Different contexts

4 Typical native varieties: the Inner Circle 69
5 Becoming an English speaker 98
6 English becoming an Asian and African language: the Outer Circle 117
7 English without the English 144
8 New sites of contact: local and global urban migration and the internet 167

Part 3 Outlook

9 Taking stock and looking ahead 185

References 204
Index 221

Preface

This book is intended to offer the reader a comprehensible and perhaps in part provocative picture of the global diffusion of English and some of the most typical linguistic consequences for the language across the range of locales where it came into use. The aim is to be reasonably complete – not encyclopaedic in scope, but contained. It should be accessible to any interested reader, but it should also offer established and emerging scholars in the field an original perspective on the varieties of English across the world, world Englishes.

I have not tried to pacify or hide some of the severe conflicts of view, nor some of the contradictory implications and consequences of how English came to be in use so widely, how the language is affected, but also how people are affected. I rely on the major models, particularly Kachru's concentric circles and Schneider's dynamic model, but go beyond their scope and intent in some respects. I have not tried to gloss over hard parts in some sober and detached academic voice, nor tame the story into something with a peaceful denouement after a plot full of crises that led to conflicts, some kind of climax and then an all-lived-happily-ever-after ending. This should not be taken as a political statement, a kind of wokeness of the type that offends people who may have a more favourable or, I'm afraid to say, triumphalist view of the global spread of English. At the same time, I am not trying to argue for an elusive multilingual dispensation in which English is cut to size and contained to its native speakers who will one day show keen awareness of the fact that English is just another good old language.

The English language presents a most intriguing societal and intellectual puzzle today, one well worth exploring. A thorough understanding, stripped of both triumphalism and defeatism, can do much to aid our understanding of ongoing relations – civil and cordial, as well as acrimonious and antagonistic – between people within and across urban, national or virtual boundaries. In a world of echo-chambers, deplatforming and exaggerated complaints thereof, fake-news and the dismissal of contrary views as fake-news, a world of ongoing violence, natural disasters, energy crises and poverty, it is more worthwhile than ever to try to understand complicated stuff, even if it brings about inconvenience and erodes comforting certainties and self-perceptions. This book represents an attempt to grapple with some of the complicated issues involving English.

My journey with world Englishes started when several fortuitous turns of events led me to the field and its potential to understand the global spread and diversification of English. These include participating in a workshop on the sociophonetics of Black South African English at the Linguistics Society of South Africa annual conference in Cape Town, January 2000, co-organising the eighth annual conference of the International Association of World Englishes in Potchefstroom in late 2001, and contributing to the first special issue of the journal *World Englishes* devoted to English in South Africa, which appeared in early 2002. From these beginnings, an affiliation with the field and a sense of affinity with the scholarly community developed, which still energises me after more than two decades. Despite severe differences of opinion, the open and engaged community of world Englishes scholars is exemplary of what academic scholarship and citizenship should be in very many ways.

Along the journey, I have benefited from the collaboration, assistance, feedback and sometimes just engaged conversation of many people that contributed to giving shape to the ideas in this book, but none of those people is responsible for the remaining oversights and other shortcomings.

First and foremost, three people have been collaborating with me closely for many years, reading my work and volunteering their time to engage me on my ideas and analyses, in addition to various pieces of research we have undertaken jointly: Susan Coetzee-Van Rooy, Haidee Kotze and Gerhard van Huyssteen. Baie dankie.

The North-West University (NWU) was my professional home for more than two decades. Much of the work and thinking that informed this book took place while I worked there. I want to thank colleagues and postgraduate students who challenged me, encouraged me and in many cases also collaborated with me and, in doing so, helped me to understand aspects of world Englishes better. Some are no longer with us, some work at other universities or in other careers, although many are still at the NWU. I would like to acknowledge my former students Debra Adeyemi (PhD 2017), Ian Bekker (PhD 2009), Lande Botha (PhD 2012), Jim D'Angelo (PhD 2016), Melanie Law (PhD 2019), Henk Louw (PhD 2012), Keoneng Magocha (PhD 2010), Ansie Maritz (PhD 2019), the late Thadeus Marungudzi (PhD 2017), the late Madoda Nkani (working on his PhD at the time of his passing in 2003), Maristi Partridge (PhD 2019), Caroline Piotrowska (PhD 2022), Karien Redelinghuys

(PhD 2019), Anke Schumacher (MA 2005), Lize Terblanche (MA 2012) and Ronel Wasserman (PhD 2014). In the same breath, I also want to acknowledge a number of current or former NWU colleagues, especially Anneke Butler, Gustav Butler, Wannie Carstens, Attie de Lange, Ulrike Janke, Johanita Kirsten, Jan-Louis Kruger, the late Themba Ngwenya, Johann van der Walt, the late Herman van Wyk and Daan Wissing, as well as Linda du Plessis, the deputy vice-chancellor of the NWU on the Vanderbijlpark campus, for her support and the space she always tried to create for me.

Beyond the NWU, I want to acknowledge colleagues from elsewhere who collaborated with me, offered feedback, and/or made the time to talk to me about world Englishes and linguistics: Lawrie Barnes, Kingsley Bolton, Werner Botha, Carrol Clarkson, Daniel Davis, Sylviane Granger, Rusandré Hendrikse, Hilton Hubbard, Christiane Meierkord, Rajend Mesthrie, Arne Peters, Josef Schmied, Edgar Schneider, the late Larry Smith, Rias van den Doel and Hans-Georg Wolf. I wrote most of the eventual manuscript while in the employment of the University of Amsterdam, which offered me space to explore world Englishes in some depth in my classes, and allowed me time (the basic unit of measurement in the Netherlands) to write this book. I thank my colleagues in English Language and Culture for their encouragement and interest in the project, and for picking up quite a few tabs in the last six months of writing. I also want to acknowledge Ellen Rutten, the chairperson of Modern Foreign Language and Cultures at the UvA, for her support during the period I was writing. The team at Edinburgh University Press did an incredible job to support and guide me through the writing process. I want to thank all of them, including Heinz Giegerich, Sam Johnson, Laura Quinn and Eliza Wright.

On a personal note, I offer my gratitude to my family and close friends. The two-year period during which I wrote this book was a tough one, in which my father-in-law, brother-in-law and mother passed away, while several family members confronted very severe health challenges. I completed the first full draft of the manuscript two days before my mother's birthday in July 2022, while I was technically on holiday with my wife, children and parents in St Francis Bay, South Africa. It cleared a few precious days without work, what turned out to be the last few days under the same roof with my mother Jacoba, who passed away six weeks later. To Susan, Jonette and Herrie, to my parents, siblings, in-laws and friends: thanks for being part of my life, and for all the encouragement and support. This book is a testimony to all of you, and I would like to dedicate it specifically to Susan and my parents.

Part 1
Perspectives

1 English going global

You must be knowing some English if you can be able to read this book, and understand it even. It may very well be self-evident to you; why would you read a book in English if you don't know English. It may also be self-evident in another sense: why wouldn't a book about English not be in English? Actually, why wouldn't a book about more or less anything not be in English, you know covering topics like *A Brief History of Time* (Hawking, 1988) or *A Short History of Nearly Everything* (Bryson, 2003), for instance, inclusive of the neat hedging through *brief* and *short*?

Some of this might actually not be all that self-evident. Historically, English did not dominate publication, and without apparent harm to the reputation of the non-English authors: Galileo Galilei (1564–1642) wrote much of his work in Italian, but some in Latin, while René Descartes (1596–1650) mostly wrote in Latin, but also published some work and letters in French. Isaac Newton (1642–1727) wrote some of his major works in Latin, others in English. Immanuel Kant (1724–1804) wrote mainly in German, although his early works include a master's and a doctoral thesis in Latin. These figures, who are still influential in some ways into the present, managed to get by with a lot of Latin and a fair helping of their home languages, which happened to be English for Newton only. Later in the nineteenth century, Karl Marx (1818–1883) continued to rely more on German than English for his influential books, while Sigmund Freud (1856–1939) did likewise. Ferdinand de Saussure (1857–1913) and Jacques Derrida (1930–2004) continue to be influential in some lines of linguistic research, yet they both wrote mainly in French.

Nonetheless, this is increasingly less likely to be the case today – continental Europeans who feel like sharing something with the larger world are very likely to write in English or have their work translated almost straight away (as one sees in the publication strategy of Thomas Piketty, born 1971 – from French to English within a year usually) if they aim for wider impact; and this is not very different for Asians, Africans or Latin Americans with similar aspirations today. This is not necessary and not everybody plays along, as articulated very forcefully (in English, ironically) by Ngũgĩ wa Thiong'o in *Decolonising the Mind* (1986), to take one compelling example. There are those who choose to let translation do the work, and there are still many multilinguals that can and do read in multiple languages, but the central position of English in the World Language System (De Swaan, 2010) is a given.

You may be a little concerned, though, or more than a little, about the language in paragraph one. Maybe you were not worried (bless your soul, dear reader who read for content without activating your inner grammar nazi), but these are the possible reasons to worry, if you want to: the in-your-face use of 'must' isn't very polite, is it, but you can agree to let it go – the author may not be fully familiar with the conventions of politeness in English, coming from a non-English background. Much more worrying, though, is that he ought to know that one doesn't use 'knowing' in a sentence like the first one at the top of the page, or use that horribly tautologous combination of 'can be able to'.

It depends. In some parts of the world, users of English are not so scared by 'must', and in many parts of the world, using 'knowing' like this is actually quite common. 'Can be able to' is a thing that many users of English actually say, if not always write, and there are a couple of examples of this in the King James Bible translation too. All of these might be so, you could counter, but that doesn't make it right, does it? Sure, but then again, it depends.

1.1 English all over the place

The worry about the use of the English language has a bit of history. There are people who have raised their concerns about the state of the language for a long time – people who should know, one might add. The author Jonathan Swift (1667–1745) raised his concern to the British prime minister in 1712 in a pamphlet entitled 'A proposal for the correction, improving and ascertaining the English Tongue', as follows:

> My Lord; I do here in the Name of all the Learned and Polite Persons of the Nation, complain to Your Lordship, as First Minister, that our Language is extremely imperfect; that its daily Improvements are by no means in proportion to its daily Corruptions; and the Pretenders to polish and refine it, have chiefly multiplied Abuses and Absurdities; and, that in many Instances, it offends against every Part of Grammar. (p. 8)

The worry got amplified over time as the English language came into use in so many places beyond the British Isles. In the mid-nineteenth century, another well-regarded English writer, Samuel Coleridge, penned the following judgement of English as it was used in the United States of America:

> An American by his boasting of the superiority of the Americans generally, but more especially in their language, once provoked me to tell him that 'on that head the least said the better, as the Americans presented the extraordinary phenomenon of a people without a language. That they had mistaken the English language for baggage (which is called plunder in America), and had stolen it.' (as cited in Nelson, 2008, p. 298)

The concern about the threat to 'proper English' posed by American corruptions of the language was at least one of the matters that weighed heavily on the mind of His Royal Highness the Prince of Wales, when he was the speaker at a launching event for the British Council's *English 2000* project in 1995. He 'stressed the need to maintain the quality of the language' in the face of the American influence, which he described as follows:

> People tend to invent all sorts of nouns and verbs, and make words that shouldn't be. I think we have to be a bit careful, otherwise the whole thing can get rather a mess. (O'Leary, 1995, p. 2)

For better or for worse, these are the worries about English as spoken in eighteenth-century Britain or nineteenth- and twentieth-century America. It gets worse, though. A decade before he turned to the history of nearly everything, Bill Bryson bowed his head over the English language, and confided as follows to his readership in the opening lines of his book *Mother Tongue* (1990):

> More than 300 million people in the world speak English and the rest, it sometimes seems, try to. It would be charitable to say that the results are sometimes mixed. (p. 1)

These mixed results are cause for graver concern to some than the Americans were to the then Prince Charles in 1995. For one, Sir Randolph Quirk, president of the British Academy from 1985 to 1989, made a presentation to the Japanese Association for Language Teachers in 1988. In this talk, he warned of the dangers in overemphasising variation in the English language to the point where teachers become reluctant to correct the mistakes of their learners. He reflected on the difficulties encountered in teaching English all over the world, which led him to the insight:

> No one should underestimate the problem of teaching English in such countries as India and Nigeria, where the English of the teachers themselves inevitably bears the stamp of locally acquired deviation from the

> standard language ('You are knowing my father, isn't it?'). The temptation is great to accept the situation and even to justify it in euphemistically sociolinguistic terms. (p. 22)

After commenting on the bad advice of consultants to not correct the intelligible but deviant English of learners in the Philippines, he concluded that:

> It is neither liberal nor liberating to permit learners to settle for lower standards than the best, and it is a travesty of liberalism to tolerate low standards which will lock the least fortunate into the least rewarding careers. (pp. 22–23)

Non-native-English-speaking academics are likely to encounter advice, with a stylistically intriguing selection of modal auxiliaries, telling them to have their manuscripts edited by a native speaker before submission, seemingly premised on the fact that they cannot all be able to write well enough in English. For instance:

- Very politely: 'Authors, particularly those whose first language is not English, *may* wish to have their English-language manuscripts checked by a native speaker before submission.'
- Somewhat hedged: 'It is important that authors whose first language is not English *should* have the paper checked by a native English speaker before submission.'
- More forcefully: 'Authors whose native language is not English *MUST* have the manuscript edited for language accuracy prior to submission.'

If the English language is such a difficult thing to master, and if mastery at any level rather than the 'best' (Sir Randolph, later Lord Quirk) or the 'Britishest' (the Prince of Wales, later King Charles III) is not really worth much, one is left with a puzzle. Why should those souls who are not among the 300 million preordained, anointed native speakers who can call English their 'mother tongue' with Bryson (and Lord Quirk and King Charles) continue to revere the language so much that they invest the time and effort in mastering it, well knowing that at the end of the day, they will need native speakers to (may wish to/should/must) check their writing, and find the means to satisfy 'the need for non-native teachers to be in constant touch with the native language' (Quirk, 1988, p. 19)? The challenge to the English language is really getting out of hand, it seems; things are only getting worser and worser. One of the participants in the study of Edwards (2010) remarks:

> I have noticed that international journals frequently publish papers that do still have Dutch (or other 'foreign') features in them. I attribute this not to

'acceptance' of these features as a special form of English, but to the fact that not all journal editors are equally language-conscious. In fact, many editors of international journals are not necessarily native speakers themselves and may not be able to judge the linguistic quality of papers. (p. 22)

How do you keep the world whole if even international journals now have non-native speakers as editors! The hidden synonymy of international and English, as well as the uncontested need for the English to be native English, could not escape me, especially since the participant quoted here, according to the information provided by Edwards, is a Dutch national and not, by the look of things, an English native speaker.

Native speakers of English do not generally have this kind of trouble with English, and as a rule do not impose similar demands on themselves as far as the command of other languages is concerned. In entertaining his readership with anecdotes from his travels in continental Europe in *Neither Here Nor There*, Bryson (1991) recounts how he struggled to order in a German restaurant where the waitress spoke no English. He had to resort to German, using the words on the menu, and only after a lot of to-ing and fro-ing, he got his message across. '"Ah, *beer*," she said, with a private tut, as if I had been intentionally misleading her. I felt abashed for not speaking German . . .' (p. 89). All the while, on the other hand, the English-speaking traveller managed quite well with his home language throughout Europe. He felt taken aback when he encountered someone selling train tickets in Gothenburg who didn't speak English, and he drew on the full range of stereotypes when representing the attempts of the seller to direct him to another ticket booth where the seller did speak English (p. 150). He was mighty pleased when travelling through Antwerp, about which he remarks that the locals speak English that is 'nearly always perfect' (p. 71) – nearly: nativespeakerness being the norm and standard, speaking another language being a source of amusement.

If one reflects on this asymmetry for any length of time, one inevitably has to take very seriously the conclusion of Phillipson (1992): English is an imperial language with a knack for killing off others. The widespread and exclusive use of the English language threatens to exclude people from participation; it is in fact a continuation of imperialism in a different guise – linguistic imperialism, the successor of the British Empire that managed to cover the world more thoroughly than its predecessor, according to him.

This book offers an attempt at understanding the position of English in the world today, despite the apparent odds, while also advocating a more nuanced look at what type of English is 'worth settling for', and what happens to the language when one stops looking for amusement or opportunities to make money by selling your brand of best English. This book is written from the perspective known as world Englishes,[1] with a deviant plural that works on the nerves of my word processor and makes it scribble red, a perspective that accepts the worldwide diversity of the English language and aims to understand it in historical and social context. Work in world Englishes combines linguistic description with contextual interpretation, and an activist stance is part of the way in which some of the scholars in world Englishes approach their craft.

There are three major puzzles that this book tries to solve:

- How did the position of the English language in the world today come about?
- What are the linguistic consequences of the worldwide uses of English?
- What does the foreseeable future have in store for the English language?

Part 1 of the book introduces three complementary perspectives on English: the history of the spread of English, alongside the two core models of the field (this chapter), followed by the social forces shaping the use of English (Chapter 2), and the linguistic features of varieties of English across the world (Chapter 3).

Part 2 takes a closer look at the historical and contemporary contexts in which English came into use in terms of the three perspectives introduced in Part 1, considering the earlier colonial expansion of the language alongside contemporary globalised expansion. Settlement colonisation resulted in new native varieties of English developing in countries like Northern Ireland, the United States, Canada, Australia, New Zealand and South Africa (Chapter 4). Language shift under influence of either plantation colonisation or settlement colonisation gave rise to new native speakers of English, among people whose forebears were from West Africa or India or who continued to live in their ancestral land as minorities among the offspring of English-speaking settlers, for example in Ireland, Australia or New Zealand (Chapter 5). Exploitation colonisation in Asia and Africa gave rise to distinctive non-native varieties of English in widespread use, enhanced and developed further by the ongoing use of English in most of these countries after political independence from their colonial masters (Chapter 6). Coca-colonisation, or post-Second World War globalisation is presented as the main driver of the extended use of English beyond the geographical control of British and American colonisation, resulting in the use of English beyond the scope of what one would traditionally call a foreign language (Chapter 7). Migration and the internet provide new

---

1. Usually spelled *world Englishes* with lower case 'w' as well, except at the beginning of a sentence.

contact settings and new channels for the transmission of English, resulting in the consolidation of the worldwide position and affecting the shape of the language on an ongoing basis (Chapter 8).

Part 3 consists of a single concluding chapter, which looks at the cumulative effects of the spread of the English language represented in Part 2, and projects into the future. Major issues for discussion are identified and the points of debate set out.

1.2 The spread of English – by people

Britain used to be part of the European continent, not only in political terms before Brexit but also in geographical terms. The present-day islands were part of the European continental landmass until about 10,000 years ago, but then rising sea levels caused the area linking the present-day islands to the continent, known as Doggerland, to be submerged under water (Walker et al., 2020). Several millennia later, in the fifth century CE, Germanic tribes from the European continent settled in the British Isles: Saxons, Angles, Frisians and Jutes invaded and colonised the main island (Nielsen, 1998, p. 65). By the eighth and ninth centuries, the various Germanic dialects spoken by the continental settlers grew into a new language with a fair degree of homogeneity, although not without residual variability that can be ascribed to the varied input (Nielsen, 1998, pp. 78–80; Trudgill, 2004, p. 11).

English came into being through the migration of people, and not without much warfare and colonising activity. Much of this continued for the first millennium after the Germanic tribes colonised parts of Britain, as the Celtic inhabitants of the island came increasingly under the linguistic influence of English and language shift continued. Further colonisations, by the Norse (late eighth to eleventh centuries) and the Normans (eleventh century), further impacted on the shape of English and also on the composition of its speakers.

The English started colonising the island of Ireland in the Middle Ages, in ways reasonably similar to their gradual expansion of influence over Wales and Scotland on the island of Britain. However, a major settlement in the seventeenth century changed the course of history on Ireland more than the smaller-scale incursions that preceded it, when English-speaking Scottish Protestants, alongside speakers of Scots Gaelic, settled permanently in the North of Ireland from the beginning of the seventeenth century. These ancestral speakers of English continued to use a dialect of English called Ulster Scots. The majority of contemporary speakers of English in Ireland are native Irish people whose forebears shifted to English over the last few centuries (Hickey, 2012).

Coinciding with the settlement and colonisation of Ireland, the British also settled on some Caribbean islands and a few areas of the east coast of the North American continent. Over time, these endeavours reached other parts of the world, in Africa, Asia and Australasia, which all added up to the extensive geographical transplantation of the language through speaker movement and the adoption of English by others. British colonisation in the rest of the world can be viewed in terms of a number of colonisation types: trade, settlement, plantation and exploitation colonisation, as proposed by Mufwene (2001) and expanded by Schneider (2007), which sometimes followed in successive phases and sometimes coincided. These processes involved English speakers travelling long distances across the oceans and living, for longer or shorter periods, on other continents. They carried the English language in them to the new place, and in various ways, English became a part of the linguistic ecology of the new place.

In the case of settlement colonisation, the English speakers became permanent inhabitants of the new locations and thus continued using English in the new place, in much the same way that the earliest Germanic settlers in Britain did when they colonised the island. Trade contact often implied very limited settlement at the geographical edges of foreign territories – in fortified or unfortified trade stations, called factories. In these settings, pidginised varieties of English usually developed to facilitate trade contact, for instance along the coast of West Africa, India and Southern China. A few of the pidgins subsequently became languages of wider communication for the non-English speakers who found further use for them beyond contact with the English traders. In plantation colonisation, a much smaller number of English speakers settled, alongside a large number of slaves who were forcibly settled in the same area. These slaves spoke multiple languages, many of which were not mutually intelligible and thus shifted to English over a very short period of time. A typical consequence of this form of colonisation was the development of creole varieties of English, especially in the Caribbean. Exploitation colonisation usually went hand in hand with a small number of temporary English-speaking settlers, most of whom returned to Britain after a period of 'service', or after a couple of generations. While they used English amongst themselves, they also used English with a small number of indigenous intermediaries, supported by English-language teaching by missionaries in schools and some workplace acquisition. Gradually, the English language also came into wider use by the indigenous populations of the exploitation colonies, and such use continued after the English colonial settlers left the occupied territories. In these contexts, the indigenous inhabitants added English to their linguistic repertoires without shifting from their earlier community languages, as was the case in the plantation colonies.

Since the end of the Second World War, English has steadily become the undisputed language of wider communication in the world. Political and economic factors all play a role, and thus the spread of the language is now carried by education systems right across the world, together with ever-increasing opportunities to use the language for business exchange, academic interaction, international tourism and entertainment. English has reached a point where the language spreads independently of the people speaking it and carrying it to new places.

The position of English in the world today is not the result of a coherent or planned process but the outcome of multiple events and types of events that had partially independent motivations. To understand the current worldwide spread and use of English, let us turn to each of these types of colonial and contemporary events that contributed to the spread of English.

1.2.1 Trade colonisation

The earliest way in which English spread beyond the British Isles was through trade, starting in the sixteenth century. The British followed the Spanish, Portuguese and Dutch in establishing trade contacts and trading posts along the west coast of Africa and various parts of Asia, and established themselves as a global economic force by the latter part of the seventeenth century (Frankopan, 2015). The trade happened with limited contact and often through intermediaries, who needed only enough mastery of English (or earlier Portuguese-based contact languages) to enable successful trade. Early trade gave rise to contact varieties of English that later came to be called pidgins in West Africa (Huber, 1999), India (Sharma, 2012) and South China (Bolton, 2002), and also served as initial mediums of interchange in the Caribbean and North American mainland before more complete language acquisition replaced pidgins (Dillard, 1992).

Pidgin English varieties still in use today, for example in West Africa or the Pacific Islands, have their origins in plantation colonisation and subsequent migration of former slaves or indentured plantation workers, rather than the early trade. Thus, in the case of West Africa, Huber (1999) records evidence of early trade pidgin use by Africans from the seventeenth century onwards, but the stabilisation of West African Pidgin English in the twentieth century followed only after the migration of Krio speakers from Sierra Leone throughout West Africa, whose English had its roots in Caribbean plantation colonisation rather than trade colonisation.

The trade pidgins in India (Sharma, 2012) and China (Bolton, 2002) fell into disuse from the end of the nineteenth century, although some extant use was recorded into the middle of the twentieth century. There is a suggestion of Chinese Pidgin English also supporting the later development of Pacific Island pidgins, but mostly in indirect ways (Mühlhäusler, 1985). In the United States, pidgin English gave way to 'more ordinary' English by the second half of the seventeenth century already in the settled parts of the East Coast, but its continued use in contact with new slaves and indigenous peoples in the ever-shifting frontier of the colonial United States is recorded until the nineteenth century (Dillard, 1992).

1.2.2 Settlement colonisation

The diffusion of English to other parts of the world through the migration of English speakers is responsible for the English-speaking majority living in a number of countries across the world today, noticeably millions in the United States and Canada in North America, and in Australia and New Zealand in the Southern Hemisphere. It is also due to migration of English speakers that English is spoken natively by sizeable numbers of people in Northern Ireland and South Africa, although language shift and other factors played a role to expand the influence of English far beyond the contribution of the original settlers in these countries. On a much smaller scale, the English speakers on the Atlantic islands of Tristan da Cunha, St Helena and the Falklands are also there due to settlement of previously uninhabited territories.

The same process of native-speaker migration also resulted in numerically smaller settlements of English speakers in present-day Zimbabwe, Zambia and Kenya in Africa, as well as Singapore and Hong Kong and some Indian cities in Asia. These settlements were less permanent. There are still resident native speakers who trace their ancestry to migration from Britain in some of these places, but in relatively small numbers today. Zimbabwe, the country that historically had the largest number of English-speaking settlers of this group, with an average settler population of 270,833 for the years 1973–1979 (Brownell, 2008) was down to a tenth of that at 28,732 in the 2012 census.

Yet, as a detailed comparison of settler arrivals between Zimbabwe and earlier settlements will show, it was not inevitable that the settlement in Zimbabwe would ultimately not yield a permanent speech community. Early attempts at settlement in South Africa and New Zealand, antedating Zimbabwe by less than a century, also remained small for several decades, until the discovery of precious metals in both cases. In Australia, convicts and their children outnumbered people who went there out of their own accord and their descendants for the first forty years of settlement (Kiesling, 2004, p. 419). The first attempted settlement in what became the United States of America, the Roanoke Colony, failed and the 115 settlers disappeared from history without a trace, while the first settlement that became permanent, in Jamestown, Virginia, had very high mortality – only 38 of the initial 104 settlers survived the first year, and 4,800 of the 6,000 settlers to Jamestown between 1607 and 1625 died, ultimately very likely because of an extreme drought during the period (Stahle et al., 1998). Inauspicious as it was, Zimbabwe still had a better start than some of its predecessor settlement colonies, and its British emigrants didn't know what history had in store for them or their descendants when they left the island.

The attempted settlements in Zimbabwe and Kenya came at the tail end of a phase in history when the British did not regard the inhabitants of other places as their equals – many territories were claimed as *terra nullius*, unoccupied land under international law, as if indigenous inhabitants didn't count. This was not uniquely British, but a widespread European attitude that found its first expression in the Portuguese and Spanish conquest and colonisation of West Africa and the Americas in the fifteenth and sixteenth centuries. Europeans at that juncture in history came to dominate the world through their military and naval advantages, and regarded themselves as superior to the Native Americans and Africans in particular (their attitude towards Asians and Muslim North Africans was somewhat ambiguous but for a long time, they did engage in trade rather than conquest with such major powers as the Ottoman, Persian and Chinese empires, and for a period also with India).

The reasons for emigration from Britain and settlement in a colony were quite diverse. Most of the settlers did not leave Britain as part of a government-sponsored or planned settlement, although such organised settlement took place after the Napoleonic Wars in the 1820s to the Eastern Cape in South Africa (Lanham, 1996, p. 20) and to Canada (Dollinger, 2008, p. 78). In both cases, territories that were previously under the control of other European colonial powers – the Netherlands and France – and already settled by non-English Europeans came under British control. Settlement followed in order to anglicise these territories and solidify British rule. Commercially organised settlement also took place to New Zealand in the 1840s and 1850s (Gordon & Trudgill, 2004).

Broadly speaking, there were push and pull factors. Push factors were either political or economic. Religious dissenters sought freedom from persecution, including the Puritans who settled in Massachusetts in the early seventeenth century and the Quakers who settled in Pennsylvania late in the seventeenth century. Roman Catholics from Britain and Ireland sought their freedom in the United States in subsequent centuries (Hickey, 2020, p. 27).

Economic push factors were extensive, and revolved around poverty and lack of employment opportunity. Since the changes in agricultural production during the reign of Elizabeth I in the early seventeenth century, the rural poor lost access to land and needed a place to live and work. This included the clearance of the Scottish Highlands in the eighteenth and early nineteenth centuries, as well as the Irish potato famine of the mid-nineteenth century (Bauer, 2002, pp. 15–16). As a result, many of the settlers leaving Britain and Ireland were from rural and urban working-class backgrounds, and not highly educated.

A much more literal push factor was being forced off the British Isles, with poverty being an underlying factor here too. Britons in financial trouble were compelled into indentured labour contracts, and many were sent to North America in particular, including the Caribbean (Schneider, 2011, p. 47). The deportation of mainly petty criminals to the penal colony in Australia formed the foundations of the early settlement there – in total almost 700,000 people were transported as convicts to New South Wales between 1788 and 1840, and another almost 70,000 to Tasmania. These were mostly English, with a strong representation of Londoners, but about a third were from Ireland (Kiesling, 2004).

The pull factors were either adventure or economic gain. The idea of a new life in *terra nullius*, the opportunity to make a fresh start, served as an enticement for some – amply supported by the emerging genre of the imperial romance novel in the nineteenth century, glorifying the adventures of big-game hunting in Africa or the Wild West in the United States. Reports of life in the new colonies, reaching relatives and acquaintances in Britain and Ireland via letters, enhanced the pull factor.

Economic gain came in the form of various gold rushes and other sudden opportunities arising from the discovery of resources, especially during the nineteenth century, in America, South Africa, Australia and New Zealand, with accounts of fortune seekers travelling from one discovery to the next.

1.2.3 Plantation colonisation

Plantation colonisation developed in the second half of the seventeenth century in the Caribbean islands. The early settlement of some of these islands, for example Barbados in 1627 and Jamaica in 1655, coincided with the settlement of continental North America. During this period, a settler majority was established, together with some slaves and indentured servants, which initiated the formation of a koine of the settler input. However, before that process had been completed, the economies of these islands changed drastically as sugar cane plantations were established and a sudden demographic change occurred with the extensive forced settlement of slaves bought along the West African coast and transported across the Atlantic Ocean. Economic opportunity – making big profits on sugar cane and other crops – led to the continued occupation and exploitation of the Caribbean islands, but went hand in hand with the large-scale importation of slaves from West Africa, rather than the exploitation of indigenous labour.

The conditions on the plantations were such that slaves who arrived spoke multiple different West African languages, which were from different families. There was a deliberate policy of keeping the slave population on ships and in different plantations linguistically heterogenous, to avoid a situation where an African language could serve as a lingua franca and enable slaves to organise a revolt, a policy also adopted in the plantation economy of the United States (Dillard, 1992, p. 61). During the homestead phase that preceded the plantation phase, slaves and English settlers lived in close contact, and thus the settler variety served as input for the acquisition of English by slaves, resulting in less divergence. Once the plantations got off the ground, strict segregation ensued, together with ongoing importation of slaves continuing for more than a century. Imported slaves outnumbered locally born slaves until the end of the eighteenth century, and these newcomers had to continue learning the local form of English from other slaves in the main, rather than through contact with the small number of settlers. Nevertheless, for lack of alternatives, the slaves shifted to English as their main language, whether acquired as an additional language as adults or acquired as a native language when born in bondage. Stabilisation of the English used among the slave community followed only in the nineteenth century, as the locally born members of the community outnumbered imported slaves and children did their bit to organise the input into focused varieties – not unlike the children in settler communities, but in a context where they were confronted by much more variability and under very different social and material conditions, including limited formal education and literacy (Mufwene, 2001, pp. 50–51).

From the middle of the nineteenth century, new plantation economies were developed in Queensland, Australia and the Pacific Islands to the north and east of Australia, in which new contact Englishes developed. By this time, slavery had been abolished, but indentured labourers occupied a similar position in the linguistic ecologies, and pidgin Englishes developed amongst them. One important difference from earlier slave plantations was that there was a degree of voluntariness among the labourers and they had the option to return after serving their indentured contracts. The development of more stable contact-influenced Englishes as a native language was thus not a general outcome of all these new plantations. Nevertheless, some of the contact Englishes from these plantations also stabilised and became native languages to inhabitants of some of the Pacific Islands, the most widely used of which was Tok Pisin in Papua New Guinea, spoken as a native language by about half a million, alongside several million second-language users (Mühlhäusler, 1985; Velupillai, 2015, p. 37).

1.2.4 Exploitation colonisation

Trade, rather than settlement, was the principal concern of British engagement with Africa and Asia throughout the seventeenth century and well into the eighteenth century. The British established trading posts along the African west coast, sometimes on islands just off the coast, sometimes on the mainland, often fortified in order to defend their interests, especially against other European trading nations. The same thing happened in Asia, with trade concessions negotiated in India and later also in South China, Singapore and other parts of Asia. Nominally, there were agreements with local rulers to set up such trading posts, although the arrangements in Asia were typically more formalised, as if in some kind of partnership, while for those in Africa often there was the thinnest veneer of legality over a massive imbalance in military force. Missionary activity followed in the wake of longer-term trading posts, but activities remained restricted to small coastal areas with few territorial claims by the British Crown until later in the eighteenth century. The contact with China, even towards the late nineteenth century, cannot be distinguished all that clearly from the (colonial) trade engagements with other parts of Asia.

The historian Peter Frankopan (2015) notes that in the eighteenth century, 'Attitudes towards Asia were changing from excitement about profits to be made to thoughts of brute exploitation' (p. 275). He pinpoints the tipping point to 1757 when a protectorate came into being after a British military expedition went to support the rulers of Calcutta against an attack by the Nawab of Bengal. Robert Clive, leader of the expedition, soon found himself in control of the territory and began taxing the local rulers for the British Crown. British exploitation resulted in human catastrophe after a mere decade, as millions of pounds were taken from Bengal to line the pockets of East India Company employees. The price of grain had been driven so high that it became unaffordable, and several million Indians died in the resulting famine by 1770 (Frankopan, 2015, p. 277).

It is worth quoting Frankopan (2015) at length here, lest there be a misunderstanding of the nature of colonial exploitation:

> The situation was entirely avoidable. The suffering of the many had been sacrificed for personal gain. To howls of derision, Clive simply answered – like the chief executive of a distressed bank – that his priorities had been to protect the interests of the shareholders, not those of the local population; he deserved no criticism, surely, for doing his job. (p. 277)

After the bankruptcy of the East India Company, the British government took control and bailed it out (Frankopan, 2015, p. 277). To fund the bail-out, the government in London passed the Tea Act of 1773, in part to raise more taxes from its American colony on the opposite side of the world. This was one of the contributing factors to the eventual revolution of the American colonies and their battle for independence from Britain, which in turn resulted in Britain becoming all the more possessive of its Indian territory, although India was occupied mainly without clear plans to also establish a British settlement in the territory (Frankopan, 2015, pp. 278–279).

Ruling over people, exploiting their resources but also expanding commercial activity to include more intensive methods of production required much closer engagement with the indigenous populations than trade did. This necessitated the development of a larger class of indigenous intermediaries, and initiated a much more concerted effort to teach English to a small but not insignificant class of the indigenous population to ensure that the messages of the rulers were conveyed to the people, and to have this class act as clerks and overseers beyond the hands made available by colonial officials. The more widespread use of English was thus set in motion in Asia by the end of the eighteenth century and continued to grow for the next century and a half.

Trade occupation in Africa grew during the course of the eighteenth century, but so too did competition between the European occupiers. Apart from the settlement colonisation in South Africa, gradual territorial control also grew in West and East Africa. Towards the end of the nineteenth century, Africa was carved up by the European colonial powers at the Berlin Conference (1884–1885), at which point Britain was 'given control' over large expanses of African soil, and it implemented administrative control, supported by military enforcement and missionary education. A system of indirect rule developed, where a small occupying force ruled through the traditional rulers, with a similar need for intermediaries to that which had developed in Asia.

Across the occupied territories of the British Empire, until the Second World War, administration and education grew and covered larger parts of the territories. No general access to English or widespread proficiency in the language arose, but a group of English-educated indigenous people grew steadily. Members of this group gradually acquired a larger stake in the use of the English language and began using it for their own purposes, rather than merely to act as intermediaries of the British rulers. English became something of value to this relatively small group, to the point that sometime in the nineteenth century, Africans and Asians started writing books and publishing newspapers in English, with fellow colonised people as their principal audience. In some instances, books were very deliberately written for a native-speaker audience, such as Solomon Plaatje's *Native Life in South Africa* (1916). This book documented the exploitation of indigenous Africans and the resultant hardship and disruption of communities in the wake of the Land Act of 1913, which dispossessed Africans of land in 'white South Africa', forcing them to either cede possession of the livestock to white farmers and become their wage labourers or opt to relocate, with their animals and earthly possessions, to very arid and inhospitable farmland not deemed attractive enough for use by white farmers.

The end of the Second World War set in motion a process of political independence, first in Asia (and not only in the British Empire – the Indonesian War of Independence from the Dutch happened simultaneously with the Indian independence movement), and then in Africa, leading to the formal granting of independence to all these countries. At this point, many of them, and especially the majority of those in Africa, opted to continue using English in similar public functions to those under the British administration and education. With the expansion of education in the postcolonial phase, a much wider cross-section of the formerly colonised gained access to education and thereby to English-language proficiency, but under new conditions: with fellow non-native speakers as teachers rather than the English-speaking or near-native English-using teachers of the colonial era. The expediency of this choice was strongly encouraged by the colonial powers as they withdrew but sought to continue their influence in some way (Phillipson, 1992).

1.2.5 English beyond the empire: coca-colonisation

The reach or range of functions of English today is not due to colonisation only, otherwise we would not be able to account for the difference between English and other European colonial languages like French, Spanish or Portuguese. The widespread use of English in countries that were not under British or American colonial control provides the key to the difference. English reinvented itself from foreign language to international language to lingua franca in the course of the twentieth century, and then got on the wave of global telecommunications, a wave that it is still surfing with no immediate prospect of being caught by other languages or falling off this wave. What is crucial about the process is that English has become different to other foreign languages, and is used in ways that go beyond what is traditionally expected of a foreign language.

The dominant role of the United States economy, especially after the Second World War, was a catalyst, while the immediate post-war conditions also favoured the use of English in the post-war reconstruction programmes in Europe and the Far East. In these initial stages, English native speakers were often involved in the communicative interactions, but gradually as transnational exchanges increased, English came to be the preferred choice of language for exchanges not involving native English speakers too. This is true for academic exchange, for global tourism, and for global business and industry, but also for regional politics, as seen with the entrenched role of English in the European Union even after Brexit, and the even stronger position of English in ASEAN, the Association of Southeast Asian Nations. What is crucial about the spread of English in the last half century, though, is the fact that it is no longer driven by the migration of English speakers. Agency has passed to a much larger group of people across the world, albeit those who are typically the more well-off in their respective societies.

These processes together create a self-reinforcing cycle of perceived value, supporting the learning of English, yielding ever more dividends because of the ever-widening possibilities to use the language, and enhancing the perceived incentive for yet more people to learn the language and master it better and better.

1.3 Models of world Englishes

Let us consider some of the key ways in which we can make sense of the worldwide spread of English. The idea of something called 'world Englishes' was pioneered by Braj Kachru (1932–2016), an Indian-born linguist, who completed school and university education in India before continuing to doctoral research in the United Kingdom and taking up a position in the United States in the early 1960s, from which he retired four decades later. Kachru's work in the 1960s focused on Indian English and its claim to status as more than just the incomplete and error-filled approximation of British English. This early work led to the development of ideas about the use of English as the language of the former colonies with local ownership of the language, rather than continued deference to the colonial centre of control.

From the late 1970s, Kachru collaborated with the American scholar Larry Smith (1941–2014), who independently developed similar ideas about the role of English beyond the British colonial world, the countries that used English as an international auxiliary language, without the need for those learners to learn British or American culture (Bolton & Davis, 2018). When Kachru and Smith put their heads together, a model of understanding emerged in which the use and users of English came to be conceptualised as three concentric circles: an Inner, Outer and Expanding Circle (most explicitly articulated by Kachru, 1985/2015d).

The three circles refer to different countries in terms of their histories and use of English. The Inner Circle consists of the countries colonised by the British through settlement, and where native varieties of English came to be used, notably the United States, Canada, Australia and New Zealand. The Outer Circle consists of the countries of the former British Empire where English is not spoken as a native language in the main, such as India, Singapore, Kenya or Nigeria, alongside the Philippines as the one former American colony with similar characteristics. The Expanding Circle refers to those remaining countries of the world where English is adopted as a language of wider communication with the rest of the world, such as Japan, Mexico or Germany. However, the concentric circle model is not merely a model of the standing and role of English, in which case it would simply be a terminological variant of the split between English as a first/native, second and foreign language. The model is supported by further claims, which take us beyond this. The Englishes of the Outer Circle localise or indigenise – they too, like transplanted native varieties, grow local characteristics to be usable for the local landscape and serve as an expression of local culture and life, as proposed by Kachru. The Englishes of the Expanding Circle are not mere foreign languages – they are not used mainly for communicating with and about the foreign cultures that are associated with the language. Rather, the international use of English, later called the lingua franca use of the language, and the importance of communicating one's own culture to others became key hallmarks of the Expanding Circle in Smith's conceptualisation.

The model has its limits. It does not provide a clear conceptualisation of the creole and language-shift varieties of English, the 'illegitimate offspring' as framed by Mufwene (1997). It is static and treats national categories without detailed consideration of changes over time, or diversity within countries (Bruthiaux, 2003; Schneider, 2007). Yet, it serves as a convenient shorthand, with valid conceptual insights, for some of the major variety types, and will thus be used in this book, forming the basis for the conceptualisation of the varieties of English in Chapters 4, 6 and 7, while the work of Mufwene, Mesthrie and others serves as a valuable elaboration for the major varieties not made sufficiently visible in the Three Circles model in Chapter 5.

The other major model is much more recent, the dynamic model of postcolonial Englishes originally proposed in 2003 by the Austrian-born German scholar Edgar Schneider (born 1954), and expanded over time (e.g. by Schneider, 2007, 2014). Schneider focuses on the varieties of English that developed in colonial contexts, covering in detail the way settlers, indigenous people and others who moved to the same places, such as slaves, interacted to shape English in new places. Thus, dynamic and interactive dimensions of the Englishes covered in Chapters 4–6 are central to Schneider's model. His key insight is the similarities across these various settings, where contact takes place between people, where the language undergoes a process of indigenisation, and where over time, local standards develop and gain acceptance. These processes and developments are captured across five consecutive stages: foundation, exonormative stabilisation, nativisation, endonormative stabilisation and differentiation. Throughout, his model is concerned with the way the settlers and indigenous people relate, together with others who enter the same space where appropriate. Over time, he observes that the contact and interaction become closer, thus mutual influences increase and contribute to shaping the local form of English, which grows more similar across the different groups in contact until they reach reasonable homogeneity in stage four, endonormative stabilisation. A key insight is that identity reorientation typically precedes stage four; the settlers have to identify with the new land, and not conceive of themselves as representatives of Britain on foreign soil, while the indigenous people have to adopt a sense of shared nationhood that includes the descendants of the settlers.

Schneider's model has likewise been subject to criticism, refinement and extension, to which Schneider himself also contributes. The most important elaboration is to test the applicability of the dynamic model beyond the colonial context, perhaps most compellingly by Edwards (2016) for the Netherlands. Buschfeld and Kautzsch (2020) offer a very comprehensive review of the development of models for English across the world.

This book relies more on the basic conceptualisation of Kachru, with extensions from Mufwene, but the dynamic and interactive insights from Schneider inform my thinking throughout. The three-way division between historical, social and linguistic aspects I adopt is also strongly indebted to Schneider's (2007) detailed application of his model.

The next chapter turns to the social processes that affect the spread, the use and the shape of the English language in its journey from a small island to the rest of the world. This will be complemented by Chapter 3, which looks at the linguistic processes shaping English, to round off the overarching picture of Part 1 of the book, before Part 2 is devoted to the specifics of English in its various manifestations.

1.4 Note on terminology

In this book, I am not particularly dogmatic in the use of terminology, except for terms that clearly represent a reductionist view, which will be presented in quotation marks where appropriate for the context. I resist the temptation to offer long terminological discussions and reflections, but I return to some of these matters in the final chapter. There is a fair degree of terminological innovation in the field, without the rationale for not using a previous term always being made clear in a manner that convinces me, hence I often stick to the terms that enjoy widest currency among scholars of world Englishes. I also resist the temptation to put all British and other 'noble titles', Sirs, Lords, Royal Highnesses and their terminological variants in quotation marks, but the reader may well infer that I am not a royalist of any description and use these terms with a bit of a chuckle. Of course, to understand the contextual dynamics, these inherited, assigned or bought titles matter, and should therefore be taken into account, but from my side are certainly not endorsed. I apologise to all highnesses for the offence this gives, in a truly South African way. Sorry.

Equally, terms that are contested, for good reason, by scholars in world Englishes, such as 'native speaker', 'non-native speaker' or 'standard English', are used with their very typical denotations. The contestation around these terms is a productive way of dealing with their limits, but it becomes quite cumbersome to refer to sometimes very mundane classifications if one has to circumlocute or add several caveats or disclaimers like 'so-called' to these terms. For those toes that feel hurt by my persistent stepping on them, sorry too.

2 Using English

William Farquhar (1774–1839) was the first resident of Singapore, the chief colonial officer at the establishment of Singapore as a British colony. History has mostly credited Sir Stamford Raffles as the founder of Singapore, although he was not involved in the practicalities and spent little time in the city itself during the early years of British colonisation. Farquhar, a Scot, was given the affectionate nickname Raja Melaka by the early colonial subjects of the new British trading post. He was a speaker of Malay and had a half-Malay wife with whom he arrived in Singapore from Melaka in 1819. Frost and Balasingamchow (2009) write about him that, in contrast to Raffles, he 'seems to have been more sensitive to local practices and attitudes; in fact, in some respects he might have been said to have "gone native"' (p. 62). Such a disposition did not count in Farquhar's favour in the early nineteenth century, not with Raffles, nor with the overlords, the East India Company, who formally acknowledged Raffles's 'assertion that he was the sole founder of the settlement at Singapore' (p. 68), as much as the territory had already been settled prior to Raffles's arrival.

Rather than Farquhar's, the much more typical nineteenth-century attitude is portrayed by the British colonial official Thomas Babington Macaulay (1835), who opined:

> I have no knowledge of either Sanscrit or Arabic. But I have done what I could to form a correct estimate of their value. I have read translations of the most celebrated Arabic and Sanscrit works. I have conversed, both here and at home, with men distinguished by their proficiency in the Eastern tongues. I am quite ready to take the oriental learning at the valuation of the orientalists themselves. I have never found one among them who could deny that a single shelf of a good European library was worth the whole native literature of India and Arabia. The intrinsic superiority of the Western literature is indeed fully admitted by those members of the committee who support the oriental plan of education.

This view, together with the quality of its evidence, would have been neither here nor there if it had been shared on present-day social media, but it came with official clout as part of the Macaulay Minute on education for India, a recommendation that was adopted by the colonial administration and subsequently implemented in India and elsewhere in the British Empire. Macaulay was still quite a bit more enlightened by the standards of his time when compared with the protagonist Charlie Considine in the 1877 youth adventure story *The Settler and the Savage* by the Scottish writer R. M. Ballantyne. The novel is set in the early years of British colonial occupation in South Africa, around 1820. Considine encounters an indigenous San character while riding on horseback through the Karoo, an arid landscape in the interior of the Cape Colony of the time. The following exchange is reported in the opening scene of the novel:

> 'Can you speak English?' asked Considine as he rode up.
> The Bushman looked vacant and made no reply.
> 'Where is your master's house?' asked the youth.
> A stare was the only answer.
> 'Can't you speak, you dried-up essence of stupidity!' exclaimed Charlie with impatience.
> At this the Bushman uttered something with so many klicks, klucks, and gurgles in it that his interrogator at once relinquished the use of the tongue, and took to signs, but with no better success, his efforts having only the effect of causing the mouth of the Bushman to expand from ear to ear. Uttering a few more klicks and gurgles, he pointed in the direction of the setting sun. As Considine could elicit no fuller information he bade him a contemptuous farewell and rode away in the direction indicated. (p. 3)

Ballantyne is mostly remembered for his work *The Coral Island* from 1858. In an entry on Ballantyne, Encyclopaedia Britannica notes that the author was annoyed by a mistake he had made in this story, and subsequently travelled widely to do research for his books. It is also noted that he wrote from personal experience, and that his work was characterised by 'models of self-reliance and moral uprightness' (Britannica, 2022). The author visited South Africa prior to the writing of *The Settler and the Savage* and published memoires from that visit under the title *Six Months at the Cape* in 1879, making him perhaps more qualified on the subject than some contemporary 'experts' on social media.

Neither Macaulay nor Charlie Considine was quite going native in the nineteenth century. But then, in the late twentieth century, Bill Bryson (1991) wasn't quite going native in Europe either, and still exoticised other languages and their speakers in terms strikingly similar to Ballantyne's. In *Neither Here Nor There*, he shared with his reader how amusing he found it when a Dutch speaker explained the Dutch pronunciation of the artist Vincent van Gogh's surname: 'he made a sudden series of desperate hacking noises, as if a moth had lodged in his throat' (p. 104). Bryson was exaggerating for comic effect, Ballantyne maybe did likewise, but the attitude towards things that are not English is hidden in plain sight.

It is a matter of some perplexity that a language whose speakers had such dismissive attitudes towards others managed to find itself at the pinnacle of the World Language System (De Swaan, 2010). The historical route to this point has been traced in the previous chapter, and we will now continue to consider the relevant social factors that support the use of English across the world. The focus is in the first instance on contact between people that facilitated the spread and use of the language, before turning to the uses of the language, then its acquisition, and returning to attitudes in the final part of this chapter.

2.1 Contact

Contact is an important contributor to language change: one language adopts new features under the influence of another language, with influences potentially flowing in both directions, depending on the specifics of the contact situation. Language contact takes place only insofar as there is contact between people speaking these languages, though, requiring a look at people rather than languages in the first place (Clyne, 2003, p. 1; Matras, 2009, p. 3). Asymmetrical relations between speakers translate into differential effects on languages (Matras, 2009, p. 47). The present chapter focuses on contact between people, while the linguistic consequences are considered in the next chapter.

When we turn to English, there are two types of contact situations that need to be considered. The first situation is dialect contact between different transplanted varieties of English in the colonial context of the settlement colonies. Speakers of different British dialects who lived in relative geographical isolation in Britain prior to emigration to the new colony came into contact in the new setting, and over the course of a few generations, but not instantaneously, a new local dialect of English stabilised in the new setting. Furthermore, in different types of colonial settings, speakers of English also came into contact with speakers of other languages – indigenous languages, such as the Athabaskan languages of North America, or the languages of Africa, India and Australasia, but also other transported languages, including the languages of slaves and the languages of other European settlers in the same territories. In consequence, the types of English that developed in these various settings show the influence of other languages, but in different ways and to differing degrees.

2.1.1 Contact among speakers of different English dialects

Dialect contact is not unique to settlement colonisation as such. In Britain during the time of emigration to the colonies, migration also happened with the territory, bringing people from different parts of Britain into contact with one another, especially in the big cities (Britain, 2020). What made the earliest settlements in North America, Australasia and South Africa different from the migration within Britain itself was the absence of an existing, settled community into which the new inhabitants were integrated. If somebody from the North of Scotland or even the North of England moved to London in the seventeenth century, their way of using English was unlikely to have any lasting effects on London English, and their peculiarities were likely to disappear as they themselves came to the end of their lives. However, the centrality of London and the stability of its dialect does not extend all the way back to the early history of the English language. Raumolin-Brunberg (2017) identifies the North of England as another centre from where variation spread to other parts of England, including London. One clear case is the sixteenth-century spread of the third-person singular suffix [-s], a northern usage that was gradually adopted in London. However, once established in London, and once London English attained the kind of stability it did by the end of the sixteenth century, subsequent influences brought by migrants to the city were fewer.

There was no established dialect in a new colonial setting, and in this context, the speakers from various parts of Britain had to forge one – mostly unintentionally. Trudgill (2004) emphasises the *tabula rasa* context of these settings, where a new dialect emerged through a combination of the various features that settlers brought along. He finds that the outcome of the mix is broadly proportional to the specific linguistic variants in the input. This dialect does not correspond exactly to any specific input dialect – in that sense, the colonial settler varieties are not simply transplanted versions of particular dialects from Britain but new dialects that combined features from multiple British dialects, resulting in combinations within the same speaker of features that no British English speaker would combine.

This is a peculiar situation in that the usual social factors involved in language change and sociolinguistic variation, such as prestige and solidarity with some in-group, are absent or considerably weaker. Trudgill (2004) also argues that children play an important role in this context, unconsciously selecting majority variants from the much more variable input around them than the sociolinguistic environment that obtained in Britain.

However, once a local dialect is in place, this dialect becomes a point of reference and subsequent migrants have much less influence on it. For instance, despite extensive migration from Ireland in the nineteenth century, American English did not grow more like Irish English than before. Even more strongly, once a colonial dialect stabilised, this dialect was carried by in-country migrations to other parts of the same country as the European settlements expanded. This is particularly striking in the case of Australia and Canada, very large countries that have relatively homogenous forms of English spoken from East to West across several time zones. This eventuality is designated the Founder's Principle by Mufwene (2001, pp. 28–29), where a founder population has a disproportionate effect on subsequent generations of speakers, due to their being there first and having established the basic outlines of the new variety.

2.1.2 Language contact between speakers of English and speakers of other languages

Language contact contributed more to new varieties of English across the world than dialect contact. Following Schneider (2003), it is important to distinguish between two perspectives: language contact from the side of settlers, who were native speakers of English and were typically in dominant positions in contact encounters, and language contact from the side of the speakers of other languages, indigenous inhabitants or non-English speakers, such as slaves, who also entered the new linguistic ecologies, who acquired English as an additional language and in some cases shifted to English as their primary language.

Native speakers of English moved to a new territory and in most cases, encountered indigenous people who were already resident in that territory. Within a few decades, the number of indigenous inhabitants of the new territories suffered dramatic demographic decline, through the combination of European illnesses against which they had little immunity, and military force. Germs turned out to be far more lethal than guns in reducing the indigenous population of North America by an estimated 95 per cent within two centuries of the arrival of Europeans (Diamond, 1997, p. 229), and a corresponding decline of 80 per cent in Australia (Diamond, 1997, p. 350).

Contact between English speakers and indigenous populations was generally limited until the late nineteenth and early twentieth centuries.

English speakers usually did not acquire proficiency in indigenous languages, so a few indigenous intermediaries took care of the communicative needs. During these contacts, some vocabulary for the local landscape and fauna and flora was borrowed into English, but very few further influences impacted on English as a result of the contact with indigenous minorities.

Native speakers of English also encountered other Europeans in the new settlements. Lexical borrowing from the other European languages, for domestic and economic referents, testify to relatively harmonious contact among the English and non-English settler populations, for example a reasonable portion of Dutch loanwords and even placenames into American English (Dillard, 1992, pp. 23–31). Gradual assimilation of the non-English Europeans took place in the nineteenth and twentieth centuries in the United States (Mufwene, 2001) and Australia (Clyne, 2003), and the influence of these other languages on English therefore came to an end. Since the assimilation was gradual, the founder's effect of the already established settler dialects was not disrupted by the generations of shifting speakers who were absorbed.

The Québécois in Canada retain a strongly separate identity, and integration between anglophone and francophone Canadians is relatively limited, not only culturally but also geographically. The province of Quebec retains its legal status as a French enclave within the Canadian Federation, enforced by such measures as Bill 101 from 1977 that enshrines certain uses of French and prohibits particular uses of English in the province (Morton, 2000, pp. 530–531).

The English settlers have never been a majority in South Africa, but they remain a sizeable and cohesive group. They encountered the Afrikaans speakers, who, like the French speakers in Canada, have not shifted to English and have not been incorporated into the speech community. In part, the Afrikaans settler descendants are a slightly larger group than the English settler descendant group, and animosity from the nineteenth century was only resolved very gradually during the twentieth century. Nevertheless, contact between the groups has been extensive throughout the twentieth century, and bilingualism is a strong feature of both groups (Coetzee-Van Rooy, 2013, 2021), even if contemporary Afrikaans speakers tend to be stronger in English than English speakers in Afrikaans. Such a bilingual context makes for a relatively extensive exchange of vocabulary in both directions, but even sporadic evidence for grammatical influences, again running in both directions, such that South African English also shows a small number of grammatical patterns that can be traced to contact with Afrikaans (Van Rooy, 2021).

2.1.3 Language contact between speakers of other languages and speakers of English

From the opposite perspective of the non-English-speaking participants in the colonial contact encounter, a distinction should be drawn between the kinds of contact in the plantation colonies, settlement colonies and exploitation colonies.

In the early phases of the slave-holding colonies, labelled the homestead phase, a relatively small number of slaves worked on farms in close contact with their owners and in some cases also indentured labourers. Such a setting provided opportunities and reasonable input for the acquisition of English, if not ideal circumstances to adult learners of another language; some slaves were quite young, though, many under the age of fourteen even (Mufwene, 2001, p. 50), and possibly in a somewhat better position to master English. In this phase, slaves did as well as they could with the linguistic resources available. The likely outcome of the homestead phase, according to Mufwene (2001, p. 50), would have been relatively close approximation of the emerging variety of the settler community in the new setting – both on the Caribbean islands and on continental North America.

When the economy changed to labour-intensive plantations, usually sugar cane or rice, the demographics and patterns of contact changed very dramatically, with slave populations constituting more than 80 per cent of the total population in an area and very limited contact with Europeans. Older slaves served as models for newer slaves, but even fluent English speakers among the slaves became minorities in the slave community, not to mention the extremely limited input from contact with native English. This context was more conducive for influences from shared features of West African languages to come into play as selection from a much more diverse pool of inputs had to be made (Mufwene, 2001, pp. 50–59). The replacement of slaves was more through new arrivals than through slaves born locally, which resulted in what Mufwene (2001, p. 51) terms basilectalisation, the development of creole varieties of English that deviate much more from the settler varieties because of the smaller proportion of input contributed by the settler English varieties. Only a small contribution of vocabulary from West African languages survived in some of the Caribbean Englishes, but grammatical patterns can be traced more often to shared input features across several of the contact languages that speakers brought with them. The slaves were forced into making the best use of English since the alternatives were not effective, and thus became speakers of English which was transmitted to children to the extent that there were any, as well as to newcomer slaves who acquired the local varieties as additional languages.

In settlement colonies, indigenous people spoke multiple languages. Since they lived separate lives from the settlers, beyond the geographical border of the settlements and separate from the settler economies, English played a negligible role in their lives. Only insofar as they became involved as labourers in the settler economies did a need for some mastery of English arise, but to the extent that they remained integrated in their indigenous communities, they would have remained native speakers of their respective indigenous languages. Two changes in the patterns of contact occurred from the late nineteenth century. Forced assimilation meant that children were put in schools under English-only policies. Here, they came into extensive contact with English-speaking teachers and school personnel, and acquired a form of school-based English not unlike the missionary school English in the exploitation colonies in the same period. At the same time, and continuing to the present, the indigenous minorities are gradually incorporated into the mainstream economies, and the geographical separation falls away. Language shift has been happening in the wake of the forced assimilation policies, but because the social integration is incomplete in many cases, the Englishes used by descendants of native speakers of indigenous languages remain distinctive ethnolects. Recent initiatives to halt and reverse language shift may or may not have the intended effect – we are not in a position to tell at present.

The initial situation in the exploitation colonies was relatively similar to the situation of indigenous minorities of the settlement colonies, where the majority of the indigenous population had little need for English or for direct contact with English speakers. Even those who were in contact with English colonial officials, missionaries or military remained part of other linguistic communities too, and were not denied the opportunity to use their other language(s), except for periods when attending boarding schools with a strict 'English-only' policy. This context was less disruptive for the indigenous people (compared with indigenous minorities in settlement colonies or slaves in plantation colonies), and also meant that the communicative demands on English were less stressful. In consequence, restructuring of English to make the best of the available input did not occur as extensively as with plantation slavery. The amount of contact with speakers of English and the setting for the contact varied between the workplace and schools. Workplace English was necessary for only a limited part of the day but may have been somewhat similar to the workplace contact of slaves in the homestead phase. However, given more stable contacts, the opportunity to use some indigenous forms and the chance of those forms being adopted by English speakers were higher. In some cases, pidginised workplace varieties of English did develop, such as Butler English in India, but in other settings, other contact languages, such as Fanakalo in Southern African, Swahili in East Africa or Bazaar Malay in Southeast Asia, served the needs of workplace contact.

Contact between English speakers and indigenous school pupils was mostly mediated by the English language, except for a few missionaries who acquired proficiency in indigenous languages. Typical second-language features were present in the emerging English varieties of the school-educated inhabitants of the exploitation colonies, alongside some vocabulary items that came into use between native English speakers and indigenous users of the language. Several factors – especially the language input in schools and the continued opportunity to use other languages – put less strain on the need to communicate in English, allowing a longer time for proficiency to develop, while reducing the opportunity for contact-induced language forms to stabilise.

The situation changed during the twentieth century as education expanded in the former colonies without the conditions remaining as conducive to the acquisition and stabilisation of a more native-like variety. The relatively higher proportion of native-speaker teachers and indigenous teachers with advanced proficiency declined, and a higher proportion of less proficient teachers took over as principal agents of transmission. This created conditions for more extensive cross-linguistic influence to come into play.

2.1.4 Contact with English without direct contact with speakers of English

Throughout the history of trade contact, but accelerating after the Second World War, the English language came into use as contact language between English-speaking traders and others. Contact was fleeting and the linguistic consequences were slight beyond the world colonised by the English. As an interesting example, one can consider the situation in the Netherlands. In the sixteenth to eighteenth centuries, English was not taught in schools in the Netherlands; to the extent that languages were taught, Latin was central, while French was the only modern language that had been institutionalised in the education system. The opportunities to learn English were limited to personal contact. Before the middle of the seventeenth century, available material was usually multilingual manuals and translation exercises – English was not the only language included in the manuals. The first textbook specifically for the purpose of learning English (but simultaneously for the learning of Dutch by English speakers) was produced in 1646, and its contents betray a strong emphasis on the learning of phrases and expressions useful in conducting trade (Loonen, 1990). English was instituted as a school subject from the final quarter of the nineteenth century only, and superseded French and German as the first additional language in the Dutch education system from the 1970s (Wilhelm, 2018). Contact with English was in the classroom, with little contact between foreign-language learners and speakers of the language.

Since the end of the Second World War, this situation has been changing with more contact between foreigners and speakers of English. In Western Europe, this followed in the wake of a stronger orientation towards the United States, given its economic strength in the immediate post-war decades, and amplified by the Cold War and solidarity within the West at the time. Other parts of the world also came into increased contact with the United States as its economy, exports and later outsourcing of manufacturing gained prominence in the post-war world.

Even China, which had oriented itself towards Russian rather than English as the first additional language after the establishment of the People's Republic in 1949, began to reintroduce English as a school subject by 1960. Access to English was temporarily put on hold by the Cultural Revolution, but the position of English as the first additional language has been firmly entrenched since the late 1970s (Bolton, 2003). Much of the access is driven by Chinese teachers rather than face-to-face contact with English speakers.

The economic motivation for strengthening English-language teaching at some point began to reach beyond the opportunities of trade with English speakers. The utility of English played a role in trade with the United States, and also other English-speaking countries, including the United Kingdom too, but in trading with former colonies, the language had the same kind of utility value. Thus, it became equally serviceable for interactions between Ghana and Nigeria, or India and Sri Lanka, and at some point even further, for interactions among 'non-anglophone' countries without any 'anglophone' country forming part of the interaction. In parallel to the extension of worldwide trade, worldwide academic exchange and tourism also grew, offered more interaction, and increasingly, English became the principal medium for conducting such interactions, irrespective of the individual backgrounds of the interactants. Face-to-face contact in these international exchanges, what Meierkord (2012) terms 'Interactions across Englishes', increased and became a self-reinforcing cycle. School education became a preparation for such interactions across Englishes, moving beyond the traditional purpose of teaching English as a foreign language in order to interact with native English speakers.

The most recent phase of new contact is online contact – written, spoken and more dynamic blends of media, enabled by the development of the internet, ever faster connection speeds (although not equally fast and equally accessible to all in the world), and a constantly increasing range of platforms. Where the earliest contact was relatively static, apart from e-mail, the last two decades have seen an increase in synchronous interaction, enabling the citizens of the world to interact without leaving their homes or offices but yet have access to an extensive menu of interaction opportunities – online games, platforms for diasporic communities, social media, entertainment content – where English continues to be the medium for a multitude of interactions.

2.2 Uses

The uses of the English language are extensive, although not all users use English in all these functions. Uses can be divided into private uses, public uses and international uses. Private uses, with familiar people, are typically spoken and informal, although letters and mobile communication add further channels of communication to private communication. Public uses include familiar and unfamiliar individuals, and take place in transactional contexts, ranging from trade to education to government. Written and spoken channels, including online and face-to-face options, are possible. Language tends to be more formal. International uses are in a way extensions of public uses, but not all regular public uses correspond to international counterparts.

Starting from the home and the most traditional, English is used as a language for private communication, written and spoken, in the intimate and personal domains. Informal registers of the language serve these domains, which trace their continuity to the very beginnings of the language in the fifth-century transplantation of Germanic dialects to Britain. For typical native speakers who grow up in English-speaking homes, this is the first use of English in their lives as young children. As they grow older, and become members of peer groups beyond the family, they add further informal registers to their repertoire, for instance at school, in sport and leisure activities, in societies, and even for socialising at the workplace. Not all these registers are straightforward informal versions of standard native-speaker English, as the typical uses of English in private domains include those by peer groups with such shared interests as calypso or country, hip-hop or rock music; inner city or working-class peer groups who develop strong in-group identities and a sense of shared style; supporters of particular sports clubs; or political activists who share a set of ideals and socialise together.

Private uses of English are not limited to typical native speakers either. In metropolitan areas in some former British colonies, multilingual peer groups use English as part of their communicative repertoire in informal domains, from Singapore to Nairobi, and from Johannesburg to Manila. Earlier, in language shift contexts brought about by slavery, English was called into service for private use despite extremely limited proficiency on the part of some interlocutors. English is often a code that neutralises the traditional cultural associations that indigenous languages carry, as noted by Kachru (1986), a marker of modernity for upwardly mobile young people from poor backgrounds, as much as it is an emblem of modernity for those who have enjoyed elite English-medium education.

Public uses of English display a measure of similarity across the former British Empire, as well as the United States and its colonial extensions. In many of these countries, English plays an important role as the language of education, government, law and business. This is self-evidently so in environments dominated demographically by native speakers of settler descent, but also applies to non-native and language-shift dominated contexts. The British colonies inherited the use of English in their public institutions from the colonial era, and in many cases, English has continued in that role after independence. S. Dasgupta (2014) speaks of the dual need for a break at the point of independence alongside a need for continuity to maintain public order through the administrative infrastructure that was already in place at that point in time – with the English language then being part of that continuity.[1] J. Das Gupta (1970) emphasises the delicate balancing act among local languages, questions of language rivalry that merge with ethnic and political conflicts, where the use of the colonial language offered a way to defuse the tensions. He notes that some of the earlier attempts to replace English with one or more indigenous languages did not go as far as envisaged during the early postcolonial period, and in some cases, earlier decisions were later reversed. The case of the Indian constitution that provided for the complete phasing out of English, which was ultimately reversed, is perhaps the most celebrated case, in the most populous former colony, but indigenisation policies were implemented with more practical success in some of the Indian neighbours – Sinhala in Sri Lanka, Malay in Malaysia, Urdu in Pakistan and after some conflict with Pakistan, Bengali in an independent Bangladesh.

In some settings, especially on the Caribbean islands, the English of the general population is not the variety used in prestigious public roles such as government and education, where a standard variety is used. This is in

---

1. Such continuity is not a logical necessity, at least not linguistically, but a choice, as shown by the very different choice of Indonesia to do away with Dutch completely and install Bahasa Indonesian, with Malay roots, as its national language at the same time that India developed its constitution (J. Das Gupta, 1970, p. 23).

part true for non-standard dialect users across the native English-speaking world, but the distance, and hence the adjustment required, tends to be more extensive for some (with a language-shift background) than others.

Public uses of English are becoming somewhat more prevalent in a number of European countries, especially in multinational companies and academia where internationalisation infiltrates the local public use. Thus, a colonial history that included English is no longer a requirement for the use of English in certain public roles. Even in South Korea, where the use of English is not nearly as extensive as in Northern Europe, an English language test score is a recommendation for certain employment opportunities within the country. This indicates an anticipation that internationalisation is going to impact the daily language use in business more and more. Korean parents, living in a largely monolingual country, even invest in English-language pre-school education for their young children, or extended living-abroad experiences for older children (Park, 2011).

International uses of English are central to the current global use; they are the most important reason for the difference in the global distribution and usefulness of English. Through the confluence of colonialism and the global British influence of the nineteenth century, its commercial and industrial success during this period and into the twentieth century, expanded considerably by the export and industrial success of the United States in the twentieth century, combined with political forces, English came to be the most widely used international language. There are several prominent international uses. A very prominent one is trade contact – which is not new, and has been happening since the seventeenth century at least, but the scale of such contact and the depth of penetration into societies changed after the Second World War. In the twenty-first-century world of distributed production, the communicative needs of the coordination of global supply and production chains and distribution of finished products to end users involve many more parties in a communicative exchange than the one-on-one context of seventeenth-century trade, where a small fleet of European traders didn't require many contact people to negotiate the deal with African or Asian traders, who likewise only needed a few middlemen (they were mostly men way back then).

The internationalisation of academia is a further impetus, where English is not only the dominant language of international conferences and international scholarly publication, but it also has a disproportionate share of the university textbook market. Textbooks are produced in many languages and are easily translated across languages, but these remain labour-intensive processes, whether writing new textbooks or even translating existing ones. In consequence, economy of scale considerations often lead to non-anglophone universities prescribing English-language textbooks, further enhancing the perceived importance of English as the carrier of the world's knowledge. That this is not a fundamental truth but a secondary association is not in question. Nevertheless, this is the kind of perception that drives marketing strategies and strengthens perceptions that young, upwardly mobile students, from affluent and impoverished backgrounds, may have when entering university.

Traders, industrialists and academics are seasoned global travellers, the former in business class and the latter in economy class, perhaps, but they are not the only globe trotters these days. With the increase in the reach of long-haul air travel and the frequency of flights, only temporarily halted by COVID-19, international tourism has been on the rise ever since the global economic recovery after the Second World War. To be sure, it is not a new phenomenon; Frankopan (2015, p. 263) notes that the concept of a Grand Tour was used in as early as 1670 by affluent Northern Europeans for a holiday trip to the cities of Italy, where the buying of curios (if often of the somewhat more expensive kind than present-day hand-carved miniature wild animals from OR Tambo airport in Johannesburg or informal markets outside the Serengeti National Park) was already a thing. Whether travelling to immerse oneself in the culture of Old Europe, or the animals of Africa, or the beaches of Indian Ocean islands, or the night life of New York, or many other stereotypical and less stereotypical destinations and purposes, English is far more likely to be used, for face-to-face interactions, but also on restaurant menus, public notices, and in airport and train station announcements.

The global reach of English-language entertainment and electronic media further strengthens the position and perceived utility of English. Such uses have received a very strong boost from the internet as dissemination and access route, while the rise of social media created yet another profile for global connectivity, which conspired to promote English even more, despite the many possibilities of online contact to support the use of many languages – possibilities that are also cultivated and exploited, but not in competition with the ongoing growth in the use of English.

The confluence of these various uses is to position English as 'the global language', with associations of affluence, modernity and upward mobility, as attested by government policy and choices made by parents and members of civil society in Korea as much as in India, and in Denmark as much as in Botswana, irrespective of the country's historical background. Local factors play a significant role in the variations, leading a country like Rwanda to replace its colonial language, French, with English, in order to strengthen regional connectivity within East Africa, or leading ASEAN to adopt English as its sole working language.

This should not be taken as an endorsement, nor should any student investigating English see the outcome as something to be celebrated, but probably also not as the outcome of some grand conspiracy by 'Big Angla'. There are certainly political actors involved and commercial interests at stake, and the computer algorithms as well as human metrics in weighing things like university rankings show very clear 'Anglo bias', but there is much happening by way of extending the use of other languages to new domains and revitalising languages under threat. We will return to the likely futures of English in the final chapter; for now, the focus is on understanding how the current position of English came about and what the worldwide use of English entails.

2.3 Acquisition

In order to use English, one has to acquire it. Like so many statements in this book, this is as self-evident as can be, except that in the case of English it isn't always. The users of English don't fall neatly into two categories of people who acquired the language as their 'mother tongue' and those who acquired it as a foreign or additional language in a classroom. There are indeed a very large number of English speakers who do acquire the language as their mother tongue from their own mothers, an experience of such lasting inspiration for some of these individuals that they write books on the topic, such as Bryson's *Mother Tongue* (1990), billed as a 'hymn to the mother tongue' on the blurb on the back cover of the edition on my bookshelf. This scenario is just as typical for many other languages of the world, large and small. The only issue one needs to raise is that English isn't the valuable resource it is across the globe because of this, because as a mother tongue, English is one among a good number of rather big languages with more than 100 million native speakers, but not the biggest – Mandarin Chinese has considerably more speakers, Spanish a few more, and English, Arabic and Hindi are relatively close (English being slightly larger if one disaggregates Urdu and Hindi, and there are challenges to drawing simple boundaries within Arabic).

Mother tongue acquisition, in the case of English, is rather diversified in terms of the input and the context, because a number of present-day Englishes were acquired in the context of language shift. These present-day varieties of English were acquired as a first language by children whose parents were not native speakers of English in the usual sense of being the children of native speakers themselves. Earlier (or current) generations of Irish speakers of English, South African Englishes in the Indian and Coloured communities, and Singaporean native speakers of English acquired their first language from their mothers, and other caregivers, and from their peers in the playground without the mothers having acquired English from their mothers. This is equally true for slave children who acquired English from their parents on the plantations. Several linguistic features of those present-day varieties can be traced to their language-shift history, but other than as an expression of cultural chauvinism, it makes little sense to regard such Englishes as belonging to the second league of native varieties, not quite in the 'league' of the 'actual' mother tongue varieties, or as 'illegitimate offspring', as Mufwene (1997) argues. Yet, the government of Thailand, for instance, decided in 2012 to remove the Republic of Ireland and South Africa from the list of countries of 'native speakers' who would be allowed to teach English in Thailand without the requirement of a language proficiency test (Van Zyl, 2016) – conveying exactly that sense of second-league Englishes to these teachers: multilingual backgrounds can be a legal barrier to native-speaker status.

Nor do all non-mother tongue speakers of English acquire their English in the idealised classroom setting, as one subject among many, while happily acquiring literacy in their mother tongue and mastering the world of knowledge through some other language. The latter is the case to a considerable degree for learners of English in continental Europe and the Far East, but for many other children, especially in parts of Sub-Saharan Africa and South and Southeast Asia, English is the medium of instruction from early on, a language that is not only a subject but also the means through which they acquire other knowledge. Yet, given the conditions of overcrowding prevailing in many classrooms in the developing world, including those countries historically part of the British Empire, and the problems with qualified teachers, many students leave the system without attaining very high proficiency in English. Conversely, though, for many present-day learners of English, privileged or poor, the school is no longer the sole context of acquisition. Out-of-class experience with English – through entertainment or advertising, for instance – is common rather than extra-ordinary.

Workplace acquisition was historically an important alternative to school education as a way of gaining proficiency in English. The historical results were typically at the lower end of the proficiency scale, with terms like 'broken', 'pidgin' and various synonyms used to describe the outcome; alternatively, a contextual label such as Butler English (also known as Kitchen English) or Boxwallah English indicated the professional context of the users, described by Kachru (1994, pp. 511–512) as Indian domestic servants of native English speakers in colonial India and as door-to-door sellers carrying their wares in boxes ([box] with [-*wallah*], a Hindi–Urdu suffix denoting owner or possessor). Modern-day workplaces may well provide the opportunity for more advanced proficiency than did being a domestic servant or vendor, but tourism is a new kind of context that demands relatively less from users of English (Schneider, 2016) than finalising a distributed supply chain arrangement across multiple countries and tax regimes. Also, modern-day workplace users of English will usually have had the benefit of formal education and will therefore refine and advance their mastery of English as they continue to use it in the workplace, unlike the experience of many learners of conventional foreign languages, who may find that their mastery of the language declines during adulthood, unless they take active steps to continue their exposure to and opportunities for use of such languages.

If one insists on the use of such idealised categories of mother tongue acquisition, foreign-language learner and reduced pidgin English, as if they represent empirical truths, one is going to have a difficult task to account for the worldwide use of English, and to tell the use of English apart from the use of languages like French or Spanish that also have many native speakers and are also widely taught as foreign languages in schools. Yes, many of these foreign-language students do travel to Paris and Madrid, or Ville de Québec and Ciudad de México, and know which accent to put on which vowel when writing the names of these former colonial cities in the other two major colonial languages of North America, but many, maybe most, tourists visiting these cities do not speak much French or Spanish and would have the expectation, rightly or wrongly, that they will be helped in English somewhere, somehow, by at least some of the locals working in the tourism industry. Speakers of Spanish and French, European or North American ones, would be pleasantly surprised if they were assisted in Spanish or French on their next trip to London or Sydney, but may not have the same expectation of such service that the English speakers have when travelling in the opposite direction.

The various contexts of acquisition for English all contribute to building the strength and utility of the language. One cannot ignore that the implicit act of relegating those whose acquisition occurred in atypical contexts to a second or third league raises an important ethical question: counting 'them' IN when it is about the superior position of English, its 'undisputed global language' status as per the blurb of *Mother Tongue*, but counting 'the rest' OUT as genuine, authentic, real speakers when claiming in the opening sentence of the book:

> More than 300 million people in the world **speak** English and the **rest**, it sometimes seems, try to. It would be **charitable** to say that the results are sometimes mixed. (Bryson, 1990, p. 1, emphases added)

The othering is quite obvious, but charitable much?

2.4 Attitudes

Attitudes towards the spread, use and type of English vary considerably. At the level of overall use, there are those who celebrate the connecting role of English and those who regard it as a killer language, and are able to provide clear reasons. At the level of when to use English, there are those who argue for an extended role of English in education, the odd debate about elevating English to the status of national language or official language in some unexpected quarter of the world, as much as there are efforts to curtail the use of English, sometimes through national legislation that requires signage to give a more prominent position to the national or some indigenous language, and to prohibit the supply of more information in English than in other languages. These kinds of attitudes have a strong political dimension, and to the extent that linguists contribute to such discussions, they often act in their capacity as citizens rather than as disciplinary experts, joining the democratic trend to 'do their own research' as many of the self-taught experts on COVID-19 and its treatment did in the period 2020–2022, not to mention the emerging specialists in election fraud worldwide. Much of what is written for general audiences relies more on the catchy headline that serves as clickbait than the substance of the research and argumentation – although of course, many popular works are as substantive and well researched as the best scholarly work, despite being well-written and a pleasure to read. If people are generally confident about making medical judgements based on what they read online, without training in medicine, then why should people feel any less hesitant about making linguistic judgements, given that they speak a language, after all, and all the more so if they speak English natively? They are entitled to have views on the matter, and if they can find others to agree with them, they may feel they have the start of what has been termed 'the weight of informed opinion'.[2]

Attitudes about the desirability of English cover a range of possibilities, and often generate strong reaction. One dimension concerns the effect that English has on the space for other languages, the idea that English takes up the space of other languages and leads to the death of languages. This is not something we need to speculate about; it happens, it has happened in the past – much of the content of Chapter 5 deals with this. The more difficult question is how to balance the value of a language of wider

---

2. I'm quoting, not out of context, but against the grain of the argument, from an author who passed away several decades ago, so let me not name the writer. Google tells me that several others writing in the English language have found occasion to use the expression, so it is probably not a violation of fair usage or anti-plagiarism restrictions.

use against the effect this has on other languages to serve their speakers well, and ultimately on the fairness towards speakers to participate in the world around them. This is more a debate about politics and ethics and less a question of attitudes that language users have, and will not be the central concern of this book, although I will return to some of the ethical concerns in the final chapter.

This book is more concerned with two attitudes among language users: why they choose the English language at all, and what their attitudes are towards different varieties of English. Native speakers do not choose English initially, they just get it from their parents. For some, the parents may have made a deliberate choice to replace another language with English as the language of the home, and their motivation is usually grounded in its perceived utility to enhance their children's opportunities in life. Non-native speakers today choose English in part because they get it in school, but more so because they get it outside school and can see that it is useful. Ordinary people are often less concerned than linguists with such choices, although as Bryson (1990) quite rightly observes, English is pretty useful and one can do many things with it. Kachru (1986) speaks of the alchemy of English, its uncanny attractiveness despite its history. Attitudes towards English as such are usually more instrumental than directed at integrating into the native English-speaking communities (Sridhar & Sridhar, 1986; Coetzee-Van Rooy, 2006). Yet, it signals a world-mindedness for many who view it favourably – positive associations with global citizenship and participation (Coetzee-Van Rooy, 2006), which is exactly why certain segments of societies want to keep the influence of English at bay – through restricting its use in society, even through legislation on advertising and public signage, or through protecting other languages against the influence that English might have on their vocabulary or grammar, under the banner of the fight against anglicisms (Gottlieb, 2020; Van Rooy, 2020). In the past, as will be made very clear in Chapter 5, the choice was not entirely free, and it is a matter of serious debate whether the choice made in the past century is without undue, if hidden, coercion (Phillipson, 1992, versus Spolsky, 2004). The voices of people on the ground are not always as salient in these debates, so there remains considerable room for research into the attitudes of ordinary language users, ideally research that asks open-ended questions rather than aiming to confirm 'research hypotheses based on the extant literature'.

Varieties of English are the subject of two kinds of attitudinal responses. One set of responses concern matters of right and wrong, or standard and non-standard. The other set of responses are concerned with the relative prestige of intuitively or overtly identifiable varieties or dialects of the language.

The debates about standards concern attitudes that take the idea of a standard variety as a given and something empowering for those who acquire it, in opposition to a view of the standard as something exclusive and discriminatory. Alternatives are either multiple standards or a rejection of standardising practices in favour of an inclusive ethos, blending into an everything-goes attitude in its most extreme guise. These discussions often mix political and power dimensions with educational dimensions, ideas of authority and privilege on the one hand, and ideas about educational goals and aspirations on the other. Kachru (1986) speaks of the schizophrenia that many users of English experience: they tend to aspire towards traditional prestige varieties as a mark of attainment in their mastery of English, yet their own practice is not aligned with their aspirations and does not seem to converge on their aspirations.

Prestige debates concern the acceptance of forms in everyday contexts, public more than private, but certainly not limited to the public use of language. The growing prestige of American English (but not all its manifestations), alongside certain non-standard or traditionally less prestigious varieties such as African American, Jamaican and Nigerian Englishes (Mair, 2013a), is one contemporary manifestation of these attitudes, but further back, the very acceptance of American or Australian English in the eyes of their own native speakers already constituted a landmark of linguistic liberation from the central control (if imaginary, perhaps) of British English – as richly documented by Schneider (2007), and much to the horror of Prince Charles and Samuel Coleridge, as noted in Chapter 1.

In the next chapter, we will look at how diverse varieties of English actually are, and why, before we consider the spectrum of world Englishes in Part 2 of the book.

3 Reshaping English

Ongoing change is inevitable in all languages, at least for as long as they remain in use – dead languages have been known to be less susceptible to change. This was an unpleasant thought for the likes of Jonathan Swift ('daily Corruptions') and Prince Charles ('make words that shouldn't be'), and a reason to take up the pen for many a twentieth-century contributor of letters to newspaper editors. One such gem, quoted by Milroy and Milroy (1991) from an anonymous writer in Northern Ireland, reads thus:

> For many years, I have been disgusted with the bad grammar used by school-leavers and teachers too sometimes, but recently on the lunch-time news, when a secretary, who had just started work with a firm, was interviewed her first words were 'I looked up and seen two men' etc. It's unbelievable to think, with so many young people out of work, that she could get such a job, but perhaps 'I seen' and 'I done' etc., is the usual grammar nowadays for office staff and business training colleges. (p. 38)

Moving across to the Outer Circle, the following complaint made its way to a newspaper in South Africa in 1994:

> When my eight-year-old daughter asked what the SAfm [radio station] newsreader meant by 'cow pools', it was the last straw! Here was more proof of SAfm's propagation of English errors. As an English teacher (MA, HED) and concerned parent, I was obliged to make my humble protest. [. . .]
>
> English is the lingua franca, so why not present this wonderful globally dominant language to the people within a paradigm of acceptable grammar and pronunciation.

Behind this anxiety is an unspoken belief that a language is a reified instrument, an object that can be improved or damaged, and therefore rendered more or less useful to perform its function. Furthermore, as any artisan or chef knows, one gets attached to one's tools, takes care of them polishes them, even sometimes displays them for their own sake. Another metaphor underpinning this set of beliefs is that language is a container, used to convey a message from sender to receiver, which raises the fear that if the container is damaged, the entire message may not be conveyed – parts of it might fall out in the act of transferring it.

English has changed and diversified in its pronunciation, grammatical forms, vocabulary and registers. This chapter introduces the levels of description very briefly, to pave the way for a more detailed examination of some changes in Part 2 of the book, before attending to some of the main underlying factors responsible for diversification and ongoing change in English.

3.1 Linguistic variants in English

English varies from one place to the next, from one speaker to the next, and from one situation to the next. Such variation can be observed in all components of the language. The range of variants are described in general terms in this chapter, while characteristic features of different contexts of use are presented in more specific terms in Part 2 of this book. The discussion will start with variability in vocabulary and pronunciation, before proceeding to the less salient but still pervasive variation that can be found in the grammar and style of English usage across the world. It is often helpful for our understanding to distinguish between the ways in which the native speakers of English and the (historically) non-native speakers participated in contributing the variants.

3.1.1 Vocabulary

Vocabulary is noticeably different in English right across the world, although one should not forget the considerable shared vocabulary of most users of the language. Borrowing and transfer from the indigenous languages are an important factor contributing to worldwide diversification, since the other languages that come into contact with English are different from place to place. Speakers of English who moved to new places borrowed nomenclature from speakers of indigenous languages or other settler languages to refer to the local landscape, fauna and flora. Relatively little contact is required for such vocabulary adoptions to take place. Place names and names for major landmarks are the most typical and often the only borrowings taking place in the earliest phases of contact (Schneider, 2007, p. 36), for instance the names of American states with indigenous origins, such as *Alaska*, *Kentucky* or *Massachusetts*, or the endemic Australian *kangaroo* and New Zealand *kiwi* are names borrowed from indigenous languages. Such borrowing usually involves heavy phonological adjustment, even distortion, as the English speakers seldom acquire sufficient proficiency in the indigenous languages to borrow terms in a phonologically or grammatically faithful way. Speakers of indigenous languages can also contribute, by transferring words to English when they do not find a suitable English form to express the meaning they have in mind. In this book, despite limitations of the metaphors, borrowing is used to describe what native speakers do when they take words from indigenous languages, and transfer to describe what speakers of indigenous languages do when they carry words across to English.

English vocabulary is extended through coinage as well, if usually on the basis of existing word-formation processes such as compounding, and using native English morphemes. English speakers can form new compounds that describe the denoted object or idea, for example *Blue Mountains* (Australia), *Rocky Mountains* (USA) and *Table Mountain* (South Africa), although in the latter two cases, other languages already had designations with similar meanings which were adopted (in loan translation) by English speakers when they first encountered these landmarks.

A vocabulary strategy that also contributes new words is the **naming** of places or other salient landmarks in the new space after people or places from the geographical and political heritage of the English speakers, a process known as eponymy. This naming strategy accounts for the occurrence of place names from the UK and other English-sounding names in the settler-dominated colonies like Australia, Canada and New Zealand. The Canadian city *London* has about 400,000 inhabitants, a bit smaller than its English namesake, and the South African *East London*, at 300,000, a bit smaller still. Even *Derry* in Northern Ireland had *London-* attached to it, although the full name of the city is not always used, especially not in the Republic of Ireland.

Semantic change to existing English lexical items is the other major source of variation and ultimately differentiation between varieties of English across the world. These adjusted meanings – through semantic extension or by narrowing or specialising the meaning of the term – show that the speakers notice a similarity with the new concept to be designated, but the altered meaning comes to be conventionalised in that place and is not necessarily understood in exactly the same way elsewhere in the English-speaking world. This is evident in the extended way the term 'bush' is used in Australia, to refer to the sparsely populated areas of the country outside the major metropolitan centres, irrespective of vegetation. Thus, an arid area with rather few trees can also be called *bush* in Australia. A similar meaning is in evidence in South Africa, reinforced by the Afrikaans equivalent *bos* that differs from its Dutch cognate *bosch* in the same way that the colonial bushes differ from British bushes. Yet, in Australia and South Africa, *bush* is still used in the sense that corresponds to the uses of the term in the Northern Hemisphere, becoming slightly more polysemous, therefore. As an example of specialisation, the South African term *cubbyhole* denotes the glove compartment of a car (on the passenger seat side), a much more specialised use of the term than elsewhere in the world (Silva, 1996, p. 200).

3.1.2 Pronunciation

New varieties of English sound different from their input varieties in a number of ways. Native varieties often contain sounds that mostly correspond to different British varieties that served as input, but because of the diversified input, the speakers who formed the new settler communities made choices and accepted some input sounds and sound patterns, while letting go of others. In phonological terms, the settler varieties tend to have the same phonemes (contrastive underlying sounds), while the permissible combinations of sounds into syllables (their phonotactic patterns) and the effects that come about from the combinations of syllables into utterances such as rhythm, stress and intonation (their suprasegmental characteristics) are reasonably similar too. Differences are mainly in the **allophones**, the specific sounds that are spoken to give audible shape to the underlying phonemes. Thus, many speakers of American English use a flapped allophone [ɾ], a shortened version of [r] with some similarities to a very quick [d], as the realisation of phonemes /t/ and /d/ in the middle of a word between two vowels, resulting in the words *ladder* and *latter* sounding very similar – [læɾɹ], although the difference may still be signalled by a somewhat longer pronunciation of the [æ] of *ladder*.

In the case of non-native varieties, further allophones are often introduced because the languages that those speakers already spoke prior to their contact with English had slightly, or sometimes very, different allophones for the same phoneme. Since these allophones convey the same basic sound, speakers tend to take the best available form from the linguistic resources they already have, and use that to speak English. The English phoneme /r/ has a range of pronunciation variants, but for most Australian, New Zealand, British, American and Canadian speakers, the dominant allophone is vowel-like in quality, without the tongue-tip making contact with any part of the inside of the mouth, represented by the phonetic symbol [ɹ]. Speakers of Afrikaans, who are generally very fluent users of English if they complete their secondary education in South Africa or Namibia, sometimes transfer the Afrikaans allophone [r], which involves trilling, brief contact between the tongue and the alveolar ridge, usually three or four times during the articulation of the sound. It leads to no confusion, since the same phoneme is conveyed, but it is noticeably different. The same allophone is also prevalent among Indian English speakers. Likewise, Afrikaans and Indian English speakers share a propensity not to aspirate the voiceless plosives /p, t, k/. While many native speakers have aspirated phonemes [pʰ, tʰ, kʰ] in syllable-initial position before a vowel, these second-language users tend to use the unaspirated allophones [p, t, k], but for different reasons. Afrikaans has no aspirated allophones in widespread use, while many of the North Indian languages have a phonemic contrast between aspirated and unaspirated voiceless plosives, and to their ears, the English plosives sound more similar to the unaspirated than aspirated variants in their prior linguistic background, which is then their preferred allophone when speaking English (Gargesh, 2008; Watermeyer, 1996).

Non-native varieties in many parts of the world also make use of suprasegmental features from their prior languages when speaking English. This inclination is likely strengthened by the important role that school education plays in the acquisition, since a lot of the input is written, without being linked to pronunciation immediately, and to the extent that most teachers are native speakers of similar languages to the learners, there is constant reinforcement of syllable-timed rhythm – where each syllable attracts almost equal force and duration, and often also different stress-placement patterns for some words.

A final source of difference between English varieties in different places is the adoption into English of phonemes from loan words, which then become available for even wider use in the language. One such example is the incorporation of the velar fricative /x/ in South African English, originally in loanwords from Afrikaans, such as *gogga* [xɔxa] 'small bug' and *gatvol* [xatfɔl] 'fed up', but also in use for newer borrowings from indigenous languages, such as the name of the most populous province *Gauteng* [xaʊtɛŋ], from the Sotho languages, meaning 'place of gold', with the stem *gaut-* in turn borrowed from Afrikaans *goud* by the Sotho languages earlier. Given the widespread use of loanwords in South African English in which the /x/ occurs, most native speakers of English also show the ability to pronounce the phoneme in a way that corresponds to the source words, with only a few speakers persisting with an anglified pronunciation of *Gauteng* as [haʊtɛŋ], marking such speakers informally as somewhat less well integrated into the broader society.

3.1.3 Grammar

New grammatical patterns can arise in a number of ways. Existing patterns can be tweaked or used in different ways, which will over time lead to grammatical changes (Leech et al., 2009), as is usual for grammatical change in any language. In the case of world Englishes, the transportation of English to new places brings two further sources of new grammatical constructions into play. Speakers of other languages can transfer in less or more transparent ways patterns from these other languages to their own English, and if others do the same, there is the possibility that these grammatical patterns become stable features of English in that place. Alongside possible transfer, speakers of other languages can create new constructions that are not (in the main) based on examples of their other languages, but simply new ways of combining words in English, since as adult speakers of an additional language, they do not have the same grammatical representations that a native speaker acquired as a child (Hoffmann, 2021; Van Rooy, 2010). This could be in the form of reanalysis, or new generalisations that are wider or narrower than similar ones among native speakers. Both these types of sources of new constructions are in a sense expected, one could say inevitable, in the context of language contact.

To the extent that access to English-language input is limited and the communicative demands for the use of English are extensive, as was the case in the plantation settings in particular, the input is very likely to be analysed and cognitively interpreted in different constructional patterns than those current among native speakers: the input is insufficient for close approximation of 'old speakers' of English, and 'new speakers' of English have to be creative to make the language useful to their communicative purposes, thereby making their own creative generalisations. Of course, the outcome of these processes can be interpreted as errors, as a failure to master English – as is done by the two complaint writers at the beginning of this chapter. Such a judgement is true to the extent that English is a thing that is cast in stone, or at least relatively fixed and stable, but such is the case only for already established contexts of use among typical ('old') native speakers. If (the) English (the language and its ancestral speakers) had stayed at home in Britain and hadn't spread to other places in the world, then we would not be having this discussion. It seems prudent to make sense of the process of change without being judgemental about it, while dealing with the judgements as separate facts about language users in an appropriate place.[1]

---

1. If we want to be judgemental, we should talk about colonialism first, and then about language change following from colonial conquest, domination and occupation. But since both these things happened, it is sensible to understand them as well, which is what this book is about.

One example of a grammatical construction based on transfer is the *after* perfect of Irish English ('You're after ruinin' me' in the meaning of 'You have just ruined me', Filppula, 2008, p. 330), modelled after a corresponding construction in Irish. Another example from South African English is the use of *and them* to indicate a group of people associated with the noun preceding the conjunction *and*, for example 'my brother and them' or 'Kobie and them', based on the Afrikaans pattern (Branford & Venter, 2016, p. 170), where the 3rd person plural pronoun (*hulle* 'they/them/their' – Afrikaans uses a single form for all cases) is attached to a proper noun or a noun denoting a relation to the speaker. In Afrikaans, no conjunction is used, so the English form is not a direct translation but a construction influenced by the option in Afrikaans. The crucial point about both examples in this paragraph is that they are being used by native speakers of English alongside the (native) speakers of Irish or Afrikaans who coined the original pattern by analogy to their other language.

3.1.4 Discourse and pragmatics

Variation in English comes about when it is used by new users or in new uses. The new users may have particular ideas or particular ways of phrasing things that have not been expressed through English before, and hence they add elements from their linguistic repertoire when using English. This might not necessarily imply new vocabulary or grammar but new combinations of elements that gradually become established as conventional usage patterns. New elements may well be added as English comes to be used by more people who contribute to it.

An example of such a style difference is provided by the Nigerian author Chinua Achebe (1965) when reflecting on his own writing. He offers the following passage from his own writing in *Arrow of God*, which can be contrasted to a version written by an imaginary native speaker from the colonial centre:

> I want one of my sons to join these people and be my eyes there. If there is nothing in it you will come back. But if there is something there you will bring home my share. The world is like a Mask, dancing. If you want to see it well you do not stand in one place. My spirit tells me that those who do not befriend the white man today will be saying had we known tomorrow. (p. 29)

The imaginary alternative could have been:

> I am sending you as my representative among those people – just to be on the safe side in case the new religion develops. One has to move with the

times or else one is left behind. I have a hunch that those who fail to come to terms with the white man may well regret their lack of foresight. (p. 29)

Such uses and innovations are not limited to literary writing. Conventional African metaphors, rooted in notions of family and mutual obligations, pervade corpora of African English, as shown by Wolf and Polzenhagen (2009). Mutual obligations within society, as well as transgressions of those obligations, are conveyed in food metaphors, for instance, as the following extracts show (Wolf & Polzenhagen, 2009, p. 93).

(1) You eat money the way locusts eat tons of green.
(2) ... members fed fat on gifts destined for disaster victims.
(3) I didn't open treasury for people to chop money.

The food metaphors are widely shared by the indigenous languages of West and East Africa, where the data analysed by Wolf and Polzenhagen (2009) come from, and are put to use in English too.

In a few cases, the cultural context in which English is used gives rise to very different kinds of English-language communication. A celebrated case for world Englishes scholars is matrimonial advertisements in India, published in the matrimonials section of English-language newspapers. Kachru (1982/2015b, pp. 95–101) speaks of the transformation of text types, drawing on lexical and grammatical options but particularly innovating at the discourse level, in the case of matrimonial advertisements where educated, English-using families with traditional views on social arrangements in the Indian society seek matches for their children. This practice continues into the present, as Polzenhagen and Frey (2017) show in their analysis of a corpus of matrimonial advertisements from 2010. They show that such advertisements also occur elsewhere in the English-using world, but the English used in the British and Indian advertisements have very different rhetorical styles and use different vocabularies. Such common English words as *boy* and *girl* carry different meanings in Indian English – they may be used for adults approaching forty even, as long as they are not married, for example 'Boy up to 40 Yrs reply'. The interpretation of such words is premised on a world-view that full mature adulthood requires marriage, hence one remains a boy or girl, at least in some respects, even in one's late thirties if one is not married (Polzenhagen & Frey, 2017, p. 180). An extensive vocabulary for caste and related requirements, for example 'clean shaven' in the context of unconventional Sikh men who cut their hair and shave their beard, is another such culturally embedded expression that is easily understood in the Indian context but not beyond without acquired cultural knowledge (Polzenhagen & Frey, 2017, p. 181). This is not peculiar to India, and should not be exoticised. The expression

OHAC for 'own house and car' in dating advertisements in other parts of the English-using world, inhabited by native speakers, equally requires intimate contextual knowledge to recognise but especially to make sense of – where a particular type of financial and social independence is a desirable quality in a potential partner.[2]

3.2 General processes reshaping English worldwide

English displays variation across the world, as illustrated by the examples in this chapter so far. To understand the variability better, the remainder of this chapter is devoted to understanding the processes giving rise to it. The starting point for such an understanding is to make a clear distinction between the **sources of variation** and the **processes of selection** among the variants available to speakers and writers. This distinction follows the evolutionary metaphor for understanding language change developed by Croft (2000), and employed in similar ways by Mufwene (2001, 2008).

Sources of variation account for the introduction of forms to the feature pool of English in a particular place – the English-language input of the speakers moving to that new place, permanently or temporarily, alongside the innovations that accrue over time, which come into competition with pre-existing forms and which may ultimately gain acceptance in the place of the pre-existing forms. Four broad sources of variation and innovation can be identified: diversity in input, localisation, contact and language learning. These sources of variation all build on a relatively stable, shared starter pack of 'English' that forms the foundation of mutual understanding, those forms that those who communicate with one another use and understand in similar enough ways to make communication possible. The starter pack is rather bigger for settlement colonies, the Inner Circle varieties, and speakers arrive with that starter pack in place. The starter pack is made available in smaller increments to learners of English who initially don't have it at all. Some of them have more time to acquire English, as their other languages continue to serve some or most of their communicative needs, but others, particularly the slaves of plantation colonies, have little time but lots of needs to be served, and thus acquire the English coming their way in a different manner. So, the starter pack is not equally accessible or available to all, and speakers will supplement it in suitable ways to serve their communicative needs best.

In the initial presentation of these four sources, the focus is on their contribution to (new) variants, without regard for the likelihood

---

2. My attention has been drawn to this example by my colleague Julia Bacskai-Atkari.

of success. The sources introduce features to a feature pool for possible selection. The processes of selection are mainly social (Croft, 2000), although certain psycholinguistic factors play a bigger role in these environments than in monolingual environments, and determine which forms gain acceptance and become relatively stable parts of the local variety of English, and which forms eventually don't make it and fade into oblivion. The selection processes are considered in the last part of this chapter.

3.2.1 Source of input and variation

The use of English anywhere requires some English-language **input**. In the earliest stages, such input came from settlers or colonial administrators who moved, temporarily or permanently, to the new place. The diversity of input is proportional to the dialect background of the individuals moving to that space. Similarities between native Australian, New Zealand and South African settler Englishes are due to the similarity in the dialects of the founding speakers – with a higher proportion of linguistic forms from speakers of Southeast English dialects than any other region in Britain, resulting in such features as non-rhoticity and higher lax front vowels in words like *kid*, *bed* and *bad* than in other parts of the native English-speaking world.

Any subsequent new groups of settlers may potentially increase the amount of variability, but if there is a strong enough founder's effect already in place, due to the demographic size of the already settled population, the effect of subsequent settler populations is ultimately less. Thus, the initial input matters more than subsequent input, unless the initial input is heavily diluted by demographic changes. This happened in the transition from the homestead phase of slavery to the plantation economies, where much larger numbers of new slaves, who were not speakers of English upon arrival, had significant effects on the development of English on the Caribbean islands and parts of the United States, as Chapter 5 sets out in more detail.

Non-native speakers are equally dependent on input, and the same dialect diversity also plays a role in the early acquisition of English by non-native speakers. Thus, there are examples where the variety that emerges among a group of second-language users displays variants that were part of their input, even though those variants did not survive in native-speaker dialects. Subsequent changes resulted in those forms getting lost among native speakers, but non-native speakers and their offspring were not affected in a similar way and thus continued the use of those forms (irrespective of whether the offspring shifted to English or continued to use English as an additional language alongside other languages in their repertoire). One such example that has been studied carefully is the English used on the Cape Flats in the Western Cape of South Africa by descendants of slaves, indigenous people and biracial people who had earlier shifted to Afrikaans and then came into contact with English since the early nineteenth century. Input retentions that did not survive among ancestral native speakers but did survive among Cape Flats users include the dative of advantage (Mesthrie & Bhatt, 2008, pp. 191–192) in example (4) and the use of unstressed *do* (Mesthrie, 1999) in example (5).

(4a) ... your memorialist then built **him** a house on a spot of Ground. [Input example from nineteenth-century South African settler English] (Mesthrie & West, 1995, p. 124)

(4b) I'm gonna buy **me** a car. [Contemporary Cape Flats English] (Mesthrie & Bhatt, 2008, p. 191)

The highlighted pronouns, *him* in (4a) and *me* in (4b) are both co-referential with the subject and are likely to be expressed with a reflexive pronoun in most other varieties, where the context demands that the beneficiary be made visible. It could also be omitted if such information is not required in context.

(5a) My men have been very refractory and **did refuse** to work for a while. [Input example from nineteenth-century South African settler English] (Mesthrie, 1999, p. 67)

(5b) It was under the English flag, you follow. That time we were all under the English flag. Now under the English flag then England ruled South Africa, you follow. England **did rule** South Africa. Now England ruled South Africa so they had to speak English too. [Contemporary Cape Flats English] (Mesthrie, 1999, pp. 62–63)

Mesthrie's claim is not that the settler input is the only source or cause, but that there is clear overlap between a variant in the input that got lost in settler English in South Africa while it remained current among Cape Flats users, who initially acquired English as a second language in a community with long-standing bilingualism to the present. He also shows in the case of unstressed *do* that there was further input of the pattern in the use of English by continental European missionaries who worked for British missionary societies in South Africa and were teachers of English and regular conversation partners of earlier generations of the present-day community during the earliest phase of contact. Mesthrie (1996a) shows that in many cases, missionaries to South Africa were themselves non-native speakers of English but nevertheless provided input in the schools, which were the principal setting for the transmission of English to non-native speakers in nineteenth-century South Africa.

In the twentieth century, input from non-native speakers became very prominent in schools as education systems across the former British exploitation colonies expanded, and likewise for native speakers of varieties of English in the former plantation colonies. Such input tended to contain many features not present in the English of ancestral native speakers, and continued to influence the forms that emerged and stabilised in these settings.

From the perspective of a social judgement made in the present, one can think of these variant forms as un-English – a case of group fossilisation, according to Selinker (1972, pp. 215–216). He is adamant, though, that from a psycholinguistic perspective, the case of Indian English (or other such non-native varieties) is not different from that of learners of English (or other languages) in contexts where the primary input is from native speakers. He does not elaborate on the point, but it seems useful to separate what is different from what is similar. From the perspective of the individuals involved, they can only acquire what they have available as input, whether they acquire English as a native language or subsequent to the acquisition of another language. Thus, in part, a closer understanding of the variability of input will contribute much to our understanding of the varieties that emerge, in ways that *a priori* judgements of error and deviations will not help to illuminate. To the extent that group fossilisation emerges from the input itself, it is no different from the acquisition of the input forms of a native language. To the extent that learners deviate from their own input, along the lines that Selinker (1972) explores, there is indeed a second-language learning phenomenon at play, which is considered below. The application of the interlanguage idea in accounting for deviant properties of non-native Englishes is not always sensitive to the difference between what is not acquired in native-like ways despite being present in the input (incomplete acquisition) and what is not acquired because it wasn't a prominent enough part of the input. Such insensitivity is often premised on an unspoken assumption that 'native English' is the input – while the overt assumption is in any case that native English is the goal of learning. If the analysis of data is methodologically grounded on a comparison between the learner's production and what a native speaker would say under the same circumstances, then the distinction between a model/goal and the actual input is not drawn, which becomes misleading if the analysis is used to explain the process of acquisition, rather than the educational 'deficit' to be overcome. The assumption is warranted in the minority case of second-language acquisition by outsiders in a settler-dominant context, the Inner Circle, but not elsewhere in the English-speaking world, the Outer and Expanding Circles where native input contributes a minority of the variants in the feature pool.

Let us not ignore the elephant in the room, though. Second-language learning (or acquisition), the elephant, is another unavoidable contributor to variation in English, and one that can be wished away as little as language contact. This factor has played an important role in the history of English since the earliest days, both when the language is acquired as a first language and when it is acquired as a second language. It acts as a selection mechanism too, in that adult second-language learners and younger children, as first-language learners, may select differently. Children tend to make fewer abstractions and thus reproduce the most dominant forms in their input more closely, which renders their role almost invisible in non-mobile contexts with limited dialect and language contact. When they are confronted with diversity in the input, they are forced to choose, and in that sense make a contribution to the selection of the most frequent input forms, as explained in Chapter 4 in more detail. The older the learner, and especially when learning a second language, the more predictable, systematic forms will be selected, those that fit better with more abstract patterns that adults are able to extract. While this is still largely a matter of selection, rather than innovation, it also potentially leads to innovation in the guise of 'overgeneralisation': adult learners see a pattern and use that pattern to formulate expressions that are not already part of their input, leading to their coining of new forms, which are deviant if judged from the perspective of the input or the perspective of the native-speaker child (Van Rooy, 2010).

The English language, like a few others, has had extensive periods of second-language acquisition in its history, and therefore tends to display more regularity and transparency than languages that are isolated and acquired by children only in relative isolation from contact with speakers of other languages, such as Icelandic, or languages of traditional hunter-gatherer communities that remained untouched by extensive contact with others for several millennia (McWhorter, 2007). Language learning does not account for all patterns in English, but it strengthens the occurrence of variants like regular past tense forms (*learned, burned, dreamed*, but also a form like *goed* which native speakers usually don't encounter or use) rather than irregular ones (*learnt, burnt, dreamt, went*), and transparent plural forms rather than lexical or other kinds of exceptions (*fishes, sheeps, luggages, informations*). The introduction and higher frequency of these more regular forms – if deviant from the perspective of the input variety grammar – may ultimately lead to the selection of these forms, since they become part of the input in the new environment.

A different source of variation, which is not always distinguished systematically from second-language learning, is localisation. When English is used in a new context, there are things to say that English has not previously been called upon to say. In order to be fully adequate as a means of communication, English has to localise. From the perspective of settlers who arrive in the new locale with a language that has served them well to communicate about life in another place, there is a need to add further features to be able to communicate effectively in the new context. Minimally, an extended vocabulary is required for the new landscape, fauna and flora of the new place, and also, to various degrees, to talk to and about the people already living there.

Non-native users of English who have an existing language acquire a new language, but this new language – either because they only acquire parts of it or because the language really has never evolved to address particular aspects of the material or social reality – does not give them the words and the strategies for combining words into discourse to talk about all aspects of their lived experience. To the extent that it becomes necessary or useful to do just that, they will draw on their other languages to expand the expressive power of English in order to serve their communicative needs adequately. This is the process of *nativisation* that Achebe illustrates with the nativised versus non-nativised passage in the novel *Arrow of God*, where the English language has to be remoulded to convey adequately a different experience and a different understanding of the world. It can take the shape of vocabulary transfer, as well as rhetorical and metaphorical transfer, but may even extend to grammatical or phonological transfer, to use patterns that serve the speakers well in other languages to also serve their communicative needs when speaking or writing English.

Language contact is related to localisation, but these two processes do not overlap in full. It works in tandem with second-language acquisition, except that it does not represent the psycholinguistic process of forming new generalisations about English, but rather the resources of the other languages that become available to either transfer directly – especially in the form of vocabulary – or provide templates for the formation of generalisations about English usage. Where localisation is in part goal-directed, the effects of language contact are largely unavoidable. In the contact situation, speakers with knowledge of other languages bring that knowledge along in their encounters with English, and can potentially introduce subconsciously elements from these other languages into the English that they speak, since the multiple languages in the minds of bilingual speakers are usually all activated, rather than sequentially activated or suppressed. Once this happens, the features and forms introduced in this manner become part of the feature pool of input forms and can potentially be selected by other users of English in that environment too.

The effects of contact range from allophones and phonemes from other languages, for example using an aspirated lateral click /ǁʰ/ to pronounce the name of the language isiXhosa in the manner that the sound represented by the letters 'xh' is pronounced by speakers of the language itself (as opposed to finding the closest English equivalent, usually [kʰ]), to vocabulary items (loanwords), to grammatical patterns or grammatical functions of patterns that correspond to indigenous grammatical patterns in some recognisable manner. The effects of language contact at the level of introducing new variants are fundamentally unavoidable, since speakers of other languages do not switch these languages off when speaking English – a multilingual person is not several separate monolinguals hosted in the same head. The fact that not all potentially contact-induced elements are ultimately present in a particular form of English is due to the way selection works, not due to different degrees of potential language contact phenomena in the linguistic feature pool.

3.2.2 Competition and selection determining the outcome

We know that variants entering the 'feature pool' of local linguistic ecologies do not all become established as new features of the local variety or varieties; the vast majority of variants come and go without leaving permanent traces. Who knows whether the readers of this book will still recall the terms *plandemic* or *covidiot* in future? They certainly still had traction at the time of writing, mid-2022, as a kind of rallying call for a particular set of ideas, but as the SARS-CoV-2 virus fades into history, one hopes, the terms may lose their currency. An invention that has not (yet) quite made it into any substantial speech community is the novel coinage *covfefe*, coined at 12.06 a.m. (Eastern Daylight Time zone in North America, to be more precise) on 31 May 2017 by a very prominent user of English, Mr Donald J. Trump, at the time the president of the most populous English-speaking country, the United States of America. Despite lots of humour, the word has not gained traction beyond self-referring to the event itself, mostly in jest, to what one can only presume to have been a typing error.

In thinking about variation in English, one has to distinguish the sources of variation, which have been reviewed in the previous section, and the actual selection of variants to become established for a group of speakers, which is done in this section. The precondition for a variant to be selected is that it has to be **present** in the linguistic feature pool of the ecology in a particular place. This is a very obvious truism, but one that is denied by the simplifying assumption that learners 'aim' to acquire the standard native variety. Reduplication of wh-interrogatives, such as *who-who*, *where-where* or *what-what*, is present in Indian South African English, with the meaning of several entities being asked about – who of several people, where of several places, what of several things. There is a potential contact source for this feature, although not a direct one, in Dravidian languages which were used alongside English in the South African community where the usage originated (Mesthrie, 1996b, p. 94). If one consults the large international corpora of contemporary English online (english-corpora.org), it is striking that in GloWbE and NOW, such duplicated forms occur exceedingly rarely, and hardly in the sense of Indian South African English, except for the form *what-what*, which has non-negligible frequencies, although its use remains limited to South Africa. This form, but not the others, has gained traction beyond the Indian community in South Africa, and is generalising to a general-purpose noun for something not labelled explicitly, as in the following report from a South African newspaper, where a politician – a black South African who speaks an indigenous African language natively – is quoted directly.

> (6) Another ANC MP, Bongani Bongo, questioned why the committee was responding to the former public protector's recommendations regarding 'the executive ethics **what-what**', but not addressing Public Protector Busisiwe Mkhwebane's recommendations for remedial action regarding the SA Reserve Bank. (https://www.news24.com/News24/we-dont-want-no-ethics-what-what-20170909, emphasis added)

If the form was not present in the first instance, it would not have been selected because it simply wasn't a candidate for selection. Once a form is present in an ecology, it is still not a given that it will be selected, as is the case for the other interrogative reduplications from Indian South African English, like *who-who* and *where-where*. Many input forms or subsequent innovations do not get selected and hence do not become stable features of a variety. The forces affecting selection can be divided into three groups: a set of conservative social forces which favour the continued selection of existing dominant or prestige variants; a set of neutral probabilistic forces whose influence is below the level of awareness and may be regarded as psycholinguistic rather than social in nature; and a set of progressive forces that favour the adoption of innovative variants, particularly attitudinal factors and social alignment with members of groups that the interlocutor seeks association with.

Standard variants that are already part of the feature pool enjoy continued selection due to **conservative** selection pressures. For some forms, the prestige associations count in favour of their selection, possibly also stimulated by the work of the education system to encourage the use of the standard variety, insofar as speakers aspire to use the prestige variety. This kind of sentiment is displayed by the character Ofilwe in the South African novel *Coconut* (Matlwa, 2007), when she explains why she doesn't inform her mother about a high-status event, the parents' evening at school.

> (7) Mama didn't go to high school, so what was the point of telling her about the parents' evenings? In theory, parents' evenings are there to give parents an opportunity to assess their children's scholastic progress, [. . .]. In practise it is an exhibition night [. . .] It is a night out at the gallery, where children, in their longest school skirts and most diligent shirts, display to each other their accomplished parents [. . .] Mama would not understand any of that. I care about her, that is why I didn't want to put her through all of that. Besides, **Mama's English is ghastly**. (p. 51, emphasis added)

Earlier in the novel, Ofilwe narrates the attempts of her white, native-speaker peers to 'correct' her pronunciation of English towards the high-status accent, while no similar attempt is made to pronounce her African name correctly – she quickly becomes *Fifi* to her teachers and peer group. The novel also shows how this goes wrong through its portrayal of another character, Uncle, who has similarly acquired the prestige variety in school, and liberally quotes Shakespeare. Uncle's mastery of the prestige form of English earns him the dubious accomplishment of doubling as a figurehead for a fake black employment company, using his accent and standard language vocabulary to portray an accomplished senior executive, while in fact he is employed as a security guard and does not carry the decision-making responsibility nor receive the remuneration consistent with his purported position as a well-to-do business associate. Yet, despite the obvious barriers to group membership, some of the characters in the novel aspire to and to various degrees succeed in acquiring and using standard English. They are guided by the aspiration towards the opportunities for socio-economic advancement that such a variety of English might bring, irrespective of whether those opportunities and membership of the standard-language user groups are genuine or not. This fictionalised scenario is supported by the findings of recent research by Mesthrie (2010, 2017) on the speech of the younger, highly educated black elite, whose speech indeed comes to resemble the speech of their white social and age peers to a considerable degree.

An important component of the conservative selection process is the stigmatisation of certain features as markers of low-status group membership. This is true for individuals from a historically native-speaker and non-native background. A feature like /h/-dropping was present in the input to South African and New Zealand English in the nineteenth century. One of the first generation of settlers, by the name of Jeremiah Goldswain, was born in Buckinghamshire, England in 1802, and arrived in the Cape Colony in 1820. In the latter years of his life, he wrote down the story of his life, in his relatively unschooled English, which turns out to be a treasure trove of information about one of the input dialects to early South African English (Siebers, 2010). Goldswain's *Chronicle* (1946) contains examples like the following.

(8) to our Great astonishment they had maid **oles** in the ice
(9) He Gave me sume Good advice and promised me that if I **beaved** as I ought to do
(10) it wold be thear **hone** faltes
(11) we waited for about half an hour wen Mr. **Hadam** Gilfillen came and informed ous

In examples (8) and (9), a word that would be pronounced with an [h] in present-day South African English is spelled without it – *holes, behaved* – whereas in examples (10) and (11), we find instances of hypercorrection, where a word pronounced without an [h] is spelled as if it should have an [h] – *own, Adam*. Jointly, such examples indicate that Goldswain did not consistently use [h] in his own pronunciation but was aware of this stigmatised feature, and in his attempt to 'spell correctly', he sometimes overdid it by inserting an extra letter *h* where none would have been present in the typical pronunciation around him. The implicit awareness of the stigmatised quality of the feature is not just a private thing among people like Goldswain. School inspectors in New Zealand were painfully aware of this, as Gordon et al. (2004) record with reference to school inspectors' reports from the 1880s until the first decade of the twentieth century, at which point they began to document that the 'sin of omission and commission' (p. 187) was receding and disappearing in New Zealand. Analysis of speaker data from the Origins of New Zealand English Corpus (ONZE), recorded in the late 1940s and representing speakers born from the middle of the nineteenth century to the beginning of the twentieth century, shows that speakers born before 1867 were more prone to h-dropping than those born later, speakers born in the next decade until 1876 showed a considerable decline among female speakers but not yet male speakers, but men born after 1876 also had relatively few instances of h-dropping if not the disappearance of the phenomenon, a pattern that is still true for present-day New Zealand English (Gordon et al., 2004, pp. 190–191). Trudgill (2004), who also analysed data from the ONZE corpus, points out that many stigmatised features tended to be lost within the first generation after transplantation of settler Englishes to a new geographical area.

The effect of the same stigmatisation is also true for non-native users, perhaps even more forcefully. Afrikaans has a trilled [r] as the principal allophone of the phoneme /r/, and usually pronounces the /r/ in syllable codas. Native-speaker South African English has an approximant [ɹ] and does not generally pronounce the /r/ in codas. Early (Hopwood, 1928) and mid-twentieth-century (Pretorius, 1953) records show that Afrikaans speakers at the time persistently used the Afrikaans phonetic realisation and phonotactic distribution when speaking English. By the end of the century, Watermeyer (1996) still recorded widespread but not consistent use of the trilled [r], but did not mention the use of /r/ in syllable codas any more. This coda-/r/, but also the trilled [r], attracted social stigma, already noted by Pretorius (1953), and both are strongly receding at present, as encounters with native speakers become more widespread for the younger generation and the previously rigid group boundaries between native speakers of Afrikaans and English in particular become less rigid.

A final conservative force that holds innovations at bay is when people interact mainly with strangers – fleeting contacts without establishing long-term relations – which often happens where English performs a lingua franca role, especially in international contact. Meierkord (2012) calls such encounters 'Interactions across Englishes', and makes the important point that when such interactions are in international contexts, people tend to select those forms of English that they anticipate will be most easily understood by their conversation partners. Thus, a safe, reduced selection is made from the variants available, rather than opting for innovative variants, on the assumption that unfamiliar interlocutors from another context will not understand all the forms that the speaker/writer understands. A feedback loop is also a likely force here, in that selections that are misunderstood are going to be avoided by a speaker in future, to enhance the changes of communicative success. If English is mainly used in such encounters within a particular ecology, then conservative choices will be reinforced and more likely to become stable features of the English evolving in these contexts.

Entrenchment, which results from the frequency of exposure and use of a variant, is a selection factor below the level of consciousness, and often neutral in respect of the prestige or stigmatisation of variants. Once a variant is available within a particular ecology, it can gain momentum through repeated use, and can also expand the contexts of use and potentially push out competing ways of saying the same thing. In sociolinguistic research on the diffusion of a variant within a speech community, the idea of an S-curve in the diffusion of a linguistic change is well established to capture this process. It is not a given that an incoming variant ends up occupying the complete space of the older variant – residual uses and typical contexts of use may remain. Social factors, such as age and gender, may continue to influence the rate of adoption of variants, as shown by Gardner et al. (2021) for the widely studied adoption of the *be like* quotative construction, illustrated by example (12) from their article. Female and younger speakers use the *be like* variant more than male and older speakers, but they find that the rate of adoption, if from different starting points, turns out to be relatively constant across very different geographical locations.

> (12) I kind of look back and **I'm like**, 'Why was I dating him for so long, I barely saw him?' (Gardner et al., 2021, p. 289)

Such processes of gradual diffusion are not limited to native speakers of English. Some incoming variants that have their origin in native-speaker usage also find their way to non-native speakers, with the quotative *be like* observed among a range of second-language users, such as German and Indian students. Davydova (2021) notes that while the frequency of occurrence of the *be like* quotative is lower in her German and Indian English user data, there is similarity to native speakers in the conditioning factors, and the variant achieved enough initial salience to be noticed and become part of the respective linguistic ecologies of the users.

Another proportional selection effect below the level of awareness is found in the kind of dialect contact situation that occurred during the early phase of settler dialect formation. Trudgill (2004) refers to the inevitability of new-dialect formation, where the relative proportion of variants, especially phonetic variants, in the sum total of settler input from different British dialects, plays a considerable role in determining which variants are eventually selected as the dominant variant of the variety of English that stabilises in each such setting. The native-language acquisition process of children in such contexts acts to support the long-term selection of the statistically most prevalent input forms as the eventual group norm.

The direction of spread is not limited to native-speaker origins, though. Variants can spread among non-native speakers, or from non-native to native speakers, where the same conditions hold in principle: something has to be part of the ecology and has to be noticed in order to be reproduced. Once such a triggering event has occurred, the spread of the variant and thereby increasing entrenchment through repeated exposure will promote the use of the new variant. In multilingual environments where many speakers of English also speak other languages, the proportions of use of constructions, pronunciation patterns or lexical items in their other languages may also exert an influence on their use of English. Different languages are not sealed off in the brains of multilingual speakers, so to the extent that some kind of match is made in the mind between elements from languages, the associations and the frequency of exposure and use in one language may exert an influence over the frequency of use in another language. Bilingual English users will be well aware of the almost unavoidable and often unintentional code-mixing that occurs in their other languages, slipping English words into their speech because those words don't disappear from the brain when one speaks another language. To the extent that native speakers of English participate in such multilingual linguistic ecologies, even if they themselves are monolingual, their regular exposure to the English used by other speakers in the environment may ultimately exert an influence on the native-speaker use in these contexts too. Jeffery and Van Rooy (2004) uncover the complex interplay of languages in Afrikaans–English bilingualism within the South African contact situation, where they analyse the use of emphasiser *now* in examples like the following.

(13) But you get a very much Grahamstown sort of English. That's **now** the proper proper English, which you don't find in Port Elizabeth. (p. 271)
(14) So that's **now** the soup (p. 272)

The syntactic pattern is *Demonstrative pronoun + Verb BE + now + (Adj. or Noun) Complement*, which is also attested in British English, but in ICE-GB such uses are limited to cases where the adverb *now* has a clear temporal meaning.[3] The point about examples (13) and (14) and many others in the data of Jeffery and Van Rooy (2004) is that there is no temporal meaning to *now*: the use corresponds to the way the Afrikaans cognate *nou* is used atemporally in the corresponding syntactic construction, as a discourse marker and not as a time adverb. Examples (13) and (14) were both recorded from Afrikaans-dominant bilinguals, and the vast majority of such examples are from Afrikaans-dominant speakers, although a small number of English-dominant/native speakers were also recorded with this usage. Another usage, which does not correspond to the usage of *nou* in Afrikaans, is illustrated by example (15).

(15) All that is hard concrete that you've got to **now** break up. (Jeffery & Van Rooy, 2004, p. 273)

---

3. ICE stands for the International Corpus of English, a major international project that collects similar corpus data from Inner and Outer Circle Englishes as well as language-shift varieties from across the world, initiated by Greenbaum (1990). See https://www.ice-corpora.uzh.ch/en.html for a current update on progress and access to many of the corpora.

This pattern is observed mainly among native speakers of English, rather than Afrikaans-dominant bilinguals. It does not correspond to British usage either. It occurs mainly in the syntactic frame *Semi-modal + to + now + VERB*. It appears from the data as if the initial trigger was a syntactic usage transferred from Afrikaans, and used by Afrikaans speakers in English more often, but not exclusively, than English native speakers. A further extension of the emphasiser use of *now* follows, where the native speakers lead the adoption. The proportional influence of Afrikaans supports the extension of an existing syntactic pattern in English to a meaning that is not conventional in other varieties of English, and in turn, builds momentum for further extension.

Progressive forces that favour the selection of new variants usually relate to attitude and in-group identities. While these two factors are closely tied, it is useful to draw a distinction between attitudes towards language forms and usage, and identity involving people and the aspirations of individuals. Schneider (2003, 2007) proposes several stages in his dynamic model of postcolonial Englishes. Stage four is labelled endonormative stabilisation, and signals a phase where indigenous forms gain overt acknowledgement as acceptable. Entry into this phase presupposes that the speakers of English in a particular place have accepted their identity as belonging to that place, rather than seeing themselves as Britons living in a foreign land. In the case of the United States, for instance, when the Declaration of Independence signalled the intent to sever the formal ties to the United Kingdom, a process followed where American forms were codified in dictionaries, spelling books and grammar books, emphasising the unique forms as a badge of honour to show the linguistic independence from the United Kingdom. Similar processes of endonormative acceptance of local forms of English can be identified in Australia, Canada and New Zealand, and to lesser degrees also in other parts of the world. However, among non-native speakers, there is often a degree of linguistic schizophrenia, as Kachru (1992) terms it. On the one hand, speakers are aware of the local innovations that have widespread currency in their environments, but on the other hand, as a sign of accomplishment, there is often an attachment to the norms of the colonisers, British English for most colonies, to distinguish the more proficient users from the less proficient users. While scholars like Kachru (1986) and Bamgbose (1998) argue that it is necessary to overcome the fear of accepting the local forms, it does not always happen, with educational and government authorities often continuing to pay lip service to the external norm. Kachru (1992) argues that it also took a long time for Americans to overcome their sense of speaking a deviant form of British English, and points to a range of attitudes and views within certain segments of the applied linguistics/TESOL community that continue to promote the notion that deviation from the external norm is a deficiency and should not be accepted.

The more general principle of alignment with others, and thereby minimising the distance between oneself and a group that one aspires to associate with, or of which one is already part and wishes to remain part of, is also at play in varieties of English. This principle forms a cornerstone of Labov's (2010) account of recent and older changes in the United States, conceptualised independently of the world Englishes framework. If others in a group use a particular variant, a particular speaker may do the same. It need not be a matter of explicit and overt choice, but simply the attitude to minimise the distance that will intuitively open the speaker up to converge on the forms used by others in the group. To various degrees of awareness, such convergence is easily seen in online communities, where innovations – be that of a lexical or typographic nature, a particular discourse marker or anything else really – tend to diffuse quite rapidly within a particular online community. There are limits, of course, as the innovation 'covfefe' shows by not diffusing among the online communities that feel close kinship with the innovator.

3.3 Conclusion

English has changed and diversified during the course of its worldwide spread. The processes that give rise to such changes are not unusual ones: people talk the way others around them talk, and they innovate or resist innovation in ways that correspond to how speakers of other languages do. However, English has many speakers who come to the language with other languages in their heads too, and these other languages influence the way they use English. One might call this interference, incomplete acquisition, or corruption of the language. It will not wish the non-native speakers away, and despite their mixed success in mastering the language, as Bill Bryson charitably credits them, there are just so many of them – in fact, the majority are like them – that their various usages rub off on the usage of others that they engage with, and ultimately contribute to ongoing change in the language.

Moreover, the world around us continues to change, faster rather than more slowly than in the past, as physical travel and online connections break down the boundaries that used to stabilise the communicative horizons of people. Hence, in this changing world, the language will continue to adapt to remain useful. Again, this is something that any living language will do, but English has come to be used in so many different contexts, by such a vast range of speakers, that these various contexts demand quite different things of the language. To the extent that speakers make the language oblige, the language will diversify. At the same time, to the extent that these various users interact in new and unexpected ways, their innovations will rub off on others and may spread, even very fast, almost like a *plandemic*, all over the world.

Part 1 of the book sets the stage for a closer look at the various waves of diffusion of English across the world. The exposition in Part 2 follows a broad historical sequence, although within chapters, similar varieties of English are brought together and compared, despite being removed in space or time. Let us embark on this journey around the world, as we follow the diffusion of English by its speakers and to new speakers, and see what they do to the language as they use it to engage with one another.

Part 2
Different contexts

4 Typical native varieties: the Inner Circle

Fifty years on from now, Britain will still be the country of long shadows on county grounds, warm beer, invincible green suburbs, dog lovers, and – as George Orwell said – old maids bicycling to Holy Communion through the morning mist.[1]

The British prime minister in 1993, John Major, wanted to assure his British audience during an address to the Conservative Group for Europe that EU membership would not cost Britain its uniqueness. Towards the end of his speech, he highlighted unique aspects of Britishness that Brussels wouldn't tamper with. Not all these allusions will be transparent to an outsider audience. For instance, you would need to know that county grounds refer to cricket grounds, but more understanding of the game is required to understand why there are long shadows: a county game lasts multiple full days of play, and at the end of such a day of typically seven hours of cricket, punctuated by a lunch break and a tea break, the trees lining the grounds cast long shadows over the ground. If Mr Major wanted to explain the uniqueness of Britain to an outside audience, such as the European Parliament, it would not have served his cause to use too much cricketing English. To be sure, cricket is not a marginal pursuit in England and certain other parts of the former Empire, and has gifted the local varieties of English a rich heritage of metaphors and idioms, but it just doesn't have the global reach of some of the other British sporting inventions, like soccer, to supply metaphors beyond certain interactions.

The American-born writer Bill Bryson found Britain a place of endless fascination, a world so different from the one he was used to, when he first set foot there as a twenty-something backpacker. He documented many of those unusual things that struck him in *Notes from a Small Island* (1995), such as the weather ('dreadful weather, – but it might brighten

---

1. https://johnmajorarchive.org.uk/1993/04/22/mr-majors-speech-to-conservative-group-for-europe-22-april-1993/

up', p. 15), customs ('I have never had tea with milk in it before or a biscuit of such rocklike cheerlessness', p. 25), geography ('the British have a totally private sense of distance', p. 32), and no less the language.

The language matter is a little messier, though. Mr Major, in the same address where he extolled the virtues of warm beer and old maids bicycling in the mists and (one suspects) mellow fruitfulness, still wanted to place Britain in a global frame, not quite resigned to Bryson's notion of a small island. While he stressed that Britain was no longer the global power of its nineteenth-century imperial past, he mentioned various advantages that Britain had in the EU and in global trade:

> Investors like our welcome. They like our tax structure. They like our industrial relations. They know that our workforce is flexible and adaptable. And we have English, – English, the world language. We should do well with such strengths.

As far as language is concerned, he was right, of course, in more than one way. The United Kingdom has English, and it is a world language to boot. However, to do well with the linguistic strength when talking to investors, the warm beer might not sell, and linguistic evocation of the shadows of the county grounds will possibly just be lost on the audience, as might a verb like 'york' or idioms like 'hit for a six', 'had a good innings' or 'bat for the other team' be – at least as far as understanding their meaning in terms of the source domain. So, the English language that will capitalise on the strengths that Mr Major envisaged might not be the variety of the language that Prince Charles had in mind when he addressed his words of encouragement to the British Academy two years later. For starters, there are those, for crying out loud, who go around selling an American brand of English, with all kinds of nouns and verbs that shouldn't be – such expressions as 'ball park', 'curveball', 'get to first base' or 'hit a home run' will be easier to interpret if one knows a little bit about baseball. Then, there are several craft brands of Englishes competing for attention among the connoisseurs, like New Zealand and Australian English, alongside several no-name brand varieties out there, house brands of supermarket chains aimed at the budget-conscious consumers of English.

If one steps back, out of the shadows surrounding the county grounds, one cannot but recognise that there is an overlooked ambiguity in the way that 'English' is used – the word and the language. When the rhetorical goal is to punt its position as 'world language', all users and the full range of usage are counted, but the local and the particular always lurk in the shadows, and at some point, the local is presented as if it the same as the global – all photocopy-machines are really xeroxes after all (or imperfect imitations of the original Xerox at best).

Typical native-speaker varieties of English – those used by descendants of the British colonial settlers – present two puzzles that will be considered in this chapter. These varieties across the world are not just transplanted British English that developed somewhat differently over the course of time, given the geographical distances from home. Instead, these settler Englishes, if not rebelling with military might or political protest against the monarch any more, at least do offer a normative challenge to the King's language.[2]

The former colonies, and the United States in particular, have come to rival and overtake the 'mother country' in terms of economic affluence and social prestige, such that American English is a bigger brand in the contemporary world than British English (Mair, 2013a), whereas Mexican or Argentinian Spanish do not enjoy a comparable prestige to Castilian Spanish. This may relate in part to the vast affluence that the English settlement colonies enjoy today, unlike most other European settlements outside of Europe. The four most typical English settlement colonies, the United States, Canada, Australia and New Zealand, are among the most affluent in the world when judged by per capita income, as seen especially in comparison with Spanish and Portuguese settlements in South and Central America.

Furthermore, beyond the challenge to the sanctity of British norms for native-speaker Englishes, the non-native forms of English also behave in an unruly manner at times (or maybe it is the speakers). In a spirit of liberal open-mindedness one shares with Sir Randolph Quirk (1988), one might accept some of the nouns and verbs they contribute to the language, but the challenges go deeper, to styles, grammar and pronunciation. This retrospectively has a bearing on the use of English by native speakers: Mr Major (later Sir John Major) will be toning down the cricket metaphors outside of Britain and will likely not expect his interlocutors to complete a course in cricket and its imagery, as part of the typical foreign-language *Landeskunde* training, as a precondition for engaging in conversation with him. If he did, one would probably have to tell him, 'Come on, Sir, that's just not cricket.'

---

2. At the time of original writing, rightful 'ownership' was still vested in Her Majesty Elizabeth II, but 'ownership' transferred to a new king before publication, someone who expressed some strong views on appropriate nouns and verbs. Together with his beloved, he seemed to do well with the strength of good old-fashioned nouns and verbs like 'living in your trousers' or 'come back as a pair of knickers', if those naughty recordings of their pillow-talk were authentic, after all. And old-fashioned these nouns are – the GloWbE corpus shows very clearly that these are Britishisms, with only Ireland, Australia and New Zealand finding occasional use for them. The rest of the world has really been converted to 'pants' and avoids too much revealing detail by talking about 'underwear', or, if one has to, 'underpants'.

The historical and social forces that shaped the settler varieties, together with the shape that English got through these forces, are presented in this chapter, within the broader frame of making sense of the implications of the linguistic variability and global contexts for the use of English by native speakers.

4.1 The transplantation of English beyond the British Isles

English was initially transplanted to other parts of the world by small groups of British settlers. Over time, some of these settlements were strengthened demographically by further waves of English-speaking immigrants, as well as settlers who initially spoke other European languages but shifted to English as their home language as they came to be absorbed in the English-speaking society through economic integration, education and social contacts. The speaker numbers of English, including its cohort of native speakers, grew even further through language shift to English by indigenous people of places colonised by English speakers, such as the Māori of New Zealand and the Aboriginals of Australia, or the slaves and their descendants in the case of the United States and to a less extensive degree in South Africa. These language-shift Englishes are considered in Chapter 5.

The new settlers came from different parts of the United Kingdom and spoke many different varieties, barring a few exceptions where the settlers came from a relatively specific area in Britain and spoke a relatively uniform English upon arrival already. The clearest case of this is the seventeenth-century settlement in Northern Ireland by speakers of Lowland and Western Scottish English, forming the foundation for present-day Ulster Scots (Hickey, 2004, p. 87), but there are also similar cases in Newfoundland, Canada, for instance. Relatively uniform new varieties of English emerged in most new locations within a few generations. In the case of Canada, Australia and New Zealand, there is an ongoing perception of the relative uniformity of these colonial varieties within the borders of the contemporary state. Despite vast distances in Canada and Australia, an early focused settlement from where other settlements stemmed contributed to the development of a relatively homogenous dialect before diffusion to other parts of the countries concerned. Only in the case of the United States do perceptions of uniformity not match the linguistic evidence so clearly, although even there, clear levelling and dialect mixing resulted in the emergence of several relatively homogenous varieties, but in different regions (Schneider, 2007, pp. 269–271). This can be accounted for on the basis of different early settlements in the USA that took place in parallel, without a subsequent merging into a single speech community. Let us turn to some of the major English-speaking settlements and their speakers.

English has been present in Ireland since the twelfth century, continuously so in the case of Dublin (Hickey, 2004, p. 83). Ireland was colonised by British settlers, but present-day Irish Englishes also owe their demographic strength to language shift from the ancestral Celtic Irish to English in the centuries after settlement. Language-shift Englishes are presented in the next chapter, but the transplanted Englishes of Ireland are similar to the colonial expansion of English through settlement colonisation elsewhere.

The twelfth-century settlement in coastal areas of the South and Southeast of Ireland led to the establishment of Dublin and several other towns as English-speaking centra. The 1172 Charter of Dublin established this city as the anglophone heartland in the South of Ireland, an area that came to be known as the Pale. 'Beyond the pale' was the Irish-speaking areas, an expression that has lost some of its historical connection in becoming the present-day means of delineating the boundaries of appropriateness. These early settlers became reasonably well integrated into the local society, though, and did not strongly represent the English Crown (Hickey, 2004, pp. 84–86). Tension rose in the latter part of the sixteenth century, and by the seventeenth century, the English reasserted their control over Ireland and established plantations with the Irish as their labourers. After James VI of Scotland ascended the English throne as James I, he encouraged settlement of Scots from the West and Lowlands to the North of Ireland, giving rise to the present-day Ulster Scots speakers, establishing Belfast and some other towns as anglophone centres (Hickey, 2004, p. 87). Smaller-scale settlement also took place in the South, where the English served as plantation owners and administrators in the main, but provided linguistic input for the shift to English by the Irish from the eighteenth to early twentieth centuries (Hickey, 2004, pp. 88–92). Irish English became not just a new settler variety, the oldest outside the British Isles, but became, alongside British varieties, an important input to colonial settlements elsewhere, as Ireland provided several million immigrants to the United States, Canada and Australia during the course of the eighteenth and nineteenth centuries.

English was transplanted to North America through two initial settlements in the early seventeenth century: Jamestown (Virginia) in 1607, and Plymouth (Massachusetts) in 1620. Between these Northern and Southern initial settlements, various non-English European settlements occurred (German, Scandinavian, Dutch), which led to largely separate developments in the two early English-speaking settlements (Kytö, 2020). From these initial settlements, occupation and settlement spread gradually, through a combination of internal migration of existing settlers and new immigrants from the British Isles. The initial settlements were dominated by settlers from the South of England (Virginia) and eastern England (Massachusetts), according to Fisher (2001). The settlement through most of the eighteenth century in the Midlands of the United States was dominated by Scots Irish speakers from Ulster (Montgomery, 2004), as well as Quakers and others from the English Midlands and North, wedging their way between the earlier settlements and moving inland into the Appalachians among others (Schneider, 2011, pp. 78–79). For the first century and until the American Revolution, contact was maintained with prestige English dialects through the education of affluent boys in English schools, but over time, this influence became increasingly distant (Hall-Lew, 2017; Kytö, 2020). Class differences remained pronounced in America for the early periods of settlement, despite better chances of class mobility than in Britain (Kytö, 2004, p. 131), unlike Australia and New Zealand, where class differences were less pronounced and social integration of most settlers was on more equal terms.

Subsequent waves of immigration had less of an influence on the development of the American dialects after the initial stabilisation. The most important historical developments in the nineteenth century were the westward expansion and the Civil War, leading to the abolition of slavery together with renewed racial segregation in the South (Schneider, 2007, pp. 282–284). The westward expansion led to renewed levelling of the dialects as they moved deeper into territories where there were no pre-established varieties of English (Schneider, 2007, p. 287). The aftermath of the Civil War led to a stronger racial split in the American Englishes, with less contact in the South between African and European Americans due to renewed residential and social segregation in the wake of the Jim Crow discriminatory legislation. African Americans who migrated to the North introduced Southern English there, where a racialised reinterpretation of the Southern English of African Americans as African American English came about (Mufwene, 2001, pp. 91–93).

Canadian English developed as an offshoot from the American settlement. Settlement by English speakers in what is today Canada started in the early eighteenth century, and was linguistically similar to the emerging varieties in what would become the United States later in the century (Chambers, 2004). Settlement increased markedly after American Independence, in the late eighteenth century, as loyalists fled the United States and settled north of the border, in most cases in much larger numbers than those settlers who had been living there already (Dollinger, 2008). However, as Chambers (2004) notes, the expectation of dialect differentiation after the erection of the border did not materialise. Rather, the continued influx of newcomers from America initiated a new-dialect contact situation with the Midlands and Northern United States dialects.

Once a reasonably stable 'loyalist' dialect was in place, the extensive immigration from Ireland and Britain to Canada during the nineteenth century did little to change the dialect, as a founder population already existed and there was a local dialect into which newcomers – or more strictly speaking, their children – were assimilated (Schneider, 2007, pp. 241–242; Dollinger, 2008, pp. 78–96). By the middle of the nineteenth century, nearly 60 per cent of the residents of Ontario (Upper Canada at the time) were born in Canada, just before the earnest onset of westward expansion and the coming of the railways (Dollinger, 2008, p. 96). The westward expansion happened in a context where there was persistent concern about control of the border between (British) Canada and America; hence, with Eastern Canada as centre from where expansion took place, a relatively uniform variety moved westward north of the American border, all along the forty-ninth parallel. The British government ensured regular contact within Canada, particularly by means of railway infrastructure, which encouraged ongoing exchange and hence promoted linguistic homogeneity (Schneider, 2007, p. 243).

The odd one out in the Canadian context is the province of Newfoundland. This province was the first transatlantic British colony, claimed for the Crown in 1583. For a long time, until the late eighteenth century, permanent settlers were relatively few, with seasonal fishermen making up a large portion of the residents. By the middle of the eighteenth century, the population was estimated at 10,000 in summer and about half that in winter, with an increase only from the early nineteenth century. Earlier and later immigrants came mainly from two areas: Southwest England and Southeast Ireland, but anglophones in the main as far as the latter is concerned, from the area of Waterford. With fishing as the principal economic activity and otherwise limited interaction, present-day Newfoundland English still has clear traces of these two founding dialects, with strong dialectal differentiation for most coastal towns (Clarke, 2010). The settlement patterns, without the kind of dialect contact situation characteristic of most other settlement colonies, together with economic activity centred around small fishing villages and limited integration, created conditions for dialect preservation more strongly than elsewhere in Canada, or North America more generally (Clarke, 2010, p. 9). Newfoundland was not politically integrated with Canada until 1949, and only very recently, traces of absorption into the mainstream Canadian English have become noticeable among younger middle-class residents of the urban centre St. John's (Hofmann, 2015).

Australian English developed from the late eighteenth century, as settlement began in Botany Bay (later called Sydney) in 1788. In the earliest years of settlement, there was a majority of convicts, since Australia was first established as a penal colony. However, Kiesling (2004) argues for the importance of the children in the earliest years of settlement in Sydney in shaping the emerging Australian variety of English. They were exposed to a wide variety of English dialects, but with the strongest representation from vernacular or working-class London and Southeast English, alongside dialects from elsewhere in England, Ireland and Scotland. Contemporary commentators reviewed by Kiesling (2004) highlighted the prestige of Cockney among the convicts but also the children of the first-generation settlers. These children likely adopted a middle road, by avoiding the most stigmatised features of the input and settling on a broadly Southeast English dialect mixture with a strong London flavour. While immigration continued, the founder's effect of the first generation of locally born children seems to have set the tone and served as the reference point to which newcomers, or otherwise their children, would have accommodated.

Kiesling (2004, pp. 423–424) points out that subsequent Australian settlements proceeded from previous ones; the settlement in Tasmania (then called Van Diemen's Land) was made by a pioneer group departing from Sydney, and from there, settlement to Victoria was made by settlers from Van Diemen's Land. Similar to the inland migration in the USA and Canada, Australian settlements thus also trace their uniformity to the continuity of speakers transplanting the previously established dialect to a new place.

New Zealand English developed from the mid-nineteenth century when European settlement of the islands took off. While a small group of Australians settled there, the majority were from England, particularly the South, but also from Ireland and Scotland. Settlers were mostly from lower middle-class backgrounds, not from the big cities, and typically young. After an early attempt at setting up relatively homogenous cities in the new settlement, called the 'planned settlements', the poor economic viability of these settlements, followed by the discovery of modest amounts of gold, led to much more extensive mixing of settlers throughout the country, which in turn gave rise to the development of a relatively focused New Zealand English by the end of the nineteenth century (Gordon & Trudgill, 2004). Being the most recent large-scale settlement of English speakers, and due to a fortunate accident of history, much more detailed knowledge is available about the development of the pronunciation of New Zealand English, to which we turn later in this chapter.

Settlement of English speakers in South Africa happened in three waves during the course of the nineteenth century. The first settlement was from 1820 onwards in the Eastern Cape, with lower middle-class and some working-class speakers from London and the Southeast of England (Lanham, 1996). The Eastern Cape settlement started less than half a century after the Australian settlement, and the subsequent Natal settlement happened at the same time as the New Zealand settlement. South African settlers had very similar regional backgrounds as Australians and New Zealanders, which is why there are such clear similarities between these varieties (Trudgill, 2004). These settlements were largely overrun in numbers by the discovery of diamonds and gold from the 1870s onwards, especially after the discovery of the Witwatersrand gold reef, which led to the influx of a very diverse collection of English speakers, absorbing the older Cape and Natal settlements (Bekker, 2012). Nevertheless, despite the vast numeric advantage of newcomers to the Witwatersrand, the Natal and Cape dialects served as input to the more prestigious and less prestigious General and Broad South African English varieties that stabilised in the course of the twentieth century (Lanham & MacDonald, 1979; Bekker, 2012).

Looking across the settlement varieties, the Irish settlement had its own characteristics, with settlement from two areas in Britain that live on in the present-day varieties of the language, much like Newfoundland English. The varieties in the Southern Hemisphere, Australia, New Zealand and South Africa, had similar input from a similar historical period and do show many similarities, except that the speakers of the settler variety in South Africa are a demographic minority in the overall context, much like the case was for Ireland outside the Ulster Scots speech community. The North American varieties, other than Newfoundland, likewise had similar origins in the same period, with various waves of later mixing taking place. In the United States of America, a completely focused variety was not attained, even among the settlers, but the other colonies did achieve that to some degree, because of the early settlement in one or a few areas, before moving from there to the rest of the country (except New Zealand, where several smaller initial settlements happened simultaneously, but where sufficient contact was maintained across individual places of settlement to enable convergence).

4.2 Social factors

History tells us how English spread through human migration and what these humans did when they arrived and settled in new places. Within this context, we now turn to the social factors that contributed to shaping the language in the new geographical spaces, leading to the present-day diversity.

4.2.1 Settler dialect contact

The settler varieties, with the exception of settlements in Northern Ireland and Newfoundland, were characterised by dialect contact between a range of British and Irish Englishes in their early years. Early records document a range of recognisable British varieties among the settlers, and in the case of at least some, there was a lingering sense that the local variety was akin to, or a transplanted version of, a particular British variety, often explicitly identified as Cockney in the case of Australia and South Africa. This continued up to Hopwood (1928) in accounting for South African English, if not with unqualified enthusiasm, while Kiesling (2004) explains the strong position of Cockney among the convicts and early lower-class settlers in Australia. Nonetheless, as Trudgill (2004) explains, this type of matching between input dialects and settler dialects is not accurate, as the settler varieties contained blends of linguistic features that were not simultaneously present in any individual input variety.

The absence of a founding population in new colonial settlements brought about a disruption of the stable linguistic patterns of interaction, within regions and within classes, that characterised the input varieties in their British and Irish home contexts. While the new societies were not classless, social stratification was less extensive, particularly in New Zealand, Australia and Canada, and social mobility was much higher, also in the United States and South Africa, even if settlers in these latter two countries retained more class differentiation in the early settlement. However, one thing that is clear for the colonial settlements is that stigmatised linguistic features with a limited demographic presence among the settlers were lost very early, suggesting a keen awareness to avoid being stigmatised. Trudgill (2004) notes that even adults, already on the boat journey, revealed some of this early social awareness, resulting in their avoidance of some of the stigmatised features by the time they set foot on shore.

Relationships with the 'mother country' remained linguistically influential for about a century, especially among the well-to-do American settlers in New England, and the affluent industrialists and capitalists in South Africa, where even in the second half of the twentieth century, Lanham and MacDonald (1979) still reference connections to England as a conservative factor influencing the shape of English in the local settler community. While settlement to South Africa did carry on into the twentieth century, and according to Bekker (2012) delayed the stabilisation of a local variety, it is unusual that the influence was felt for such an extended period in South Africa; settlement in the United States and Canada also continued for a very long period of time, ongoing immigration to

Australia, Canada and New Zealand remains an important aspect of their demographic landscape even today, and migration generates a lot of heated politics in Britain and the United States as well. It seems as if the continued connection with the United Kingdom was more important in South Africa than in other settlement colonies from an attitudinal perspective, and can likely be attributed to the different demographics, where English settler descendants formed a local minority – within the white community in a highly racialised society, but even more so within the context of the entire country.

Dialect contact led to linguistic convergence in the settlement area, which presupposes sufficient interaction among speakers. The size and geographical distances between the settlements, and patterns of social interaction, played a role in erecting some relatively sharp boundaries between communities, reinforcing linguistic distinctiveness across these boundaries but strong homogeneity within these groups. Labov (2010) accounts for the modern dialect differences in reference to the cultural differences, group interactions, and even philosophical and moral orientations of the major different settlements of the early years of the United States, reinforced with westward expansion from the late eighteenth century. In theory, then, one should not regard the internal diversification of United States varieties of English as a refutation of the expectation that settler varieties developed into relatively homogenous varieties over the course of a few generations (Schneider, 2003, 2007; Trudgill, 2004). One needs to recognise that different settlements came to co-inhabit the United States, where unity is more of a geopolitical kind than a cultural-community kind – Labov (2010, p. 216) talks of the cultural opposition of Yankees and Upland Southerners, with clear differences in political cultures and ideological oppositions that cement the boundaries within which people interact (Labov, 2010, pp. 218–235).

Among the Southern Hemisphere varieties (Australia, New Zealand and South Africa), a threefold sociolectal split emerged, cutting across input varieties. An exonormative, British standard remained influential, and a declining minority of speakers continued to use it, perhaps even to the present but at least deep into the twentieth century. This is termed the Cultivated variety by most commentators, following the original proposal of Mitchell and Delbridge (1965). A local, higher-status variety, labelled General, emerged among the middle-class, more educated speakers, while a Broad variety, with the strongest occurrence of local features (pronunciation, vocabulary and, where such choices are available, also grammatical), is characteristic of working-class or lower middle-class speakers, but also men rather than women, and younger men in particular – akin to the covert prestige of urban working-class and rural regional dialects in non-settler communities. The South African scholars Lanham and MacDonald (1979), building on work that Lanham had conducted in the preceding two decades, used the terms Conservative, Respectable and Extreme, where the idea of 'Respectable' is explained as a 'provincial standard'. There are clear value-judgements implied by these terms, but often, the actual linguistic choices are probabilistic – less versus more local, with even General/Respectable settler speakers availing themselves of such local features, but in lower proportions. Thus, the judgements often reflect a residual attitude of the provincial as somehow not quite the same as the metropolitan or authentic, diluting the authentic brand, as it were. In terms of the dynamic model of Schneider (2007), what we witness among settler varieties is the contrast between an exonormative and endonormative orientation, which are different stages in the development of local varieties of English.

4.2.2 Contact with speakers of other languages

Settlers also came into contact with speakers of other languages. These contacts showed patterns of change over time, but were also different depending on who the others were. Contact with other European settlers was generally relatively peaceful in the United States, Australia and New Zealand. After a period in which the other settlers formed communities of their own, they were typically assimilated into the anglophone community, but in a slow and piecemeal fashion, which prevented extensive linguistic transfer other than vocabulary loans (Mufwene, 2001, 2020). The descendants of the earlier settlers became assimilated as members of the English-speaking settler community, but after a founder's effect already in place. The shifting generation would have retained traces of their ancestral languages, but their children grew up as native speakers, with the peer group offsetting the effects of their parents' input, and these differences mostly dissolved (Clyne, 2003; Mufwene, 2020). To the extent that ethnic dialects of Europeans linger in the United States, such as an Italian-American or Jewish ethnolect, they testify to less than complete integration at a particular historical moment and the retention of some ethno-cultural boundaries. This may also be a deliberate choice and is not necessarily an indication of a failed social integration project, with ethnolectal features selected strategically by some speakers (to 'perform' a particular identity in the terminology current among some sociolinguists), rather than being the sum total of their linguistic repertoires (Benor, 2010).

The situation is slightly different in Canada and South Africa, where another European colonial power occupied a part of the land before the British took control – the French in Canada and the Dutch in South

Africa. Relations were tenser than in the Anglo-dominated societies; British authority was established only after a war on the colonial soil, which ended with the capitulation of New France in 1760 (Moore, 2000) and the South African Boer Republics in 1902. After this, a road of partial reconciliation or at least peaceful co-habitation followed, in which the autonomy and also linguistic rights of the other colonists' descendants were accepted. In Canada, the geographical separation of the French-speaking and English-speaking citizens made matters relatively easy to arrange, but in South Africa, the situation remained more complex, and official bilingualism was matched by more in-practice bilingualism than in Canada. In consequence, the influence of Afrikaans, the modern-day language that developed out of colonial Dutch, on English is more extensive than in other parts of the anglophone world, but still considerably less extensive than the inverse, the influence that English has on Afrikaans (Van Rooy, 2020, 2021).

Contact with indigenous languages would *a priori* have been expected to be more important linguistically, given that the indigenous people were much more numerous at the start. Yet, contact was generally limited, and usually proceeded only through a few intermediaries. In the very first years of occupation, contact was a little more extensive for the European 'pioneers', to absorb local know-how about agricultural conditions, during which much of the borrowing of topographical nomenclature took place. Pretty soon in the United States and Australia, and to a lesser extent elsewhere, the contact became acrimonious and persistent warfare followed for decades, even centuries. Competition for land meant that the Europeans forced the indigenous populations further and further away from the colonial settlements. Attempts to lure or force the indigenous people into the European economy were generally not successful, leading in the case of the United States to the widespread importation of slaves and indentured labourers. In South Africa, British settlement coincided with the abolition of slavery, while the settlements in Canada and Australia never relied extensively on slaves and New Zealand was settled after the abolition of slavery in the British Empire.

Only in South Africa, given the different demography, did the English and indigenous people come into slightly more frequent contact in the economic sphere, but even there, indentured labour from India supplied the hands that the indigenous people were not willing to provide on sugar cane plantations in the second half of the nineteenth century. Apart from agriculture in two parts of the country, the Eastern Cape and Kwa-Zulu Natal, the industrial incorporation of indigenous labour happened through intermediaries, often Afrikaans speakers, rather than through direct contact. All told, the contact with the indigenous people was generally not close enough for much linguistic influence throughout the period of colonial settlement beyond early lexical borrowing of terms for the space and local fauna and flora.

Contact with indigenous populations only increased in the twentieth century as residential and economic segregation gradually gave way, but with limited effect for the descendants of the settlers for most of the century. This follows both from the founder's effect and the demographic and socio-economic dominance of the established English-speaking community. Only towards the end of the century, starting in New Zealand in the 1970s and followed by Canada and Australia near the end of the century, were acts of restoration attempted to restore dignity and acknowledge past atrocities. Much as one may contemplate their symbolic value, there was also some linguistic consequence, in New Zealand more than elsewhere, in restoring more indigenous nomenclature, with some vocabulary making its way into the language. In New Zealand, but also in South Africa, with much more regular contact in the context of a much higher proportion of indigenous people (a sizeable minority in New Zealand, a clear majority in South Africa), renewed borrowing from the indigenous languages extending far beyond topography has been initiated from these settler–indigenous contacts.

Contact between settlers and slaves in the settler colonies affected settler language in very slight ways only. Most of the contact happened in areas where the settlers were a small minority and turned out to be temporary residents in the main. However, in the American South (Mufwene, 2001) and the remaining settler communities on Caribbean islands like Barbados, convergence between the English of the settlers and slaves, and their descendants, took place, signalling closer contact. Mufwene (2001) accounts for this with reference to the homestead phase, where a smaller number of slaves lived in the households and were in regular contact with their settler owners, unlike the plantation phase, where slaves had little interaction with settlers.

4.2.3 Use

The use of English within English-dominant countries is reasonably simple in the global perspective: most people use English all of the time in private and in public, and they speak to other English speakers, often with a similar dialectal and sociolectal background to themselves. In this sense, the experience of typical native speakers of English is reasonably similar to that of native speakers of Japanese in Japan, Russian in Russia, French in France, Spanish in Argentina or Spain, or Arabic in Saudi

Arabia to the extent that international encounters are set aside for the moment (something less easily done in some of these cases). Apart from being the dominant spoken language in private and public spaces, there is comprehensive native-language education, an ample supply of books and entertainment, a legal system, agriculture, business and industry all mainly in these dominant national languages, Japanese, Russian, French, Spanish or Arabic as much as English.

Native speakers who live in multilingual areas within these Inner Circle contexts have a somewhat different experience, in that they will regularly encounter fellow citizens who are not native speakers of English. For many, this has little impact on their own use of English but some influence on the types of English they encounter. They will hear the other languages, and to the extent that they are competent speakers of other languages, might engage in some conversation in those languages. This will be true for those Canadians living in Montreal or other areas where the French and English speakers live alongside each other, for New Zealanders in encounters with Māori, Irish encounters with Irish, and South African encounters with Afrikaans and indigenous African languages. Usually, such encounters still take place in English, but then with some participants in the encounters speaking other varieties of English than the native settler variety, introducing extra layers of variation into the linguistic ecology.

A phenomenon that has attracted attention recently is the encounter with 'super-diversity', urban multilingualism due to recent migration (Vertovec, 2007). This impacts mainly on the diversity of language exposure and interaction in private use, and is explored in more detail in Chapter 8. It stands to reason how different contemporary super-diversity is, compared with such immigration hubs as New York a century ago. However, there are potential consequences for language use in the Inner Circle that we should bear in mind.

English serves as a tool for international contact for native speakers as much as it does for non-native speakers. In international settings, either travelling beyond the anglophone world or attending gatherings (business, academic) in their home countries but with strong international participation, native speakers also need to adjust to the settings. They share the challenge of dealing with intercultural pragmatics in particular, because it is a naïve expectation that all other users of English will suspend their notions of politeness and directness, or complete a course in cricket or baseball idioms. Native speakers also need to understand that, as an international language, English is used differently than in domestic settings. They are free to choose otherwise, of course, but such a contrary choice will not necessarily engender communicative success.

There are conditions that limit the amount of exposure native speakers get to the otherness of other users of English, though. One might suspect that the extensive outsourcing of services to the Philippines, India and other countries around the world would enhance contact between native speakers and, say, Philippine teleconsultants for appliances or Indian IT-helpdesk staff. However, in practice, these users of 'foreign' Englishes are subjected to accent neutralisation training, and are trained to emulate some kind of American, British or whatever other desired accent to position them appropriately in the market in which they operate (Bolton, 2013).

Even translation, one way of enhancing cultural contact without some of the linguistic barriers that limit access to books or films produced in other languages, does not quite yield to the otherness of other languages. Translations into English tend to domesticate, to present the foreign elements in terms accessible to the target English-speaking audience, while translations from English into other languages are more prone to foreignise, to try to convey the source text and source culture as closely as possible (Gottlieb, 2020). These are not absolutes but general tendencies, which have the effect of raising more awareness of English speakers' ways among others than of others' ways among English speakers. One might sense an ethical dilemma for translators, but perceptions of the market conspire to deny English-speaking audiences a chance to learn more about others and their linguistic practices. A rather extreme example of such adjustment concerns the 'Americanisation' of English work written by other speakers of English, such as the editorial revisions of the *Harry Potter* series from its British originals to the American editions, about which Eastwood (2010) observes the following:

> All of these examples point toward a subtle cultural re-orientation that is facilitated through linguistic change, and more specifically, a haphazard attempt to regulate the text according to the standards of American English, rather than towards a telos of comprehension. (p. 3)

He includes as an example the adjustment made to the diction of Hagrid, who speaks clear dialectal British English, but suddenly slips in Americanisms, such as in a line about a new-born baby dragon, which in the original edition reads 'Bless him, look, he knows his mummy' but in the American edition uses 'mommy'. The erasure of difference, of otherness, as a kind of *cancel-culture lite*, is in evidence here, and denies some users of native varieties of English the encounter with other forms of English, which may in the long run not serve them well in intercultural encounters that, even though they are conducted in English, are not conducted in 'their English'.[3]

4.2.4 Acquisition

The varieties of English under consideration in this chapter are acquired by children in their homes, from parents who are speakers of English as well. The earliest generations of settler children acquired English in a context of extensive dialect contact, and thus had mixed input in their environments, rather than a stable variety. These children came to be the main inventors of the new varieties during the first few generations, as they selected from among the competing variants only some, which then came to define the new variety. Trudgill (2004) explains that the most frequent variants are typically selected by children over the course of the second and third generations in new colonial societies, and therefore that the outcome is deterministic at societal level, although individual children prior to the stable phase reached with the third generation display extreme variability in their own production. Once a reasonably stable local variety is in place, a founder's effect is established and subsequent generations of children continue to acquire that variety from their parents and environment. The children of newcomers converge on that variety to the extent that they are integrated into the groups, while the additional variants brought along by newcomer adults tend to die out as the speakers pass on.

One dimension of 'acquisition' that affects native speakers in a way that is similar to non-native speakers is the need to acquire skill in using English in international contexts, beyond the home country in particular. This might require some effort from native speakers who migrate to other native-speaking countries, such as the need for an Australian to adjust to American vocabulary in order to be understood in the United States. Nelson (2008) offers such an example of a misunderstanding between himself, an American, and his brother-in-law, an Australian: they used

---

3. It is too early to tell the consequences of ongoing attempts at restricting access to certain books in schools and public libraries (because they are too woke, or not sensitive enough), in conjunction with the echo-chamber effect of media houses and the algorithms involved in content selection of internet users of social media or search engines. To the extent that group boundaries are reinforced, we may see enhanced filtering of linguistic exposure and contact with new linguistic innovations. However, in principle, as argued by Labov (2010), such ideologically defined ground boundaries have been a persistent feature of American English for several centuries now, and may simply strengthen the forces of diversification that compete with the homogenising forces in shaping the Englishes of American users, as well as those who keenly engage with American content.

different words for a particular vegetable to be used in salad, 'capsicum' for the Australian, 'bell pepper' or 'green pepper' in American English more generally (or even 'mango' in Nelson's regional Indiana dialect). After they had resolved the misunderstanding, his brother-in-law, who had been living in the USA for a long time, observed, 'I know two words for some things, but I can't always remember which one is the Australian one and which one is the American one' (p. 302).

Much more effort is required from native speakers when communicating in international contexts where their conversation partners are native speakers of other languages and/or live in very different cultures. Smith and Christopher (2001) recount the misunderstanding between an Australian woman and a Turkish taxi driver – in Turkey – where the woman took the taxi back to her hotel after a social event in the evening. During the course of a 'pleasant chat', as perceived by the passenger, she asked the driver to turn off the interior light of the taxi, to which he replied 'quite sharply' with a 'No!' Assuming that her request was misunderstood, she reworded the request, but the taxi driver refused even more explicitly. Only afterwards was she informed that there is a legal requirement that taxi drivers leave the interior light on when driving around with female passengers after dark. The taxi driver must have understood her request as something quite improper, requiring him to break the law. The issue here is not the words as such, which were understood clearly by both parties, but the meaning in context – presupposition and other pragmatic aspects of the communicative act. While a native speaker may not be able to acquire such refined pragmatic competence for all possible international encounters, strategies to deal with ostensible misunderstanding and some pragmatic competence for potentially more regular encounters might well be an important acquisitional goal for a native speaker who makes use of English as an International Language. And of course, Sir John Major had to acquire the skill in translating cricket metaphors to international English as well . . ., or more generally, had to learn what is variety-specific and what has wider currency for diverse audiences.

4.2.5 Attitudes

Attitudes among native speakers towards their own and others' varieties of English show important changes over time. Schneider (2003, 2007) refers to the change in orientation from exonormative to endonormative, which is most clearly seen in the places where English is spoken by settler descendants. After an early phase where the local forms of English were still perceived as British, even saliently so in the context of multiple input dialects present in the same setting, a local variety stabilised.

This initially happened below the level of consciousness, but at some point, a perception of difference (from British English, however construed by the perceivers) arose, and possibly also of relative homogeneity of the speech in the new places. British visitors were often the earliest articulators of such perceptions, while school inspectors and other educationalists (in the case of Australia, New Zealand and South Africa) also contributed their impressions.

Outsiders, but also insiders, often articulated negative attitudes when they ventured into such evaluative lexis, which one should interpret as the observation of difference from some perceived (British) norm and a negative judgement about the fact of difference – the colonial people were unable to maintain authentic (i.e. British) norms, as if the original settlers did ... Gordon et al. (2004, p. 72) quote from a radio broadcast by Arnold Wall in 1951, at the end of a career as professor of English in New Zealand. Wall arrived from London (UK) in 1899, and recalled, half a century later, that in Canterbury (NZ) older people who were still born in England, particularly the 'best educated class', still spoke 'perfect standard English', but alas the younger generations spoke a local variety, which (heaven forbid) had clear Cockney qualities to Wall's discerning ear. These were bad qualities of course, guilty by association, although he added that this was less marked (thank heavens) than among the Australians. In Australia, as Kiesling (2004, pp. 421–422) notes, Cockney did enjoy some covert prestige in the early years, but even there, the proportion of Cockney speakers was not high enough that Australian English simply became a transplanted Cockney dialect. Even in South Africa, Hopwood (1928) remarked on the salient Cockney features. Later research has demonstrated that these early impressions were largely caricatures, as Cockney was but one contributor, and not the dominant one. These impressions represented negative value judgements – something still seen in the second half of the twentieth century when Lanham preferred the term 'respectable' South African English for the 'provincial standard', rather than the 'general' of the Australian authors Mitchell and Delbridge (1965), with which Lanham was familiar, judging by the references of his publications after 1965. They are consistent with the idea of an exonormative attitude about the English of the colonies (Schneider, 2003), traces of which could even be detected in the United States in the nineteenth century, long after independence from the British Crown.

The change in language attitude usually followed a reorientation of the identity of the settlers, from seeing themselves as Britons living in another space to being residents of that new space, that is, as Americans, Canadians, Australians or New Zealanders (Schneider, 2003, 2007). These terms, at least as they were understood in the period that led up to self-rule/political independence, denoted that they took control of their political affairs and no longer looked to London to take decisions about their affairs. They also applied quite narrowly to the settler populations: the settlers are the young Australians, for instance, who celebrate their identity with a national anthem (originally composed in 1878) that starts with the words 'Australians all let us rejoice. For we are young and free'.[4] The Americans who lived in 'the land of the free and the home of the brave', a song originally composed in 1814 to commemorate the battle of Baltimore – between the American and British forces – were certainly also of settler extraction and not indigenous at the time, the latter having been largely curtailed in their freedoms and soon to be unsettled even further by the implementation of the Indian Removal Act of 1830.

Political independence, often following a quasi-traumatic event that impressed upon the settler population that they were not so dear to Mother Britain as they thought – called event X by Schneider (2003, 2007) – initiated the move to endonormativity, where the settlers came to accept and promote their local variety as a true expression of their new identity as Americans, Australians, and so on. By this time, the new variety, in terms of its salient vocabulary and its pronunciation, was already in existence, but after event X and the identity reorientation, the attitude towards the variety changed from viewing it as deficient in respect of the authentic British English so revered by Professor Wall in New Zealand in the mid-twentieth century still, to viewing it as acceptable and as an expression of the settlers' new identity.

Yet, as Kachru's conceptualisation of world Englishes in terms of three circles suggests, the settler varieties still form part of an Inner Circle, which allows them the right of ownership of 'their variety', a right that is mostly acknowledged by the other Inner Circle countries. This is a matter of degree, depending on time depth and relative political power. Thus, Canadian English finds it hard to assert its separateness from American English, and much as this may not be factually accurate, speakers of New Zealand English also face the constant challenge of asserting their independence from Australian English once they venture beyond the Antipodes. In this mix, the degree of independence of the settler Englishes of South Africa and Ireland is even less. The very terms 'South African' or 'Irish' do not denote the settler population exclusively – the indigenous population (and in the case of South Africa, the descendants of the earlier

---

4. Incidentally, on 1 January 2021, the word 'young' was replaced by 'one', to expand the definition of the nation from the recently arrived ('young') settlers to a more inclusive 'one'. One wonders whether this was an unexpected instance of wokeness under the leadership of Prime Minister Scott Morrison.

Dutch colonists, as well as descendants of slaves and Indian indentured labourers) all lay equal claim to the national identity. These non-English, non-settler populations contribute much more to the idea of an Irish or South African English than is the case with the four more clear-cut cases of American, Canadian, Australian and New Zealand English. Let us then turn to some of the characteristic linguistic features of these varieties – what they share and what differentiate them from the others.

4.3 Linguistic differences among settler varieties

We know that English is different from one colonial setting to the next. Pronunciation is often the clearest cue, even if the levels of sophistication in telling people apart vary. For people with limited exposure, observing from a distance of several times zones, Canadian and American English are not always easy to tell apart, nor are Northern and Southern dialect speakers in the United States consistently identified by outsiders, but a Southern tends to hear another Southerner quite easily, and a Canadian can tell another Canadian without having to ask them to say *about the house* to check for possible Canadian raising (whether the diphthong is pronounced as [aʊ], with a low onset, or with a raised onset as [ʌʊ] – the form resulting from Canadian raising).

Apart from differences in pronunciation, there are also differences in vocabulary – only South Africans *braai* and cross the street when the *robot* is green; many other native speakers prefer the gentle art of *barbequing* (which in South Africa can only refer to an orderly way to wait for one's haircut, a 'barber queue') or *fire up the barby* (which has nothing to do with a doll in this version of Australian English), and rather cross the street when a *traffic light* turns green. Canadians will be happy to know that they can still park their car in a *parkade* in South Africa, but might of course need to rather ask for directions to a *car park* in Britain or a *parking garage* in the United States. Grammatical differences have also been identified that distinguish various native varieties of English in the former colonies from one another and from English in Britain, although they are generally of a proportional kind rather than a qualitative kind (Leech et al., 2009).

Once English had been transplanted to these new settings, unique changes may have occurred in British English that did not occur in the transplanted varieties. For instance, the glottal stop [ʔ] as variant for /t/ came into widespread use in Cockney and other Southeast English varieties after the North American and Southern Hemisphere varieties were established. Conversely, changes may have occurred in colonial varieties but not in Britain, and in all likelihood in only some but not all colonial varieties, since they do not form a single integrated group, given the vast distances separating Australia and North America or South Africa and New Zealand. This is the case with flapping, the North American English pronunciation of intervocalic /t/ and /d/ as [ɾ] in words like *matter* and *madder* both roughly as [mæɾɹɪ], or *better* as [bɛɾɹɪ].

The exposition of linguistic differences among Inner Circle varieties in this chapter is focused on the input and early homogenising of pronunciation, with particular attention to the development of New Zealand English. This is followed by consideration of colonial vocabulary, together with very recent developments in reversing some of the colonial naming practices.

Internal developments within English are in principle no different in colonial, transplanted varieties of English than in English in Britain or any other language. However, there is one important early factor that contributed strongly to the divergence of colonial varieties of English as they exist at present: in the early contact situation, in every new site of colonial settlement, extensive dialect contact occurred, setting in motion a process of new-dialect formation that was crucial to the subsequent shape of that new variety. This process of extensive dialect contact has been studied most thoroughly for New Zealand.

4.3.1 Pronunciation and new-dialect formation

New Zealand English is one of the most recent Inner Circle varieties to develop. Through an accident of history, extremely valuable information about the development of new varieties in the immediate aftermath of settlement and transplantation is available for this variety. In the years after the Second World War, 1946–1948, the New Zealand Broadcasting corporation had a Mobile Unit that travelled to various parts of the country, trying to discover rural musical talent. They also recorded elderly people in various towns, who were telling stories about the early years of the European settlement in New Zealand. The listening public found the stories of the early years of the New Zealand settlement gripping, leading to further recording tours. A total of almost 300 different speakers, born between 1851 and 1905, were recorded. These recordings were digitised for linguistic analysis by a team of linguists led by Elizabeth Gordon from the University of Canterbury, in Christchurch, New Zealand (see Gordon et al., 2004 for details of the recordings and data processing).

One of the biggest surprises from the recordings was that the majority of speakers born in the nineteenth century and recorded in the late 1940s did not sound like modern New Zealanders. Closer examination of the data (Gordon et al., 2004; Trudgill, 2004) revealed that the oldest speakers, the first generation of European children born in

New Zealand, sounded similar to what one would expect from mid-nineteenth-century British dialect speakers, reflecting the speech of their parents who were the original immigrants, born in Britain or Ireland before emigrating to New Zealand as young adults. The second generation of speakers, from the 1870s and 1880s, did not sound like speakers of New Zealand English either, but were particularly striking for the very extensive variability in their speech, both intra-speaker and inter-speaker. Certain speakers showed combinations of phonetic features that were completely unusual from the perspective of nineteenth-century British dialects, such as sporadic /h/-dropping in words like *house*, *Harry* and *Hagrid*, a feature transplanted from Southern English dialects, in combination with the retention of the /hw/–/w/ contrast between words such as *which* and *witch*, typical of Irish, Scottish and some Northern English dialects. These features were both variably present among speakers recorded by the Mobile Unit, although both have largely disappeared from contemporary New Zealand English. The curious observation is that there were certain early New Zealand English speakers whose speech displayed both features. Speaker-internal variability was also observed to be much more extensive than expected. Only speakers born towards the end of the nineteenth century began to sound like New Zealand speakers in a contemporary sense.

On the basis of the analysis of the Mobile Unit speakers, Trudgill (2004) developed a three-stage account of the development of a new Inner Circle dialect such as New Zealand English. Stage I is called rudimentary levelling. During this stage, adults accommodate to one another, but to the limited extent that adults are able to. They mainly weed out marginal and clearly stigmatised features. Trudgill (2004, pp. 89–91) argues that this process already started on the boat trip to New Zealand, which lasted several months. Adults may have been more sensitive to matters of prestige, but were mainly driven by the need to avoid features that could jeopardise mutual intelligibility.

Stage II is called variability and apparent levelling. The children living during this stage were still confronted with extreme variability in the input from their parents, and did not have a peer group with a stable variety to target. These children, born between 1850 and 1870, were the ones who displayed the most extreme inter- and intra-speaker variability of the speakers recorded by the Mobile Unit. They selected variants from a very diverse pool of candidate forms, and did so in ways that seem inconsistent at individual level. Crucially, according to Trudgill (2004, p. 108), there is limited evidence of accommodation through convergence to other speakers for the children born during stage II. Nevertheless, these children still weed out a large number of minor variants, variants with a frequency below 10 per cent for the larger population, according to Trudgill's (2004, pp. 110–111) estimate. They are not salient enough to be noticed by the children, and are therefore not reproduced by them. Nevertheless, the variants that remain in noticeable enough frequencies are reflected in the speech of the children, in ways that seem unpredictable at individual level, yet at societal level, the speech of the children born in this phase (and recorded in very advanced age in the late 1940s) reflects the proportional share of the variants that would have been part of their input. Trudgill (2004) terms this 'apparent levelling' (p. 109) – in a statistical but not intentional sense, levelling still takes place. Children of this generation did not stay within the boundaries of the transplanted dialects, but recombined in their individual speech all the input variants that were sufficiently salient, to lay the foundation for the third stage.

Stage III is the phase where the new dialect is formed, in a purely deterministic way, according to Trudgill (2004, pp. 113–115). The children born after the 1870s selected the majority variants from the entire feature pool of inputs inherited from stage II input, and they achieved a focused, less variable and more stable new variety. What counts as majority variant is determined per individual feature, which explains why the new variety reproduces not simply the most numerous input dialect but rather the aggregate of all the input dialects, where the majority variant per variable is selected. At this stage, children do accommodate to one another again, because the reduced pool of variants makes that feasible (Trudgill, 2004, p. 127).

Based on this account, Trudgill (2004) argues that the similarities between New Zealand English and the other Southern Hemisphere varieties can be explained too. These varieties formed on the basis of reasonably similar dialect mixtures, just not identical ones, but through the same process. Thus, he argues,

> If you bake cakes, I suggest, from roughly the same ingredients in roughly the same proportions in roughly similar conditions for roughly the same length of time, you will get roughly similar cakes. (p. 20)

Speakers of Southern Hemisphere Englishes generally have higher articulations for the front vowels in words like KIT, DRESS and TRAP (using the lexical sets from Wells, 1982, as is customary for describing vowel variation in native varieties of English), but those in New Zealand are higher still, which Trudgill (2004) finds consistent with the very high variants in the input. A New Zealander will pronounce *ten* in a way that many other speakers of English might mistakenly hear as *tin*, something like [t^{h}en], which a South African or Australian might still hear as intended, but a Southern British speaker may struggle to identify.

Once a New Zealander says [tʰɪn], though, even the South African and Australian will struggle, as [tʰen] is as high as they go. New Zealanders and South Africans share the inclination to pronounce *tin* not with a front vowel [ɪ] as Southern British speakers tend to do, nor with an [i] as some Australians do, but a more central variant, sometimes signalled by a transcription of diacritic marks to indicate centralisation, [ï], but sometimes the centralisation is so extensive that it sounds like the neutral vowel [ə], the schwa, to many, especially those outside New Zealand and South Africa. Yet, New Zealanders use this vowel in all environments, while South Africans only use it in some environments. To illustrate, the three closely related Southern Hemisphere varieties of Australian, New Zealand and South African English pronounce the word *cricket* in three different ways. An Australian, most similar to the person from the South of England, would say [kɹɪkʰɪt], a South African will have a different second vowel [kɹɪkʰət], while a New Zealander would likely say [kɹəkʰət]. These differences are very slight, and there are other clear similarities of these three Southern Hemisphere varieties that may lead outsiders to confuse them, but a small number of differences can be identified, due to different allophones, which were all likely present in the input varieties of all three but were selected differently as the modern variety came to stabilise.

4.3.2 Vocabulary

In these new settings, speakers of English were confronted by a new landscape, new animals and new plants, and came into contact with people with whom their British parents and cousins were not in contact. English speakers borrowed terms from indigenous populations to the extent that there was sufficient contact to enable access to the indigenous vocabulary. A typical example is the Canadian capital city of Ottawa, named after the Ottawa river, whose name is likely derived from a form *adawe* or *atawa* that means 'to trade' or 'to buy and sell' in several Algonquian languages (Rayburn, 2001, p. 231). It reached the English language via French, since the speakers of French already came into contact with the Algonquian tribe whose name contains this form in the seventeenth century (Rayburn, 2001, p. 232).

Other naming strategies make use of available material in the English language, such as a description of something salient about the place, for instance the *Blue Mountains* in New South Wales, Australia, or *Table Mountain* in Cape Town, South Africa (the latter representing a loan translation from the Cape Dutch coinage). In some instances, the naming of the landscape draws on the ancestral home of the settlers, where either the places themselves or names of important metropolitan or colonial figures are used, as introduced in Chapter 3 with reference to the various cities that have London as (part of) their name, but also the non-English Yorks and New Yorks, not to mention some Perths, Aberdeens and Belfasts scattered across the colonies.

Extending existing English words to new meanings is another strategy. One such adaptation that occurs quite widely in former colonies is 'bush' (*OED*, n1, sense 9). In this sense, current in Australia, New Zealand, South Africa and Canada, bush refers to a natural area, which may have trees, and these should be indigenous, but not a forest. It mainly refers to an uncultivated area. The *OED* mentions Dutch influence, which is certainly plausible for South Africa and may be a consideration in the other areas, although less probable.

While developments within English and contact with other languages are the two broad types of language change mechanisms by which English differentiated in the various places, there is nevertheless some order in all this. Vocabulary borrowings are quite common in the early contact situation, but they are usually restricted to topography, fauna and flora, and new objects and practices associated with the indigenous people (Schneider, 2007). Only in cases of much more extensive contact with speakers of other languages, such as what obtained between English speakers and Afrikaans/Cape Dutch speakers in South Africa, would the borrowing extend further than the scenarios listed above. Examples of such Afrikaans borrowings include *bakkie* ('small pick-up truck', literally a 'bowl'), *braai* (barbeque, literally 'fry') and *lekker* ('nice'), as well as a fairly extensive range of slang terms, many of which are quite offensive.

Two recent trends are potentially going to reverse some of the colonial vocabulary practices: the restoration of original indigenous names and the reconsideration of names that honour controversial colonial figures. Renaming occurs in a world where political sentiment has changed away from the glorification of the colonial achievements and an uncritical acceptance of the colonial heritage, therefore various indigenous names for places and people are being restored and English names replaced. This happened very prominently in the early years after independence in Outer Circle contexts, such as the renaming of *Rhodesia* to *Zimbabwe*, together with new names (often restoring names from the pre-colonial era) for almost all cities and towns that had received colonial names. It is also an ongoing process in post-liberation South Africa, where both colonial and apartheid era names are being replaced by indigenous names – sometimes restoring older names for the areas, sometimes assigning new names. In some cases, a compromise decision is made where the city itself retains its colonial name, but the metropolitan area of which it forms part gets a new name. The city of Port Elizabeth (originally named after the wife of the governor of the Cape Colony at the time of the establishment of the town by British settlers in 1820) is now part of the Nelson Mandela Bay Metropolitan Municipality,[5] and the city of Pretoria (originally named after the (father of the) Afrikaner leader who established the town in 1855) is now part of the Tshwane Metropolitan Municipality. In the case of Nelson Mandela Bay, the name of a contemporary leader was selected, whereas in the case of Tshwane, the choice was for a name that was current in the mid-nineteenth century, then used for the river flowing through the city and gradually also coming into use by the indigenous population for the entire city.

In (former) colonies demographically dominated by settlers, the naming practices and the appropriation of indigenous terms continued unchallenged for most of the history of these territories, because dramatic political power shifts like those in Zimbabwe and South Africa did not happen. Only in recent years, as part of nation-building processes and due to political pressure from minorities, have some of these names been reconsidered. In the case of New Zealand, active attempts at redressing historical grievances have been made since the mid-1970s, after the Treaty of Waitangi Act of 1975. Historical land rights are more central to the restoration process, but a number of steps have been taken to at least recognise dual names for a number of New Zealand places and landmarks (using both the Māori and English names), or correct spelling errors in European versions of Māori names. This concerns cases where places or landmarks had indigenous historical names. Reweti (n.d.) points out that most places visited and named by Captain Cook on his voyage already had indigenous names, and he was aware of and used some, but he also invented new names in other cases:

> Cook's chart of New Zealand has a few Māori names recorded, but the majority of landmarks are Cook's own coinages.
>
> While he gave insightful names such as 'Flat Island' to Mōtiti and 'White Island' to the active stratovolcano island of Whakaari, many of his names smothered the original ones, layering irrelevant meanings from a distant country onto a landscape already known and named. It is difficult to reconcile such a steadfast practice of disregarding Māori knowledge.

A different case, thrust into the limelight more recently, is the reconsideration of names assigned by the settlers and their descendants that

---

5. Port Elizabeth was renamed Gqeberha as of 2021, though, rescinding the earlier compromise.

commemorate historical figures or events that are viewed in a very different light today. Such a debate has been waged in Canada for some time, according to Macdougall (2018). She points to the two sides of such debates, the two different ways in which historical figures whose names are given to human institutions or new places are viewed. Oftentimes in earlier history, their noteworthy achievements were the reason for their names being used in the first place, but through a modern lens, their colonial roles, including their complicity and participation in slavery and the destruction of indigenous cultures or even killing of indigenous peoples, render their continued celebration problematic. A process of reconsidering the names with negative colonial associations is under way in both Canada and the United States, and gained extra traction with the reignition of the Black Lives Matter campaign in 2020, extending even to questions being asked of colonial symbols in the United Kingdom, not to mention the removal of statues, most famously the statue of Rhodes on the grounds of the University of Cape Town in South Africa, which generated a hashtag #Rhodesmustfall and some global appeal. Of course, these are heated debates that coincide with a period of very extreme political polarisation in the United States in the age of Twitter (also known as X) and contested election results, in Britain after Brexit, and no less in South Africa where the rainbow miracle of 1994 seems to have gone into hiding (Spencer, 2011). The linguistic consequences will become apparent in the decades ahead.

4.4 Conclusion

English has been transplanted to a number of countries by native speakers who left British shores for good. In these new places, new varieties of English developed, which are different from one another due to differences in pronunciation and vocabulary in particular, while a few grammatical and stylistic differences also exist, don't they?[6]

The contact among speakers of English and with speakers of other languages, together with the communicative needs that arose in these new settings, contributed to shaping the language in slightly different ways. Over time, these differences came to be recognised, initially without approval, but later on, they gained acceptance and the new varieties

---

6. If the tag question strikes the reader as rather old-fashioned, a ready-made Australian equivalent could be to just add 'mate' instead of the tag question, and South African English offers 'neh' as the full translation equivalent. ('Neh' should really be spelled 'nè', but hardly anyone who cares to write the word, does.) Otherwise, one can do Very Standard, and just skip such spoken-language gimmicks in a sober academic text.

became their own reference points, relinquishing the British norms that the early generations still acknowledged, at least in theory.

The world keeps changing, and the English language continues to adapt. Current changes include new forms of contact, which will be revisited in Chapter 8, but also new ideological challenges and difficult questions about the colonial past, and their linguistic consequences. Some words are just beyond the pale today, and using them in the wrong way will generate extensive public uproar, while using new forms has always been a matter of concern to the concerned segments of society, and no less so today. The work *woke* has gone from a positive encouragement for betterment to a swearword that summarises everything that is wrong (with the left) today. One fears for the day when some woke Irish troublemakers argue that the English expression 'beyond the pale' is offensive to them, as their ancestors were the original ones that were beyond the pale of the English sensitivities. To make matters worse, the language itself is now used beyond the watchful eye of its 300 million speakers, and the usage of these new users holds further consequences for the shape of the language and direction of change. Let's turn to the ones who became speakers of the language too in Chapter 5, before considering those who 'stubbornly' cling to other first languages while adding English to their repertoires in Chapters 6 and 7.

5 Becoming an English speaker

Many people living in (former) British colonies today are native speakers of English, but are not descendants of English-speaking settlers. Non-English-speaking immigrants to the British colonial settlements who became absorbed into the speech community played a limited role in shaping English, and to the extent that the assimilation has been complete, their present-day offspring do not use English differently from their settler-descendant peers (Mufwene, 2001). There was a shifting generation, but these were 'typical' immigrant language shift contexts, in the sense that the parents were second-language speakers but their children became native speakers. These children were supported to various degrees by second-language English input from their parents, but more crucially by strong community support in their peer groups, cancelling out the transfer features of their parents' shift variety.

The process of becoming an English speaker was not so smooth for many others, though, with no or limited integration into the settler English-speaking community, which in turn resulted in the emergence of varieties of English that are recognisably different to the present. There are two groups that have historically fallen into this category: non-English migrants who entered the new space as slaves or later as indentured labourers, with their descendants on the one hand, for example the Englishes spoken on many Caribbean islands and on mainland North America, or the Englishes of Indians in South Africa and Caribbean countries; and on the other hand, indigenous people who were dominated demographically by settlers and who shifted to English over time, losing their ancestral languages, such as many of the Native Americans, Aboriginal Australians and Māori New Zealanders. The historically native Irish of Ireland also resemble the minority indigenous people in most respects, despite not being a demographically marginal group; they were a socially and economically marginalised group, and breaking out of such marginalisation often went hand in hand with language shift.

At the risk of some oversimplification, the two groups are categorised as forced labour migrants and indigenous minorities. The exact nuances of the degree of force in compelling indentured labourers into migration in comparison with slaves or the degree of minoritisation of the Irish are considered in the discussion during the course of this chapter, but are not made salient by these two broad group labels. The Englishes that emerged from these two sets of conditions are often labelled creole in the case of native varieties developing in context of slavery,[1] and language-shift Englishes where a second-language variety of English itself becomes the native variety of the next generation without a significant native-speaker peer group counterweight to constrain the selection of features that diverge from typical native-speaker Englishes. Pidgin Englishes, which are usually not native-speaker varieties and developed in trade or workplace contexts without the speakers being uprooted from their native speech communities, are considered in Chapter 6 with other second-language varieties that developed in colonial contexts.

5.1 The histories of shifting communities

European imperial powers claimed territories inhabited by indigenous peoples throughout the colonial period, and then set about exploiting the opportunities that arose. In some cases, this resulted in large-scale settlement by Europeans, which turned out to become permanent settlements. In other cases, farming operations were set up to exploit favourable conditions for cash crops that earned high returns for the owners, but where settlement remained limited – which was typically the case across the Caribbean and parts of Central and South America. In many cases, the initial expectation of the Europeans was that they would force the indigenous population into the role of labourers, be that for small-scale, diversified agriculture or for large, plantation-style cultivation of sugar cane and other cash crops. However, through various factors, not least of which was poor resistance to European illnesses that delivered fatal blows to indigenous Caribbean and American populations (Diamond, 1997), the native populations did not provide the labour required by the European exploiters. The solution that 'presented itself' was slave labour, which was imported mainly from West Africa in the case of the British.

---

1. The need for a linguistic category of 'creole' languages is subject to serious debate in the field. In this book, an agnostic view is adopted, but one that includes creoles within the scope of world Englishes, and ties them to the language-shift varieties emerging in other contexts. See Velupillai (2015) for a thorough treatment of creoles in relation to pidgins and mixed languages.

Slaves were bought or captured along the African west coast by ships from Europe, which also carried some manufactured merchandise to sell at the trading ports. From these West African trading ports, ships were loaded with slaves and transported across the Atlantic to the Caribbean and Americas. Slaves were sold on markets there, and agricultural produce, such as sugar and tobacco, was bought, loaded onto the ships and sold back in Europe. This process constituted the Atlantic slave trade triangle, and lasted from the late fifteenth century until deep into the nineteenth century. Bans on slave trade in the early nineteenth century, followed by the emancipation of slaves later in the century in Britain and America put an end to the continued influx of enslaved Africans to the Caribbean and United States, but by then, the linguistic consequences were already established – founder's effects in various locations resulting in a reasonably stable variety of English. These varieties, called creoles by many, or broken English or even pidgin, should be regarded as varieties of English that reveal their origins just as much as settler Englishes reveal their origins into the present. Thus, following Mufwene (1997, 2001), these varieties will not be regarded as illegitimate offspring but as equally important parts of the broader canvas of world Englishes.

Mufwene (2001) distinguishes between the homestead phase and the plantation phase of slave labour. During the homestead phase, relatively smaller numbers of slaves worked on farms in reasonably direct contact with European owners and European labour. This was typical of the early settlements, not only in what was to become the United States but also on Caribbean islands such as Barbados and Jamaica. Once the economy changed to cash-crop plantations, the small farmers were often bought out and 'ownership' of the land became concentrated in the hands of a few landlords. This was followed by extensive importation of slaves to work on the plantations, without a concomitant increase in the number of English speakers, which changed the patterns of language contact and language acquisition. For example, while in Barbados there was a considerable proportion of European settlers, representing a 2:1 slave to settler ratio until the middle of the eighteenth century on this island, in Jamaica the corresponding ratio was 10:1 (Mufwene, 2001, pp. 38–39). In consequence, the variety of English in Barbados is less different from settler varieties than the variety in Jamaica (Mufwene, 2001; Schneider, 2007). In general, the early homestead phase resulted in varieties of English that were less divergent from the Englishes of the native speakers, while the plantation phase gave rise to more divergent varieties, those that are more typically labelled creole.

After the abolition of slavery in the British Empire, the need for labour to work on plantations did not go away, and the solution of indentured labour was exploited to fill the void. Indentured labour contracts were not a new invention subsequent to the end of slavery, but had existed side by side with slavery before the nineteenth century. The contract involved a contractual obligation to provide labour for a set period, in exchange for passage to the colony where the contract was to be served and accommodation and food for the duration of the contract. While this does not sound particularly appealing to modern judgement, it was a better option than starvation or the meagre alternatives at the time, at least in the judgement of those who elected to sign such contracts. Hence, indentured labourers, often of Irish extraction, were prominent contributors to the early American economy, and many chose to remain behind on the termination of their contracts. To various degrees, they were absorbed into the settler speech community without developing a stable, separate variety of English.

This played out differently for nineteenth-century indentured labourers, though. While economically destitute Irish and British subjects continued to take up indentured contracts, indentured labourers for the plantations of the Caribbean, and by now also South Africa and the Indian and Pacific Ocean islands, were often from British India. Thus, the present-day Indian citizens of Trinidad and Tobago, Guyana, and Jamaica trace their ancestry to the indentured labourers of the nineteenth and early twentieth centuries, as do South Africans, Fijians or Mauritians. Descendants of the Indian indentured labourers were sometimes joined by other Indians who came as voluntary migrants and were engaged mainly in trade (Mesthrie, 2014). Some present-day Indian communities retained Indian languages as their primary language, such as Hindi in Fiji – which, similar to settler Englishes, is not identical to any of the varieties of Hindi in India but a form that emerged locally through koineisation of various North Indian languages and dialects (Zipp, 2014). For a long period, a similar koineised Hindi–Bhojpuri developed as the medium of wider communication among part of the Indian communities in South Africa (Mesthrie, 1991). However, language shift to English has taken place in many settings, including most of the Caribbean (e.g. Leung & Deuber, 2014, on Trinidad) and South Africa (Mesthrie, 2014), where Indian languages are not transmitted to new generations and English has become the home language for the descendants of nineteenth- and early twentieth-century Indian immigrants.

The other language-shift English users, whose native variety of English is recognisably different from the settler native varieties, are indigenous minorities in settler-dominant settings. Through a combination of the very large scale of European immigration, alongside the devastating effect of European illnesses on indigenous populations and armed conflicts (one may say 'special military operations' in twenty-first-century lingo, as long as one keeps in mind that these were ultimately one-sided battles the outcomes of which many would, justifiably, simply call genocide), indigenous people in American, Canada, Australia and New Zealand were pushed to the margins of the social and geographical spaces, and became demographic minorities in their ancestral lands.

Until the nineteenth century, the indigenous populations lived in reservations – areas of land set aside for their exclusive habitation and cultivation – for as long as the Europeans did not need the land, though. Contact was limited, and a few intermediaries with proficiency in English – broken, competent, native-like or otherwise – were sufficient to negotiate the few points of contact. However, a measure of integration, often economic and not social, combined with attempts at forced acculturation into the dominant European culture resulted in the acquisition of English as a second language. These measures included the Residential Schools of Canada from 1876 to 1996, to which children were forcibly removed and where they were forbidden to use their home languages or adhere to indigenous practices (Miller, 2021), the boarding schools of America (Leap, 1993) and the forced assimilation programmes in Australia since 1869, yielding the so-called Stolen Generations of children who grew up in facilities of the government and missionaries to be assimilated into the mainstream culture and language (Commonwealth of Australia, 1997).

The final step came in the past century, where English replaced the indigenous languages as home languages for many individuals from these communities, particularly to the extent that they left the area of residence among fellow indigenous people and moved to the towns and cities where they became integrated into the economies. When children from indigenous backgrounds started to attend school among children from settler English dominant backgrounds, they were likely to shift to English as the dominant language and acquired the peer group variety. To the extent that the world in which they lived was dominated by contacts with fellow indigenous people, the ethnolectal characteristics of their English continued to be transmitted, but to the extent that ethnic contacts begin to fade into the background, more recent generations become increasingly less distinctive from the majority variety of the environment.

English is the native language of the majority of people living in the Republic of Ireland and the province of Northern Ireland within the United Kingdom today. Yet, historically, the settlers from Britain represent a considerable proportion but not much more than half the population in the northeast, and a minority elsewhere – most of Ireland remained beyond the pale. Language shift from Irish to English took place over a relatively long time (approximately 1600–1900); English remained a second language rather than the first language for most native Irish until the nineteenth century. Bilingualism ceded to English monolingualism only in the nineteenth century, when incorporation into the urban economies drew increasing proportions of rural Irish to the English cities, where eventually the transmission of Irish as their home language declined and children grew up as monolingual English speakers (Hickey, 2004, p. 92).

The degree of completeness of language shift within communities varies. For languages spoken by descendants of slaves, the shift to English is complete throughout the Caribbean, where African languages are no longer spoken. Alleyne and Hall-Alleyne (1982) review reports from the first half of the twentieth century and earlier, showing how the Maroon language of Jamaica, mainly a transplanted form of Twi-Asante, had by and large disappeared at that time except for a few older semi-speakers and, by the 1980s, only a few words that were still known but not used spontaneously any more. Indian languages, which were transplanted later than African languages under the system of indenture, are still in use at the time of writing, but are under severe pressure in many of the transplanted contexts because they are no longer transmitted in most Caribbean, Mauritian or South African homes. One very clear exception is Fiji, where the local form of Hindi is still alive and well, and English functions as a second language rather than the native language for most Fijians of Indian descent.

Turning to indigenous languages spoken before British occupation and settlement, the situation is often dire for many languages, but some retain a measure of vitality. Thus, many North American and Australian languages have died out, but a few are still used by indigenous communities who are generally also proficient in English. In Ireland, Irish is still used in some homes in the Gaeltacht, and Irish is taught as a second language in schools, keeping the use of the language alive, if not always in home-language functions. The same is true for the Māori language in New Zealand, although the native speakers constitute a higher proportion of the indigenous community than is the case with Irish. Māori speakers are usually proficient users of New Zealand English as a second language, with little differentiation among native and second-language speakers of the ethnolect where it concerns proficient users.

5.2 Social forces in shifting communities

5.2.1 Contact

Contact between speakers of other languages with the English language is an essential requirement for shifting to English. One would of course expect, as has been the argument in this book so far, that such contact with a language implies contact with its speakers, since languages do not exist beyond speakers. Yet, for oppressed indigenous minorities and forced labour migrants shifting to English, the contact with speakers of English was quite limited. The nature of such contact ranged from very acrimonious, oppressive and violent to barely benevolent neglect. For the slaves and indigenous minorities, especially further back in history, until the second half of the nineteenth century, the full humanity of the shifting speakers was not recognised, neither legally nor morally. Extreme power differentials resulted in limited verbal interaction, and thus reduced the amount of English input from native speakers in the shifting context.

One might ask why speakers shifted at all then, given the circumstances. The English language clearly did not come with a recommendation that mastery of the language would grant access to social acceptance by native speakers and membership of their speech community. The answers are rather straightforward for many of the shifting speakers, and only somewhat more complex for a few, particularly the Irish and Indian indentured labourers of the late nineteenth and early twentieth centuries.

Slaves had no viable alternative. With a few exceptions, the slave population had no common language with a sufficient number of speakers to make it a viable in-group code. In the context of adjustment to a traumatic new life under conditions of hardship and constant threat of violent punishment and death, wrested away from a life within a broader speech community, the first priority would have been personal safety, for which mastery of some English to understand orders and respond appropriately was essential and unavoidable. During the earliest periods when slaves were relocated to the United States, but even to the Caribbean islands, the plantations were not yet an important part of the economies. This phase, the homestead phase, was characterised by relatively fewer slaves living on farms with European masters and indentured servants – European but often not English-speaking. More extensive input from the English speakers in the environment, combined with more regular interaction, would have given rise to second-language varieties of English among the non-native speakers that bore strong resemblance to the input. If these varieties were acquired by children, of whom there were relatively more in the homestead phase, a local variety of English would have emerged that was not creole-like but reasonably similar to the emerging native variety of the English-speaking settlers (Mufwene, 2001, pp. 50, 80). What remains obvious about this phase is that the languages spoken natively by the arriving slaves had very limited currency, and no speech community developed for the African languages that the transported slaves spoke. New slaves who continued to arrive from various places learnt English mostly from slaves who were already there, alongside continued input from masters and indentured labourers, leaving no space for African languages to be used meaningfully (Mufwene, 2001, p. 51).

When the plantation phase commenced, the situation changed in several ways. Many more slaves and relatively fewer English speakers occupied the same space, with considerably less interaction. More deliberate racial segregation was also applied. Locally born slaves and old hands who had been there for several years and managed to stay alive became an important source of input for the acquisition of English by the new arrivals. Native-speaker slave children were relatively less important in the plantation phase, since 'population replacement' took place through importation rather than birth, although a relatively high proportion of children under fourteen, even under ten, were among the slaves arriving anew from Africa throughout the eighteenth century in the most severe period of slavery (Mufwene, 2001, pp. 50–51). The main linguistic consequence of the plantation phase was basilectalisation – much greater divergence between the English used among slaves and native-speaker varieties, including the variety that stabilised among slaves during the homestead phase (Mufwene, 2001, p. 51). During the plantation phase too, there was simply no meaningful use of the indigenous African languages, except for a few individuals who happened to have been part of the workforce of a particular plantation and spoke the same language. They would have been able to use the language amongst themselves, but transmission to others would not have taken place on a scale that allowed language maintenance across generations.

For indentured labourers in the early American settlements, the personal situation was potentially less dire. However, stable speech communities did not develop for Irish, German or other European languages spoken by indentured labourers, as it happened for voluntary immigrants. Those indentured labourers who stayed seem to have shifted to English within the first generation and became absorbed into the local settler community, rather than forming separate linguistic islands.

The nineteenth-century indentured labourers from India were also able to maintain their ancestral languages for longer, but apart from Fiji, most of their present-day descendants shifted to English over the course of the twentieth century. In South Africa, the fostering of a community across the different ancestral languages of India, combined with the lack of economic value and even the low prestige of the local varieties of Indian languages like Bhojpuri (in comparison with Standard Hindi), conspired to instigate language shift in the third quarter of the twentieth century (Mesthrie, 1991). A similar fate befell the Indian languages in the Caribbean. The contact with native speakers was not extensive, yet this was largely a bottom-up process of language shift driven by parents who were second-language speakers themselves and acquired some English, in the workplace, from other Indians, and some formal education in the twentieth century. Overall, the language-shift English of South African Indians is very clearly distinctive from the settler varieties, and developed its own momentum within the community.

In the Queensland plantations of the late nineteenth century, Mufwene (2020, pp. 108–109) identifies a similar contact configuration with diverse languages spoken by labourers and limited English input. The English-lexified creole named Kriol developed in this setting, which in turn had further impact on Pacific pidgin varieties of English as these labourers returned home after the conclusion of their contracts. The situation may have been less desperate for these labourers than for slaves, but the patterns of contact and the linguistic outcomes were quite similar.

The shift from Irish to English within Ireland in the seventeenth to nineteenth centuries, according to Hickey (2004), also saw the second-language English speakers do most of the work. There was little native-speaker contact and a limited role for education, but during the shift, the degree of linguistic paralysis experienced by slaves was not present, as the generation before the shift was still mostly bilingual and could communicate in Irish or English. Only from the nineteenth century did Irish gradually yield to English in the home domain as well, and did children grow up who were native speakers of English (with diminishing competence in Irish). In this sense, the shift was less traumatic and did not cut people off from their own communities, although there was a strong degree of economic coercion, with legal constraints on the use of Irish in the workplace ultimately contributing to tip the scale against the maintenance of Irish. The coercion was of course not comparable to the situation of the slaves.

For speakers of minority indigenous languages in most settlement colonies, the situation was generally more traumatic than for the Irish, but traumas were of a different kind than the situation of the slaves. After an early period of little contact, and residence on reservations, indigenous peoples in North America and Australia did not acquire much English for lack of contact and lack of need, beyond a few intermediaries. Towards the end of the nineteenth century, the situation changed and boarding schools were established where children were compelled to learn English, where the use of indigenous languages was prohibited and often punished severely. Proficiency in English ensued, as there was no alternative. In some ways, the boarding schools (or residential schools – nomenclature differed across these countries) were very similar to the missionary schools of the late nineteenth- and early twentieth-century British exploitation colonies — to be presented in Chapter 6 — with one big difference in demographics: when indigenous adults were compelled into wage labour in towns and cities, they formed minorities and over time, language shift took place. However, there were often ethnic neighbourhoods or social groups, within which ethnolectal features solidified in the language-shift variety of the indigenous people turned speakers of English. Education and workplace contact formed the main points of contact for the shifting generations (see also Schneider's, 2007, discussion of the various contexts, where language shift started typically in phase 2 and 3 already for the indigenous people of Australasia); when children acquired English as a native language from them, ethnolectal features were often selected and stabilised, as the degree of integration in the settler community remained limited.

5.2.2 Use

The use of language-shift Englishes today is similar to that of settler Englishes in terms of domains: the home and private life, as well as in the institutions of public life and international contacts. However, for most of the language-shift Englishes, the language of public life tends to be closer to a standard variety, a local one in the case of settler-dominated colonies, and a partially exonormative one in the case of most Caribbean settings and areas where descendants of indentured labourers live. A larger degree of bidialectalism is therefore required from many who want to participate in middle-class public life and be successful at higher levels of education. Adding a more standardised form of English is also quite important for international usage. A partial exception, especially in the Caribbean, is the use of the native dialect of English in entertainment, for example in music, which in turn has led to international visibility for some of the dialects. Some Caribbean cricket commentators, such as the settler-descendant Tony Couzier and the slave-descendant Michael Holding, became household names through much of the former British Empire – those parts that play competitive cricket – since the advent of international live broadcasting of cricket in the late 1970s. These commentators may perhaps style-shift when broadcasting for an international audience, but similarities remain across different Caribbean commentators, irrespective of heritage, especially as far as pronunciation is concerned.

5.2.3 Acquisition

Given these contact conditions, one can pick out how acquisition proceeded. Adults or older children acquired English in limited contact with settlers, and had to do some work to craft a language from the input within a peer group of similar non-native speakers. These second-language learners were speakers of the same language in the case of indigenous minority contexts, such as Irish or Māori; but among slaves and some indentured labourers, the linguistic background consisted of several languages that were not mutually intelligible. At some point, for reasons of survival, parents began using English with their children – immediately, if there were no other languages that the parents could sensibly use, as was the case in conditions of slavery. Shared or similar features of the various languages that the slaves brought to the contact setting, together with the sparse input of mainly non-standard native speakers, provided a backdrop for the slaves and the children born in bondage to reconstruct a language with the available means – competition and selection among a feature pool that consisted of features not present in the input to settler children's language acquisition, as proposed by Mufwene (2001).

Language shift took longer in the case where the family structure was not broken up to the same degree, especially in the case of indigenous minorities then. In the case of the assimilation projects in the Inner Circle countries, particularly the United States, Canada and Australia, children were forced into boarding schools, removed from their families, and compelled to learn English in schools with an English-only policy. This had the 'desired' linguistic effect in most cases: children became fluent speakers of English, although some features of their other languages remained. In other cases, the schools, with strong emphasis on English, had the same effect, if in less oppressive contexts, accounting for the advanced acquisition of English by the Māori and South African Indians, who then over time came to use the coloniser's language in the home with the next generation of children.

The children acquired their parents' English as a native language, like any other native speaker, but their parents' input variety, which corresponded to the input from the rest of the community, was in origin a variety quite different from the settler varieties of the broader environment. In such a context, properties of second-language acquisition, such as regularisation and simplification, which became entrenched in the English of the shifting generation, were adopted by the children (Mesthrie, 1992). Apart from the formal school context of boarding/residential schools from the late nineteenth century for indigenous minorities, much of the reshaping of English took place among adults outside the school context, and thus the formal, standard variety of English played a limited role in the development of language-shift Englishes.

5.2.4 Attitudes

Attitudes towards English and the local varieties of English are quite complex for most communities whose ancestors shifted to English under the less than favourable conditions covered in this chapter. The act of shifting was a survival strategy for those in bondage, as there was no serious alternative, not even for personal use. For the communities that shifted under less dire circumstances, like indigenous minorities or the Indians of South Africa and the Irish, a sense of attachment to the ancestral language remains and the degree of ownership claims on English remains ambivalent (see Hickey, 2009, for Irish as a good case in point). Such unfavourable self-perceptions of the 'ethnolect' of English are reinforced by the generally low socio-economic status of the speakers and their minoritisation within settler-dominant communities, resulting in unfavourable attitudes towards such non-standard varieties in the larger society.

In almost all the cases considered in this chapter, the outcome of language shift was a 'non-standard' variety, in which adult second-language acquisition played a larger role and formal education, a minimal or no role. In many Caribbean contexts, this non-standard variety enjoys considerable covert prestige (see Schneider, 2007, on Barbados and Jamaica), but for a long time, the exonormative British standard was the prestige variety, promoted by the education system and demanded in public, apart from some latitude for local pronunciation. More favourable attitudes towards wider contexts of use are emerging in the Caribbean at present.

Indian South African English likewise continues to enjoy covert prestige, and while greater linguistic convergence with the native variety of the descendants of settlers is emerging as a consequence of greater social interaction after apartheid, the covert prestige is not diminished and the variety remains in use in personal interaction, as a strategic resource, and remains a vibrant resource for navigating the social dynamics in the country (Mesthrie, forthcoming). Recent changes in South Africa result in wider tolerance for diversity, especially at the level of pronunciation, resulting in more widespread favourable attitudes towards Indian South African English beyond its primary speech community (Coetzee-Van Rooy & Van Rooy, 2005). Overall, Indian South African English, while spoken by a demographic minority, does enjoy relatively high socio-economic prestige, and its speakers are among the most highly educated social groups in the country as a whole.

An important recent change in the global attitudes towards non-standard language-shift varieties is the fame of African American and Jamaican English in the entertainment and online sphere. These varieties are the carriers of particular styles of entertainment and the (perhaps subversive) cultural value that the entertainment represents (e.g. hip-hop or reggae, together with the cultures surrounding them), which has seen them grow in prestige. Mair (2013a) points out that it is the non-standard varieties, more divergent and distinctive from the standard varieties, that enjoy such global fame, not the more standardised English of Jamaica, for instance. However, this global entertainment phenomenon should not be confused with a favourable society-wide revaluation of African American English in the United States, or any other such ethnolects, as linguistic profiling and consequent discrimination continue to be rife (Baugh, 2016).

5.3 Linguistic characteristics of language-shift Englishes

The language-shift Englishes have in common influences from the other contact languages (in pronunciation, grammar and vocabulary), as well as general properties of second-language acquisition. The less contact there was with English during the period of shift and the quicker the shift, the more pronounced these features, alongside a number of features in the Caribbean, shared with creole varieties of diverse languages, where dependent morphemes of any sort tend to be avoided and replaced by separate morphemes with lexical roots – such as pre-verbal markers of tense and aspect, rather than inflections. A combined effect of many of these processes is the simplification of irregularity and greater explicitness and transparency in the form-to-function mappings. Because of the wide range of contact languages involved, over and above the differences in patterns of contact and access to English input, the varieties in this chapter do not exhibit uniformity at a more detailed level. Detailed reviews of linguistic features of groups of varieties, such as the Caribbean Englishes (Aceto, 2020) or pidgins and creoles more widely with ample attention to the Caribbean ones (Velupillai, 2015), Irish English (Hickey, 2007) and Indian South African English (Mesthrie, 1992), can be found alongside pointed, concise treatment in the *Handbook of Varieties of English* (Kortmann & Schneider, 2004). In this section, features are selected to illustrate typical characteristics, rather than trying to offer a comprehensive review of all features or give a detailed sketch of a selection of varieties.

5.3.1 Pronunciation

The input forms, for instance whether or not they were rhotic, played an important part in the development of language-shift Englishes – Irish

English is rhotic, and its input was rhotic too, and Indian South African English followed its non-rhotic input. However, transfer of phonological and phonetic forms from the contact languages is a more prominent source of diversification of language-shift Englishes amongst themselves, or in comparison with typical native varieties, which also reflect their phonological input. Hickey (2008) identifies the transfer of Irish features in Irish English pronunciation such as the use of coronal stops [t, d] or [t̪, d̪] for the fricatives /ð, θ/ in the input, intervocalic and pre-pausal lenition of /t/, and restricting the realisation of /l/ to only the alveolar [l], without the velarised allophone [ɫ]. He also indicates that in a number of cases, there is convergence between Irish itself and features of the English input in Ireland. Mesthrie (2008) likewise identifies a number of possible transfer features from Indian languages into South African English – some of which are shared by speakers across the ancestral languages in their background, such as optional retroflection of the plosives /t, d/ to [ʈ, ɖ], and others are specific to speakers with a particular linguistic background, such as the realisation of the glottal fricative /h/ as voiced [ɦ] or breathy voiced [ɦ̤] which only occurs among speakers with a North Indian background, in contrast to South Indian backgrounds, especially Tamil, where the realisation is weakened and sometimes perceived as /h/-dropping.

With the extensive linguistic diversity in the contact languages of varieties that emerged in plantations, it is harder to track individual pronunciation features resulting from the contact or language-learning situation. Velupillai (2015, p. 301) reports that creoles tend to have somewhat smaller phoneme inventories than their lexifiers, but did not, as a whole, end up as considerably simplified languages from a phonological perspective.

Given the important role of adults learning English as a second language, and in turn providing the input to their children who acquired English as a first language, pronunciation patterns with extensive influence from contact languages and some simplification should be expected. Once these features have stabilised, they remain fairly persistent, and a recognisable accent is a feature of highly educated speakers from these backgrounds even when they also use standard English as a second dialect – hence no Caribbean cricket commentator ever sounds British, even if they share the register of cricket English with their British, Australian or Indian fellow commentators, nor do Irish English speakers outside the Ulster Scots or Mid-Ulster speaking areas converge on the English pronunciation of the neighbours to their immediate east.

Ongoing changes affect language-shift varieties as much as any other variety of English, and some of these changes do show convergence with other varieties of English in the local ecologies, but even in South Africa where middle-class Indian English users are in regular contact with settler English users, residual differences resist levelling, such as the non-rounding of the NURSE vowel in Indian South African English (Mesthrie & Chevalier, 2014).

5.3.2 Grammar

Language-shift varieties are usually clearly distinctive from typical native varieties in their grammar too. Transfer plays an important role here, given the origins of these varieties in adult second-language acquisition. A very clear example of this is the *after* perfect of Irish English, modelled after a corresponding construction in Irish, as in example (1).

(1) You're after ruinin' me. [To mean 'You have just ruined me.']

This form, to a larger extent than other Irish English perfect innovations, is stigmatised and sometimes avoided by more educated speakers (Filppula, 2008, p. 330).

Mesthrie (1992, pp. 105–106) shows similar patterns of transfer, but also convergence on typical native English patterns from his data, covering a range of speakers from basilectal, non-native-speaking Indian South Africans to native speakers of English with clear acrolectal English. Non-native speakers rely more extensively on direct syntactic replicas from ancestral languages when speaking English, such as a rare object–verb word order structure, illustrated in examples (2) and (3), found among only a few basilectal speakers.

(2) It's in the garden planted.
(3) She her own-house got.

More widespread among Indian South Africans is coordination that patterns like some of the ancestral languages, as in example (4), with the conjunct *too* used at the end of both clauses.

(4) I made rice too, I made roti too.

In the Caribbean, given the considerably more difficult early circumstances in which English was acquired by the plantation slaves, restructuring was more extensive – hence the idea that 'Creoles' represent a different type of language. This notion is not supported universally among scholars of varieties so designated, since there are neither diagnostic features that exclusively characterise creoles but no other varieties, nor features that all creoles share. It is important that the varieties in this group have seen the stabilisation of a number of features that are relatively limited elsewhere, so at least in proportional terms, it makes sense to treat them as a linguistic group. There are also obvious historical similarities, but the view of Mufwene (1997, 2020) is heeded, that they should be treated as varieties of English all the same. They form an important part of the picture of global English, as they represent an early example of highly multilingual contact, typically much more super-diverse than these present-day contact settings that carry this designation (see Chapter 8).

Among the most salient of features that many Caribbean varieties display, and that also occur in some forms of African American English (with a similar contribution from slaves undergoing language shift), are the pre-verbal markers. Aceto (2020) identifies a number of independent morphemes that typically precede the main verb and encode tense and aspect meanings. Where the settler and British varieties encode many of these meanings through a verbal inflection, supported in some cases by an auxiliary verb, the Caribbean language-shift varieties encode such meanings with forms derived from lexical verbs. The choice of the lexical verb is often similar across spatially distant varieties, and may relate to similar patterns in the West African input forms, but also adhere to widely observed patterns in languages that developed under less unfavourable conditions. Unmarked verb forms, with context or adverbial support supplying the temporal information also occurs widely. Examples of preverbal markers are:

(5) Past: often derived from BE, e.g. /bin, di(d), woz, min/, e.g. *mi bin iit, mi woz iit*, 'I have eaten/I ate'.

(6) Future: often derived from GO, e.g. /go a go, goin, wi/, e.g. *dem go dans, dem wi dans, dem a go dans*, 'They are going to dance'.

(7) Progressive: /de, da, a/, e.g. *di gyul a kaal yu, di gyal de kaal yu*, 'the girl is calling you'.

Daleszynska (2015) looks at ongoing variation in the preverbal markers for past tense *bin* and *did* in Bequia Creole from St Vincent and the Grenadines. She finds that unmarked verb forms are the most frequent choices, but both *bin* and *did*, as unstressed preverbal markers, are attested. Comparing older and younger speakers in two different settlements of the island of Bequia, she notes that older speakers make more use of the *did* form, but younger speakers have come to favour *bin*, which obviously differs more from standard English usage. The purpose of *bin* as identity marker is a key aspect of her explanation: under strain from influx to the island, speakers find it useful to mark their authentic local status by selecting the more deviant marker, as the following example from Daleszynska (2015, p. 54) illustrates.

(8) It had a woman from Southside, one time she **bin come** harbour. So I **bin stand up** talking to his boy and she go down and tell my mother how some boy give me hug up in the harbour.

Unmarked verbs with past denotation (*go*, *give*) also occur in this extract, alongside *bin*.

5.3.3 Vocabulary

Vocabulary variation in the language-shift Englishes is in part due to vocabulary items that speakers already know from other languages and transferred to English. Such transfer is widely attested in Indian South African English, where vocabulary from the ancestral Indian languages is used in English. The range includes words for ingredients and preparation of food: *dhania* (coriander), *karo, karum, thikku, thitta, thikka* (from different languages to denote spicy-hot food), words for cultural practices and religious ceremonies: *nikah* (Islamic wedding ceremony), *thanni* (card game) and *jhanda* (flag hoisted by some Hindus after prayers) (Mesthrie, 2002). Most of these words, except for a few cooking items, are in use and properly understood only within the Indian community of South Africa. A few culinary terms from Asian varieties of English have made their way into more general use in English, but largely on the back of the actual food ingredients or dishes making their way into the culinary experience of people from across the world, such as *biryani, ghee, korma, masala, naan, tandoor/tandoori* or *vindaloo*. The store of transferred vocabulary is not closed, though. Given some residual competence, even passively, in the ancestral languages, Mesthrie (forthcoming) identifies a number of recent, very creative, vocabulary borrowings by present-day speakers of Indian South African English, more in line with the playfulness and creativity of language and dialect contact in 'super-diverse' contexts, which are considered in Chapter 8.

Caribbean varieties show limited but some transfer from African languages, such as the following terms from Twi (spoken in Ghana): *kongosa* 'gossip', *fufu* 'common food of yam and plantains', *mumu* 'dull, dumb, silent' and *potopoto* 'mud, muddy' (Aceto, 2020, p. 196). Multiple varieties even include a 2nd person plural pronoun *unu*, borrowed from Igbo. However, Aceto (2020, p. 196) also points to distinctive lexis that represent retentions of the English input that subsequently got lost in settler Englishes, for example *krabit* 'mean, disagreeable, rough, cruel', *beks* (from vex) 'to anger', and *fieba* (from favour) 'to resemble'.

One case of a language-shift variety of English that has not transferred extensive vocabulary from the erstwhile community language is Irish English. Hickey (2004) explains this as a consequence of the long period of bilingualism between English and Irish, where there did not arise vocabulary gaps, since speakers could continue using Irish for their expressive needs otherwise and could continue learning English all the same, so that by the time language shift took place, little Irish vocabulary transfer took place. Nonetheless, at a deeper level, conceptualisations from Irish did make their way into Irish English, as shown by Peters (2017). He uncovers how various supernatural and religious concepts emerge in Irish English, with sources in the Irish Celtic language and culture, setting Irish English apart from British English. The following example that Peters (2017, p. 138) reports would not be found in English usage elsewhere, in part because of the transferred lexeme *banshee* (from Irish *bean sídhe*), but in part because of the (conceptual) presence of this intermediary between the material and supernatural worlds in the daily experience of the speech community.

> (9) Several people have heard the Banshee in Enniscoe, and a few of seen her in the evenings. My mother saw her years ago. She is a small woman clothed with straw having a shawl on her head. The Banshee is still believed in and only one person at the time will hear her. [. . .] The cry is heard usually the night before the death and the relatives of the sick person will not believe that the sick person will die till the Banshee is heard.

In the twentieth century, but after language shift had already run its course, the Republic of Ireland deliberately selected Irish terms for some of its legislative and executive political institutions and office bearers, which are now fully part of the vocabulary of Irish English. The head of government is known as the *Taoiseach* [tiːʃəx], the deputy head as *Tánaiste* [tɔːnɪʃtə], while the legislative body, the *Oireachtas* [ɛrəktəs], consists of an upper house, *Seanad Éireann* [ʃænəd ɛərən], and the lower house, *Dáil Éireann* [dɔɪl ɛərən]. These terms are used in both the Irish- and English-language versions of the Irish constitution, without having (other) English equivalents.

5.4 Conclusion

Language shift to English as a native language has occurred for speakers from indigenous minorities (including the Irish, who were not an absolute minority but a minoritised class of people), as well as the descendants of slaves and indentured labourers. They typically had few viable alternatives, or at least did not perceive the alternatives as viable, and were coerced into using English in many situations, leaving fewer situations where the other languages had a role to play.

While English has come to perform similar roles for the descendants of these language-shift speakers, their varieties tend to be regarded as non-standard and of low prestige. There are indications that the global and local fortunes of some of these varieties are changing, but an extensive revaluation of these varieties as the social equals of the prestigious typical native-speaker varieties has not yet occurred.

The linguistic features of these varieties reveal influence of their original English input, alongside transfer from other languages in the original ecologies, mediated by simplification processes that are typical of second-language learning.

6 English becoming an Asian and African language: the Outer Circle

One has to convey in a language that is not one's own the spirit that is one's own. One has to convey the various shades and omissions of a certain thought-movement that looks maltreated in an alien language. I use the word 'alien', yet English is not really an alien language to us. It is the language of our intellectual make-up – like Sanskrit or Persian was before – but not of our emotional make-up. We are all instinctively bilingual, many of us writing in our own language and in English. We cannot write like the English. We should not. We cannot write only as Indians. We have grown to look at the large world as part of us. Our method of expression therefore has to be a dialect which will someday prove to be as distinctive and colorful as the Irish or the American. (Rao, 1938, foreword)

What I do see is a new voice coming out of Africa, speaking of African experience in a world-wide language. So my answer to the question, Can an African ever learn English well enough to be able to use it effectively in creative writing? is certainly yes. If on the other hand you ask: Can he ever learn to use it like a native speaker? I should say, I hope not. It is neither necessary nor desirable for him to be able to do so. The price a world language must be prepared to pay is submission to many different kinds of use. The African writer should aim to use English in a way that brings out his message best without altering the language to the extent that its value as a medium of international exchange will be lost. He should aim at fashioning out an English which is at once universal and able to carry his peculiar experience. (Achebe, 1965, p. 29)

Raja Rao and Chinua Achebe thought that English became a language of Indian and African expression, a tool to say something, to speak about themselves and their world, and to reach a wider world with their message. English was a second language to them, yet they claimed it as one of theirs. The question is what to make of this. Does it make sense to lay a claim to English without being an English speaker? It would appear not to for Bill Bryson, if one draws any inferences from his opening line to *Mother Tongue*, as English was not the tongue of Rao's or Achebe's mother, after all. They were merely trying to use English.

This chapter examines the history of English transplantation within the former British Empire and surveys the social and linguistic consequences thereof. The goal is to establish the extent to which it makes sense to recognise, or to continue to recognise, an Outer Circle of English varieties different from other non-native varieties. This is how Kachru conceptualised it in the 1970s and 1980s, but ever since Quirk (1988), the meaningfulness of the distinction has been challenged on conceptual and empirical grounds. Thus, after consideration of the context, we turn to linguistic differences and the conflicting ways in which potentially unique linguistic characteristics are interpreted and explained. The Englishes of the Outer Circle have been central to the development of the world Englishes framework, and raise critical questions that need answers, but which will in turn help us understand aspects of English across the world better.

6.1 The transplantation of English to the Outer Circle

The English language made its way to the Outer Circle in four consecutive phases, with remarkable similarities across different parts of the world, despite local variations and differences in the starting points and subsequent timelines:

- trade contact (sixteenth and seventeenth centuries), blending into the workplace contact of unskilled workers within the colonial economies, yielding pidgin varieties of English
- colonial occupation (late eighteenth to mid-twentieth centuries), yielding the forerunners to present-day educated and elite varieties
- postcolonial liberation (second half of the twentieth century), yielding second-language varieties with more extensive grammatical transfer
- globalisation (since the late twentieth century), characterised by hybridity on top of the heritage of the past.

6.1.1 Trade contact

The first phase was trade contact. British trade along the west coast of Africa, India and South China commenced in the second half of the sixteenth and early seventeenth centuries, and in all three locations, a form of pidgin English developed. The trade pidgins were restricted in their context of use, mainly serving to negotiate the trading of goods. It was acquired by a relatively small number of indigenous intermediaries, and likewise only by those British traders who regularly sailed those routes, alongside the factors – temporary settlers at the trading factories set up along the coastline of the three regions. In other parts of what become British colonies by the nineteenth century, such as South and East Africa and Southeast Asia, there is no evidence for an English pidgin that stabilised.

By the middle of the sixteenth century, the British traded regularly along the west coast of Africa, and they started establishing forts and trading posts from the early seventeenth century. Huber (1999) reports that English ships traded along the coast that was called the Gold Coast and later Ghana from 1553 to the 1570s, but lost interest before they resumed trade and set up the first trading post on the mainland of the continent in 1632, with expansion to many more trading posts and forts during the second half of the seventeenth century – culminating in an average of one trading post for every ten kilometres of coastal strip. No territorial claims were made by the British in this period, although education and missionary activity started before the territorial claims and administrative control that developed in the nineteenth century. According to Huber (1999), a form of pidgin English developed in the seventeenth century along the coast and started to stabilise in the eighteenth century, but this form was simpler and more variable than the form that stabilised in the twentieth century. The eventual stabilisation of West African Pidgin English, in a fairly homogenous way across the region, is attributed to the influence of Krio speakers, native speakers of a Caribbean Creole English from Sierra Leone, who were resettled there after the abolition of slavery, and then travelled throughout the West African region as missionaries or labourers.

Likewise, after trade started in India at the beginning of the seventeenth century, an English pidgin developed for the purposes of the limited interaction that was required. This early pidgin formed the basis for the later stabilisation of Butler English, a more enduring pidgin that emerged among Indians working as domestic servants for British who resided in India while performing their colonial duties, even into the twentieth century (Sharma, 2012). Hosali (2005) reports evidence of the continued survival of Butler English up to the final decade of the twentieth century when there were still a few living speakers who had been domestic servants of the British before Indian independence in 1947.

An early trade pidgin also developed in South China, with earliest attestations of its use dating from the 1740s (Bolton, 2002, p. 184). When an imperial decree restricted European trade to the port of Canton (present-day Guangzhou) after 1755, a certain continuity developed in the use of this pidgin for trade between the Chinese and British, and it remained in use after the expansion of trading ports in the nineteenth century, even occasionally serving as the contact language for Chinese speaking mutually unintelligible Chinese languages, according to nineteenth-century observers reviewed by Bolton (2002, p. 186). Bolton (2002) refers to the nineteenth-century treaty ports as semi-colonialism imposed by the British, but in the wake of missionaries and schools arriving towards the end of the nineteenth century, the Chinese-English pidgin began to be ousted by school-learnt varieties of English. The last traces are reported to have disappeared soon after the middle of the twentieth century.

Apart from West African Pidgin English, which acquired a fresh stimulus from Krio in the late nineteenth and early twentieth centuries, the other English-based trade pidgins, in Asia, have disappeared in the wake of the British leaving the area and the availability of a more standard-like variety taught in schools. West African Pidgin English continues to interact with other varieties of English throughout the West African region, and gained a new lease of life as a marker of identity in the West African diaspora and online communities as well.

6.1.2 Colonial occupation

The second phase, during which the English language spread more extensively, was the phase of colonial occupation, from the late eighteenth century to the mid-twentieth century. In this period, the British flag was hoisted and territories were claimed for the British Crown, to enable more extensive resource exploitation over and above the ongoing trading activities. In most cases, it happened quite gradually. British control over territories surrounding the trading ports gradually increased, followed by some triggering events that prompted a response, which culminated in a territorial claim over a large stretch of land. In India and elsewhere in Asia, there was a gradual process that solidified the territorial claims and administrative control throughout the eighteenth century (Kachru, 1994). The administration of further Asian territories such as Singapore was often still directed from India, and stronger local authority followed only later in the nineteenth century. In Africa, the Berlin Conference of 1884–1885 resulted in the partitioning of Africa among the European colonial authorities, after which administrative control over the territories was finalised.

This endeavour brought many more British administrators and soldiers, but also missionaries, educators and merchants, who stayed for longer or shorter periods. Intentional settlement with a possible indefinite duration was limited to a few areas, particularly South Africa and less enduringly so in Zimbabwe and Kenya. The reasons for people moving to the occupied territories varied, which in turn had a considerable impact on the kind of English usage that their presence brought about. In the early phases of colonial occupation, like the phase of trade contact, English was a foreign language that served purely practical interactive purposes for a small number of the indigenous population, but had not yet made its way into the broader society.

The British administrators needed a group of intermediaries, but for the interaction, the choice of language was not particularly important – getting the message across was. English could do much of the administrative job at hand in some colonies, for instance in the Cape Colony of South Africa, where some of the long-term Dutch settlers already had some command of English, and Dutch was gradually replaced with English as the language of administration over the course of more than a decade (Steyn, 1980, pp. 126–131). More often than not, local translators and interpreters, such as Munshi Abdullah in Singapore, conveyed the message to the local population, while early heads of administration, such as Raffles and Farquhar in the 1820s, had some competence in Malay to conduct their business (Frost & Balasingamchow, 2009, pp. 49–81). Afeadi (2015) describes the 'political agent', a messenger-interpreter, in Northern Nigeria in the late nineteenth and early twentieth centuries, who played an important role as the intermediary conveying messages between the British colonial authorities and the local traditional rulers, whom the British continued to support to govern the people. Only towards the latter years of the Northern Nigeria protectorate, after 1906, as administration intensified, did command of Standard English (as assessed by a written test) also become part of the requirements for the highest level of political agents. Elsewhere, the early colonial administrators made use of indigenous languages more extensively, if through interpreters, for example the case of Kiswahili in East Africa (Schmied, 2017, pp. 473–474) or Hausa in Northern Nigeria (Afeadi, 2015). For the indigenous people of the occupied territories, English remained a transactional language and not a language they made their own during the early period of colonial occupation.

Until the early nineteenth century in India and the rest of Asia, and later in the century in Africa, almost all Western-style education for the indigenous people was left in the hands of the missionaries. As the administrations became more complex and the interests expanded from only creating a secure space for trade to resource exploitation, the demand for English intermediaries and lower-level clerical officials among the indigenous population expanded. Therefore, the colonial administrators asked the mission schools to train a larger cohort of English-speaking indigenous people, and some government schools were also established for the same purpose.

Mission education was the mainstay of education during the period of colonial occupation. The first priority of missions was to evangelise, and education was a means to an end in that quest. Training a literate cohort of indigenous people was done to create a multiplication effect: more missionaries, preachers and teachers could be sent into the field if the indigenous people contributed to this group, and of course the indigenous people had the advantage of thorough knowledge of the languages of the people being missioned to, unlike the European missionaries who had to acquire such knowledge with more effort.

There were several schools of thought about the purpose of education in the colonised world. In India, as reviewed by Kachru (1994), there was a debate between two camps labelled Orientalists and Anglicists, respectively. The Orientalists advocated for the indigenous tradition of education to be supported, drawing on a number of indigenous languages as media of instruction, alongside the existing religious instruction in which classical languages like Arabic and Sanskrit also played significant roles. The Anglicists advocated for teaching in English and imparting Western knowledge, in the sciences and humanities. Kachru (1994, pp. 502–503) points to the existence of several schools in British India and Ceylon (Sri Lanka) that used English as the medium of instruction, alongside many using indigenous languages while the debate was still ongoing. The resolution of the debate in India followed the Macaulay Minute of 1835, which recommended the use of English for the instruction of a local elite, who would be English in their intellectual and cultural tastes, rather than oriental, and act as intermediaries between the British governing class and the Indian population being governed:

> I feel with them that it is impossible for us, with our limited means, to attempt to educate the body of the people. We must at present do our best to form a class who may be interpreters between us and the millions whom we govern, – a class of persons Indian in blood and colour, but English in tastes, in opinions, in morals and in intellect. To that class we may leave it to refine the vernacular dialects of the country, to enrich those dialects with terms of science borrowed from the Western nomenclature, and to render them by degrees fit vehicles for conveying knowledge to the great mass of the population. (Macaulay, 1835)

Teaching in indigenous languages did not stop at this point, but the most desirable education that gave access to the most rewarding employment, with government funding, was in the English language.

In Africa, apart from Islamic religious education at Madrassas, there was no system of formal education comparable in structure to nineteenth-century European education (elitist as it was in Britain at the time too and far from being the universal education that was in place by the twentieth century) prior to the beginnings of mission school education. In part, the Christian missions had similar educational goals to the Islamic education, religious rather than academic, but a liberal tradition influenced some mission schools to provide a British-style general education for the few, which included the full range of natural and social sciences taught in Britain, alongside Latin and Greek (De Kock, 1996). These elite institutions, sponsored by missions or governments by the twentieth century, like Lovedale College in South Africa and Government College Umuahia in Nigeria, came to be extremely influential through the impact of their students. Achebe (1993/2009, p. 21), a student in Umuahia in the 1940s, notes how most of the oldest generation of Nigerian authors in English hailed from the same school. Lovedale was the school attended by the first ordained African minister of the Presbyterian Church, first university professors and several twentieth-century leaders of the liberation struggle against the apartheid government (De Kock, 1996).

A debate ensued across many of the African countries between the proponents of the liberal tradition and a utilitarian, industrial orientation for education, where the purpose was not so much to cultivate the mind as to train labourers to work in the emerging industries. Thus, very similar to Macaulay's views, the first headmaster of Lovedale at the opening of the school in 1841, Rev. James Lang, defended the principle of 'allowing and enabling the educated native to drink at the English fountains of literature, science and practical godliness' (Hodgson, 1997, p. 80). Subsequently, the new governor of the Cape Colony, Sir George Grey, proclaimed in 1854 that missionary education was 'too bookish', and rather emphasised industrial education and practical subjects (Hodgson, 1997, p. 81). Over the course of the nineteenth century, with a small number of exceptions, industrial education became the norm in South Africa. Similar trajectories, of a small layer of elite institutions with a liberal academic curriculum and a larger group of primary and industrial schools, developed in the rest of Africa – on similar time scale in Ghana, but later in the rest of the continent.

One Outer Circle colony has a very different colonial history and thus a different manner of dissemination for English in its early years: the Philippines. Unlike all other Outer Circle settings, which were colonised by the British, the Philippines was surrendered to the United States of America by Spain in 1898. The Americans set about differently from the British, by sending a large group of teachers to anglicise the territory in a short space of time. Access to English was not a matter for the elite only in the Philippines, and English became accessible to a large segment of the population within a few decades of American control (Wee, 2020, p. 267).

6.1.3 Postcolonial liberation

The third phase was the postcolonial phase in the second half of the twentieth century as former British colonies and the Philippines gained their independence and were free to set their own course. In most of these countries, the new governments opted to retain the prominent place that English had occupied during the colonial period. The choice was not the result of a uniform policy across the Empire, although the long-term outcomes turned out to correspond in a number of ways in most African countries and some Asian countries. This is a strongly contested area; Phillipson (1992) and Pennycook (1994) assert that British and American government agencies played a strong role in the decision, by providing training, resources and encouragement for the teaching of English, and particularly within a teaching philosophy that was grounded in a monolingual mindset: the second language should be taught in the second language and competes with the native language. The kind of immersion models of teaching English on British and American soil got exported as common sense, and had detrimental effects on the use of other languages. There are many who disagree with Phillipson and Pennycook, but the disagreement is about the degree of detailed and intentional planning, and the extent to which these British and American initiatives were the sole or prime driver of the postcolonial expansion of English (e.g. Spolsky, 2004).

The fact that the ruling elite at the point of liberation in most countries had considerable competence in the use of English for the purposes of government administration made it an easy initial option, despite the adoption of indigenisation policies in India, Pakistan, Malaysia, Tanzania and elsewhere to replace English over time with major indigenous languages. In countries with multiple indigenous languages and a risk of exclusion of some citizens if only one or a few languages were utilised in national roles, English also received a boost from its perceived neutrality (J. Das Gupta, 1970).

Countries that adopted a policy that relied strongly on English include the countries of West Africa, although in Cameroon, English and French share the public roles; Southern Africa, including Namibia which became independent via South Africa and not directly via the United Kingdom; Uganda and Kenya in East Africa; and Singapore in Southeast Asia. In these countries, English is usually the sole medium of education after the early years of primary school, with national languages taken as subjects but not used for upper primary and secondary education. In other countries, English shared its role with one or more indigenous languages, such as Kiswahili in Tanzania, Hindi and, to a lesser degree, regional languages in India, and Filipino in the Philippines. Secondary and university education in English remains an option in these countries, either through the government or through private institutions. In other Asian countries, the (major or important) indigenous languages have a stronger role in education and government, to the extent that in countries like Malaysia and Bangladesh, a national language did come to function as the principal vehicle for administration and education, while Pakistan also relies very strongly on Urdu and other indigenous languages. Yet, even in countries with a national language as the medium of school education, English continues to be taught as the first additional language in schools and occupies a very different status from other 'foreign languages' in the education system.

6.1.4 Globalisation

The fourth phase is the current phase, the world of globalisation and transnational connectivity, where the use of English for international contact becomes increasingly accessible to a larger number of people in the Outer Circle. This expansion is facilitated by changes in worldwide production and distribution of goods, together with the internet that opens up new modes of communication. In part, these processes affect all countries of the world in similar ways, and differences are not in the first instance related to the history of colonisation of individual countries, but to economic factors such as the availability of raw products to cultivate particular industries. Thus, the clothing and textile industry in Bangladesh is not founded on its ability in the English language any more than China's clothing and textile industry is. Most of the factory workers in both countries get by without much need for English on the workfloor, and only the marketing and salespeople need to engage, usually in English, with their export markets.

However, because of the prior establishment of English in former colonies, they can access opportunities in tourism especially that require more effort in countries without the same breadth of English usage, and opportunities for call centres that are simply not possible on a large scale in countries without a sizeable English-using population. Tourism is also affected strongly by non-linguistic factors, so language makes only a small contribution, but Okafor et al. (2022) report that countries with a common official language share more tourism exchange, and this is particularly so for Sub-Saharan African and Asian countries – those areas where the former English colonies are located. When one also considers that, according to numbers from the World Tourism Organization, four English-speaking (Inner Circle) countries count among the top eight tourism spenders in the world – United States (2), United Kingdom (4), Australia (7) and Canada (8) in 2019, the last year before the interruption of international tourism by the coronavirus pandemic – then there is good money to be made through the use of English, over and above the fact that non-English-speaking tourists are most likely to use English if they do not share a common language with their destination countries.

The call centre industry, within the broader context of business process outsourcing, has developed very strongly in the Philippines and India since the start of the current century. These countries offer the possibility of finding a large pool of competent English speakers, who are able, through some on-the-job accent and language training, to do the invisible work for international, as well as American and British companies (Bolton, 2013). Bolton (2016) reports that Philippine call centre workers, despite accent neutralisation training, continue to speak a comprehensible but recognisably Filipino variety of English, although his analysis of transcripts shows that the American customers they talk to often avail themselves of more non-standard English features than the Filipino call centre agents.

6.2 Social factors

6.2.1 Contact

Indigenous people from the exploitation colonies have had limited initial contact with English-speaking colonial representatives, but the contact increased over time until the end of the colonial period. In the earliest period, a few intermediaries sufficed to make the necessary arrangements, while the indigenous people carried on with their lives in the indigenous languages.

When missionaries arrived, the contact increased for a small number of indigenous people, often children rather than adults, who attended school and acquired English from their teachers. There were a few elite boarding schools that were established in various places during the nineteenth century, with less elite institutions being added as the century progressed to meet the increased need for literate workers in the colonial administration. Some workplace contact provided further exposure to English for adults who were servants or manual labourers, but the use of and need for English was quite limited for this group.

Later in the nineteenth century, as an indigenous speech community came into being, a further contact factor became more important – contact in English among members of indigenous communities with different language backgrounds. Where indigenous languages for wider communication were available, they were used too, but in some contexts, English served as a lingua franca for the indigenous elite who mastered English at the missionary schools. The use of written English among the indigenous elite set up a further contact site within the local community.

As the education system expanded, more indigenous teachers were employed in the system, and thus contact with native speakers diminished, except for the very elite schools and most senior positions within the colonial administration, who remained in some form of regular interaction with English speakers – missionaries, administrators, educators or military officers. By the end of the period of colonial control, these last few contacts with native speakers came to an end as the representatives of the empire returned to Britain. Since the middle of the twentieth century, contact has been among indigenous people, although much of it has taken place in English in the public domain. Societies differ in the extent to which there is access to and mastery of English, but the local contact is definitive as far as the English language and its continued development is concerned.

International contact became a new avenue as the twentieth century drew to an end, in some ways similar to the Expanding Circle, although within the post-independence Commonwealth context, English speakers were a much more regular presence in the former colonies than they were in other parts of the world, while international exchange and periods of study or work abroad continued after independence, which led to contact with native speakers for a small number of the elite, many of whom returned to senior government or academic positions subsequent to such international studies.

6.2.2 Use

The use of English in the Outer Circle changed extensively over the course of time. At the beginning, only a small number of indigenous people acted as intermediaries between the local population and the colonial occupiers, and the purpose of the interactions was limited to arranging activities. To the extent that the colonisers did not intervene in the lives of the indigenous people, other languages continued to perform the private and public functions for them.

Uses of English accumulated over time. The missionaries brought Christianity and with that religious practice, but they also brought formal education. Such contact was not limited to English, but often involved the use of an indigenous language for the majority of people, if mediated by interpreters. For the select few, the intermediaries who were roped into formal education, English played a larger role, as the language of literacy and Western-style education.

Two subsequent developments added to the uses: employment and expansion of administrative control. Employment meant contact with English-speaking employers for some, which added a workplace use for English, although to the extent that the employment was in manual, supervised positions, the need for English remained limited and workplace pidgins developed. Expansion of administrative control meant that more indigenous intermediaries and clerical workers became necessary, which resulted in more employment opportunities and more use of English in organisational contexts – as was explained earlier in this chapter with reference to the replacing of Pidgin and Hausa by English as the language of administration in the early twentieth century in Nigeria.

Over time, the use of English expanded further. The teaching of English in the colonial period had the effect of establishing a small but highly literate and educated elite next to the larger group of people with some workplace English from their manual jobs. The elite were supposed to be the intermediaries between the colonial governments and the local populations, but as the reach of the colonial institutions expanded, the intermediaries' roles extended to being teachers and preachers. These roles they did indeed perform, by and large, but an unanticipated consequence also resulted: the English-using, highly educated elite began to use the English language to voice their protest against the inequality and oppression of the indigenous people. They also began to use English to tell the rest of the world about their world, which had hitherto been interpreted by outsiders who ranged from paternalistic to downright racist – as shown in Macaulay's dismissal of Indian learning without actually having read the original works. When these uses for the English language became apparent to its colonised users, the first steps towards the indigenisation of the language were taken, and English started down the road of becoming an Asian and an African language – at least for some. The indigenisation strategies are presented later in this chapter as part of the consideration of the linguistic features of Outer Circle varieties.

The public uses of English expanded further after independence to the extent that English was retained in the public functions that it had under British colonial rule. Kachru (1965, pp. 393–396) proposed to make sense of the observed variation within the Indian context through the notion of a cline of bilingualism. At the bottom, he identified minimal command of English in a limited range of interactional settings, within a larger repertoire of languages. At the opposite end, he identified ambilingualism, command of English similar to the command such speakers have of one or more indigenous languages, rounded off by a central point on the scale of adequate competence in English for some purposes. In the same period, a similar construal was developed in Nigeria, starting with Brosnahan (1958), who proposed a scale of proficiency based on education, and developed further by Banjo (1971) in terms of extent of intelligibility and linguistic difference from standard English rather than just education; Brosnahan used numbered Levels and Banjo adjusted that to numbered Varieties. Schmied (1991, pp. 47–49) proposed to use the labels basilect, mesolect and acrolect for the reference points on the continuum.

It is important to bear in mind that English is not the sole language in use in the Outer Circle contexts. In private use, other languages dominate, although English is used for socialisation and within the domestic space by some of the elite (i.e. educated middle-class professionals), especially to the extent that the contact involves speakers of multiple indigenous languages. In institutionalised public use, English is often dominant, in African former colonies and Singapore more so than in the other Asian former colonies, but to various degrees, English still shares the public space with other languages, especially in spoken interaction. Government, higher education and commerce are dominated by English, whereas primary education, entertainment and religion often see a much more extensive role for indigenous languages.

International uses of English in the Outer Circle are largely similar to the international uses of English in the Expanding Circle, which are covered in more detail in Chapter 7. Trade, tourism, diplomacy and academia are some of the domains in which English is the principal linguistic resource.

6.2.3 Acquisition

The acquisition of English in the Outer Circle traditionally occurred in two settings: formal education and the workplace. Formal education in the earliest phases of access to English was a relatively exclusive affair, with only a few missionary schools, close to the main trading ports, providing education for a select few. Over time, missionaries went further inland to set up more schools.

The early contexts provided substantial input from teachers who were native speakers or otherwise very proficient users, which resulted in advanced bi- or multilingualism for an emerging indigenous elite under colonial rule. Over time, as more educational institutions were set up, the provisioning was not kept at the same level as the early mission schools and their elite continuations. This process of expanded provision with poorer resources – infrastructure and trained teachers – was accelerated after independence to extend education as widely as possible. The constraints on provision are a concern documented widely across space and time, for example in Nigeria (Brosnahan, 1958), South Africa (Lanham, 1967), Zimbabwe (McGinley, 1987) or Bangladesh (Hamid, 2010). Pupils who completed primary education were sent directly to teacher-training colleges to be trained as teachers themselves, rather than completing secondary education first, for instance in Ghana in the period after independence, but continuing until the 1990s in Uganda (Huber, 2008; Tembe, 2006). The scale of expansion of the system can be seen when considering that in the 1920s, only 20 per cent of all black South African children attended school at all, and only one child in every thousand went on to secondary education (Hirson, 1981), whereas after the 1950s, the system expanded to almost universal education. In Nigeria, there had been about 4,000 children in forty schools by the late nineteenth century, but by the middle of the twentieth century, that number had grown to 600,000 (Brosnahan, 1958). More recently, in Zimbabwe, secondary enrolment amounted to 73,540 by the end of the liberation war in 1979, and exploded to 417,450 over the next five years (McGinley, 1987).

A major corollary of the rapid expansion of education under severe resource and capacity constraints has been that teachers were themselves not very proficient speakers of English, the language they had to teach and in which they had to teach. Nonetheless, their non-elite variety of English served as an important input to the acquisition of English by their pupils. Massification of education, with a very important role for English in it, brought about a clear differentiation in the English commanded by the populations of the Outer Circle countries: an educated variety associated with the mission-educated elite, perpetuated by elite schools that continued to provide high-quality education by highly proficient teachers, in contrast to the variety acquired in non-elite education under the tutelage of less qualified and proficient staff. A lively complaint tradition, especially among applied linguists, university staff and governments, arose in respect of the 'poor' and 'ever deteriorating' English of learners, but actual historical data are usually absent from these discussions. In a context of massification, with a growing base of learners entering universities, more selective cohorts from years gone by (such as when the complainants themselves studied) may well be the intuitive basis of comparison.

Beside these formally educated users of English, some other members of these societies with limited formal education acquired some English in the workplace. This was the case for the earlier servants of 'colonials' in India, who used Butler English or Boxwallah English, with similarities elsewhere, but it has continued throughout the period of industrialisation since the late nineteenth century. At present, the workplace provides supplemental opportunities for further acquisition of English, but to the extent that universal education is realised, there is an improved starting point for workplace acquisition after some education.

The most recent change to the acquisition of English is the out-of-classroom availability of exposure through entertainment and mobile communication. While the Outer Circle countries are in general poorer than the Expanding Circle countries where there are documented influences of out-of-class exposure (see Chapter 7), Africa and Asia are not left behind. Deumert (2014) speaks of the internet on a shoestring – not using smart devices that are dependent on lots of bandwidth and unlimited access to data – but the users of mobile communication gain further exposure nonetheless. Some of these recent influences are considered in Chapter 8.

6.2.4 Attitudes

English was used as the medium of communication by colonial English speakers – administrators, missionaries, soldiers – to communicate information and instruction to intermediaries, who were in turn expected to pass the message on to the indigenous population at large. It had instrumental value for a few, and was an imposition and invader for many. At some point, the indigenous English users came to use the English language as a vehicle for their opposition to the way they had been made subjects to the empire and to the language of the empire; 'the empire writes back with a vengeance', as Salman Rushdie (1982) framed this, by analogy to the *Star Wars* film title, but the idea of those in the margins of the empire challenging it goes back much further. The contact situation changed for some colonised users of English, who began using the language of the coloniser to articulate their condition of oppression, usually with the oppressors as the primary audience. Such writing took the shape of letters to the editors of settler- and empire-controlled newspapers, and later also indigenously produced and edited newspapers, works of non-fiction and later fiction and other literary forms. In parallel, many of the articulations were simultaneous directed at an audience of fellow colonised peoples. The process of claiming the English language and infusing it deliberately with elements from the culture and languages of the colonised is termed nativisation by Kachru (1986) from the vantage point of world Englishes, or appropriation by Ashcroft et al. (1989), writing from the perspective of postcolonial literary theory.

Favourable attitudes often hold at present for those users of English who regard it as a way out of poverty, the language of employment in decent-paying jobs. Coetzee-Van Rooy (2006) finds that a strong instrumental motivation is characteristic of these learners of English.

English also functions as an instrument for interaction beyond the workplace, a linking language in multilingual societies, in a function it shares with indigenous languages of wider communication but performs more often than not the higher one moves up the social ladder.

Favourable attitudes also develop around the possibilities of English as a vehicle for the expression of modernity in contrast to the traditional society, especially for those who are constrained in the traditional society. By way of exemplification, Kachru (1986, pp. 59–60) notes how English can be used to neutralise regional, social or caste associations of words from indigenous Indian languages when speakers would like to avoid such connotations, while De Kadt (2004) observes that English does the same job for women who want to avoid the stratified gendered concepts of their primary indigenous language. De Kadt (2004) further observes how upwardly mobile female university students from non-elite backgrounds use English more often for social interaction than men, because it signals their modern identity and their protest against the subservient position they feel their indigenous culture, encoded by the language, imposes on them.

Attitudes towards an indigenised, or endonormative, variety of English are less clear-cut. Often, as Kachru (1977/2015a) observed, there are clear signs of linguistic schizophrenia in that Outer Circle users show more favourable attitudes towards a British or some other external variety and reveal negative attitudes towards the local forms, even if their own usage also reveals clear signs of the local. This is evident, for instance, in the Speak Good English Campaign in Singapore (Wee, 2018), which aims to discourage (or even eradicate) the local colloquial form of English often called Singlish. This has also long been evident in language attitude surveys in South Africa, where the native variety of settler descendants tended to be regarded more highly than indigenised forms until signs of incipient shift in the early twenty-first century (Coetzee-Van Rooy & Van Rooy, 2005, 2021). However, even at the time of writing, early in the third decade of the twenty-first century, pressure remains on users from indigenised variety backgrounds to adjust to settler norms. This is illustrated poignantly by a series of tweets from the South African journalist Abra Barbier on 18 October 2022,[1] who recounts her experience as somebody not from a settler native-speaker background but a bilingual background, working in both English and Afrikaans in public broadcasting. The pressure for a long period to accommodate to settler norms (not usually formulated as such, but in the technical sense of the Schneider

---

1. https://twitter.com/BarbierAbra/status/1582294820810522624, referenced with permission.

model) got her to adjust her pronunciation and her lexical choice. Only in later years, and following the example of other journalists, did she manage to pluck up the courage to use her primary dialect of English in her professional role. In private communication, she maintains that in both English and Afrikaans, the other colonial language in South Africa, pressure to conform remains.

6.3 Linguistic features

6.3.1 Pronunciation

Outer Circle varieties are consistently differentiated from other varieties of English in terms of pronunciation. While the earlier speakers who acquired elite varieties in mission schools had contact with native speakers, such contact declined over time, and fellow non-native speakers, often with a similar linguistic background to new generations of learners, provided the main oral input in the classroom, as is set out earlier in this chapter. Transfer of pronunciation from the other languages in the local ecologies is therefore widespread. At the same time, there are considerable similarities between second-language users across larger regions, because often the other languages have phonological and phonetic similarities insofar as the mapping to English is concerned, while differences (such as the contrasts among aspirated and unaspirated voiced plosives, or the presence of clicks) do not have implications for the pronunciation of English, since such sounds are not called upon. In addition, to the extent that contact sites are multilingual, the various users of English may influence one another and converge on possible emerging communal norms, precisely because English is widely used in the Outer Circle societies and exposure is not restricted to the classroom only.

To illustrate the kinds of transfer, let as look at the pronunciation of Black South African English, which shows some similarities to the rest of Southern Africa and beyond. The indigenous Bantu languages in the local ecology have similar five or seven vowel systems, with peripheral vowels only, and without phonemic length or tenseness contrasts. There are allophonic differences in the exact height of vowels, and there are phonological differences in how extensive vowel raising as a subtype of vowel harmony takes place for some environments. In consequence, the varieties of English in this broader region are characterised by a marginal or no tense/lax contrast in English, no centring diphthongs, and usually limited to no vowel reduction in unstressed syllables. In consequence, a similar vowel is used in the words corresponding to the pairs KIT/FLEECE – [i], FOOT/GOOSE – [u] (without noticeable centralisation but a clear back-vowel articulation), DRESS/NURSE both [ɛ], STRUT/START, CLOTH/THOUGHT all a relatively central [a], with some front or back vowel articulation, and LOT/FORCE [ɔ] (Van Rooy & Van Huyssteen, 2000; Van Rooy, 2008; Mesthrie & Van Rooy, forthcoming). Where native varieties would use a schwa, a range of allophones are used, in different phonological environments, but also in part influenced by the spelling. Mesthrie (2005) shows clearly that spelling is not the principal determinant, but it does play a role for speakers who do not have a schwa in their set of phones, which in turn reflects the input from formal education, where words are encountered in writing before they are heard in the spoken form.

The indigenous languages share a syllable-timed rhythm and do not use lexical stress patterns, but make use of distinctive tone. The contrastive tones are not transferred systematically to English. The nett effect of the suprasegmental organisation is that syllable-timing, rather than stress-timing, constitutes the basic rhythm (Coetzee & Wissing, 2007). There is tension between replication of the variable stress patterns of native-speaker varieties and a preference for consistent prefinal stress, which seems to be transferred from the phrase-level penult lengthening of the indigenous languages. Very often, the tension has no effect on bisyllabic words with initial stress, since the competing systems converge on the same stress placement. However, in three-syllabic words with initial stress, differences begin to appear, for example 'seventy' where initial stress *séventy* and medial/prefinal stress *sevénty* both occur. If speakers communicate mainly among others with strong transfer patterns, the deviant forms are reinforced, but if they are in contact with other interlocutors too, variation might occur and ultimately shift to the native-like pattern. Van Rooy (2002) shows that syllable weight plays a role in attracting stress to the final syllable for superheavy syllables – closed syllables with diphthongs and tense vowels or syllables with coda consonant clusters, for example *about, around, contrast, debate* – which usually converge on native stress patterns too, but this means that these varieties do not show a contrasting noun/verb stress pattern for forms like *transport* or *campaign*. To the extent that speakers select a tense vowel in a closed final syllable, as in *javelin*, stress placement on the final syllable becomes possible and likely.

Speakers closer to the elite of the spectrum often resemble the phonological contrasts of typical native speakers, and differ in the actual articulation of some sounds, for example contrasting /p, t, k/ to /b, d, g/, but without using aspiration (long-lag onset of voicing) versus short-lag voicing onset, but rather using prevoicing in contrast to voicing lag of an intermediate range. Such speakers are typically perceived as more intelligible by outsiders than those who also differ in the number of phonological contrasts. For insiders, the challenge of understanding Outer Circle speakers is usually less severe. Mesthrie (2017) notes that at the contemporary elite end of the spectrum, particularly in South Africa where such elite status implies interaction with white native-speaking peers in schools and universities, there is even more alignment of the pronunciation, including the use of schwa. Women move closer to the prestige (white/native) norm while black men retain, on average, dual loyalty to the prestige variety and the one associated with their multilingual background. They choose variants that index difference from the prestige norms more often than women.[2]

Pronunciation in the Outer Circle is typically caught up in the tension of its context of acquisition and its identity function, with the degree of wider currency a further consideration. The context of acquisition inherently favours transfer from other languages and simplification. One can call this outcome fossilisation at group level, as Selinker (1972) does, and can see this as confirmation of Quirk's (1988) call for being in constant touch with the native language. However, the reality is such that these speakers, beyond Bryson's chosen 300 million native speakers, who are trying to learn English with mixed success, will continue to try, and native speakers will not become part of their daily linguistic reality anytime ever – not just anytime soon. Worldwide demographics do not favour the strategic dispersion of native speakers to all countries of the world to serve as role models. Hence, a more realistic way is to understand what happens, rather than judge what does not happen. The notions of a *been-to* in West Africa, a *coconut* in South Africa, or a *Brown Sahib* (*persons Indian-in-blood-and-colour,-but-English-in-tastes,-in-opinions,-in-morals-and-in-intellect* à la Macaulay) in any case suggest that it is not desirable in a local context for an African or Asian to be mistaken for an outsider or being too close to a native speaker on the basis of their speech (or other aspects of their English).

---

2. Designating a variety with an ethnic association prestige may not sound all that sensitive. The reality on the ground is that the speakers' behaviour suggests an affirmation of the prestige status of the native variety in the context of interaction. Mesthrie (2010) describes this as a case of deracialising, which is helpful to understand the outcome of the process, but it has to be borne in mind that there remains a kind of founder's effect in place, where the already established native variety remains a key force of linguistic assimilation, rather than a more hybrid linguistic outcome that combines pronunciation variables extensively from the backgrounds of the various speakers in the contact setting. South Africa is atypical for an Outer Circle setting precisely because of the extensive presence of the minority of native speakers from settler origin, unlike the almost complete absence of a similar segment of the local speech community in such Outer Circle contexts as India or Nigeria.

6.3.2 Grammar

Grammatical features of Outer Circle Englishes come about through a combination of transfer and innovation, often in combination, while, depending on proficiency level, residual variability due to incomplete language learning also remains. Transfer is not so straightforward in grammar as in pronunciation or vocabulary, since patterns with varying degrees of abstractness rather than words or sounds come into play in grammar. A speaker may hear an English expression, intuitively infer an underlying pattern in the usage, and match that pattern to a pattern that they already know in another language. Subsequently, they can then use their version of the reconstructed pattern in English in similar ways to how they would use the familiar pattern in the language used to make that match.

The syntactic patterns associated with adverbial placement by Afrikaans speakers, when speaking English, can serve as a first illustration.[3] The conventional sequence of adverbials is not the same: the default order for multiple circumstance adverbs in Afrikaans is time–manner–place, whereas the English native-speaker sequence is manner–place–time (Watermeyer, 1996, pp. 111–112). Afrikaans typically places adverbials before objects or subject predicates, rather than after them, unless they are clausal. Sentences like the following are used by Afrikaans speakers of English, but not by native speakers in South Africa.

(1) For women there is not actually **in South Africa** a career. ↔ ... a career in South Africa
(2) There's a bus going **every morning to town**. ↔ ... to town every morning

Watermeyer points out, correctly, that this is an option, not invariable, so in the majority of cases, Afrikaans speakers do not use a different word order pattern in English, and of course, the English pattern is sometimes seen in the Afrikaans of Afrikaans speakers: cross-linguistic influence between the two languages tends to cut both ways. Patterns are sometimes rather more subtle, and would not even strike a casual reader as unusual, until one examines the matter in more detail. The following

---

3. Afrikaans speakers are sufficiently similar for the purposes of argument to the Outer Circle context, because they have not shifted to become native speakers of English as a group, live in an Outer Circle dominant context, and have typically also acquired their English first in the school context with other Afrikaans speakers as their teachers. The contexts are changing today, but for speakers who acquired English in the nineteenth century and all but the last few years of the twentieth century, this sketch places them sufficiently close to Outer Circle speakers.

two examples from short stories (named in brackets after the examples, and taken from Bosman, 2013) by the South African author Herman Charles Bosman (1905–1951) show native-like and Afrikaans-like uses of the adverb *also*, where example (4) is a direct equivalent of the Afrikaans adverbial pattern, in contrast to native English that would more typically restrict the options to examples like (3) only, and would rather use *too* than *also* in examples like (4). Bosman uses Afrikaans characters as internal narrators in many of his stories, and occasionally puts the idiom of typical Afrikaans speakers in their wording, although the short stories are generally written in a variety that is grammatically consistent with native rather than second-language English.

(3) Often after I have thought of Karel Flysman and of the way he died. I have **also** thought of that girl he spoke about. ('Karel Flysman', p. 64)

(4) His name is actually Hendrik de Waal, of course. But we still call him Le Valois in the Marico. And I wonder what his wife, Susannah, thinks of it **also**. ('Susannah and the Play-Actor', p. 285)

A case of abstract transfer of a different pattern, involving morphology rather than syntax, is the extended use of the progressive in many Outer Circle Englishes. The languages of people acquiring English often contain a more extended range of imperfective aspect constructions, encoded morphosyntactically by very different means than in English; for instance, one of these structural encodings in several Southern Bantu languages is a verbal prefix *sa-*, the persistitive, which has the meaning of an event with long duration, often translated with the adverb *still* in English – thus nowhere near the structural template of the English progressive. Speakers may perceive a semantic similarity – different kinds of imperfective meanings, ongoing and incomplete events (Sharma, 2009; Van Rooy, 2006), and on that basis, employ the English progressive form with a similarly extended semantic range to other imperfective types too. The following two examples (taken from Kruger & Van Rooy, 2017) from Black South African English show progressives that would not be typical in native varieties.

(5) Care of patients **is** basically **depending** on the 24-hour services rendered by nurses. (p. 36)

(6) ... not willing to work in areas believed **to be having** high HIV prevalence ... (p. 37)

The semantic prototype of the Black South African English progressive is a sense of incompleteness and ongoingness, without restriction of the temporariness of native-speaker varieties. In example (5), the stative use of the verb *depend* is not bounded in time but denotes an ongoing state of dependence. One particular usage, though, with the verb *having*, illustrated by example (6), is particularly salient and stigmatised, and is often targeted for correction by editors of published texts written by black South African authors – while other extended uses such as (5) are not (Kruger & Van Rooy, 2017). Van Rooy and Piotrowska (2015), in analysing historical data, show that the transfer took place in the very early stages of the emergence of Black South African English, such that the extended semantics is clearly present in corpus material from the nineteenth century already. Over time, there is slight convergence with native-speaker usage, but the core sense of incompleteness without the temporary restriction remains valid, and is rather straightforwardly a case of transfer of imperfective semantics from the other languages in the ecology.

These examples show that transfer is not merely a mechanical thing: speakers convey meanings that they find useful, and try to continue getting those useful meanings across with the available grammatical and lexical resources of English. Ndebele (1987) spoke of the inevitability of the English language changing because of its proximity to indigenous languages, in terms not all that different from how Trudgill (2004) saw the inevitability of multiple input forms contributing to alter the shape of New Zealand English in comparison with British English that served as input.

The users' creativity can extend beyond transfer, to discover and use patterns in English unrelated to the other languages in their repertoires. Such innovations are particularly noticeable at the crossroads of grammatical patterns and lexical items, which Schneider (2007) identifies as particularly characteristic of the third phase of nativisation in his detailed exposition of the dynamic model. By way of example, some English verbs are syntactically not simple transitives, but take a preposition alongside the verb to mark the affected theme of the verb, for instance one can *talk to* someone, but when the verb is *tell*, most English native speakers do not add a preposition and simply *tell* someone. Likewise, it is common to *talk about* something, but one tends to *discuss* something without the supportive link of a preposition. There are several partial regularities in the grammars of native speakers, but no very general principle that consistently guides the user in the selection of verb themes or addressees with or without a preposition. It should come as no surprise that second-language users seek regularity, and sometimes generalise different patterns (Van Rooy, 2010). Second-language speakers of English in East Africa do just that: they use prepositions with verbs that correspond to nouns that are more consistent in taking prepositions, for instance the following sets (taken from Schmied, 2008, p. 453).

(7) Noun+preposition   Verb+preposition
    talk about   talk about
    discussion about   discuss about
    emphasis on   emphasize on
    demand for   demand for
    stress on   stress on

Another East African generalisation that shows a slightly different way of making sense of a pattern is the choice of the causative verb *enable* without the infinitive particle *to* (Van Rooy, 2011). Some (native) English infinitives invariably take the infinitive particle when they are complements to verbs like *require, cause, allow* or *force*, shown by example (8); the verb *let* takes only a bare infinitive complement, without the particle *to* as shown by example (9), and the verb *help* varies between cases with and without the particle *to*, as illustrated by example (10), all taken from ICE-East Africa.

(8a) No other vehicle was therefore **allowed to precede** the one in which the deceased was carried. (W2F008K)
(8b) ... it is not something that maybe he **caused to happen** ... (S1A014K)
(9) It should **let** them **continue**. (S1B012K)
(10a) ... it's not only the context that can **help** a child **to get** the meaning ... (S1B006K)
(10b) Which language will **help** Tanzanians **achieve** their political goals ... (S1B011K)

With *enable*, in East African English, the patterning is like *help*, in that speakers use the forms with and without the particle *to*, whereas native speakers typically restrict themselves to the variant with *to* overtly present, as shown in (11).

(11a) It **enables** the teacher **to know** to handle such children ... (S1A021K)
(11b) Yeah It could **enable** him **pass** even with very minimal efforts (S1A020T)

It might seem like East African speakers get it wrong and do something strange, but actually, if one looks at the bigger picture, the grammatical choices of native English speakers are not all that consistent, and the East African speakers who allow themselves both options don't do something drastically different. Instead of treating *enable* as similar to *allow* and *cause*, they treat it as similar to *help*. These are all causative verbs in two very similar constructions, after all.

The use of the English grammar in the Outer Circle is of course also characterised by variability, and some of the variability results from attempts made by learners. Not all variability is due to learner error – the variable choice between *help* with and without an infinitive particle has little to do with incomplete learning; even attempts at finding the pattern in native-speaker English come up with probabilistic generalisations, better than chance, but not clear-cut and inviolable patterns. Nonetheless learner error, learner uncertainty, overgeneralisations and the like certainly all occur. These are more prevalent at lower levels of proficiency, as is almost self-evident, and tend to disappear at higher levels of proficiency. Often, commentators (and researchers) do not draw clear boundaries in what they take as evidence for what. Using student writing as the source of evidence for a variety risks equating learner features and variety features, conceptually. It is possible, though, to some degree, to disentangle the errors from other types of variability, if one has sufficient corpus data to represent less and more proficient users. Several purported features of Black South African English, for instance, have been shown to be restricted to users with less proficiency (Minow, 2010; Siebers, 2007; Van Rooy & Kruger, 2016). These features may still be characteristic of the variety, but they are not likely to stabilise and remain part of the feature pool to the extent that access to English and quality of educational provisioning improves. Features not holding up to closer scrutiny include the variable use of 3rd person singular pronouns (*he* and *she* used interchangeably to refer to female and male referents, respectively), the absence of the auxiliary verb *be* in progressive aspect constructions, the absence of the adverbialiser *-ly* after adjectives like *quick*, variable use of *-self* and *-selves* in plural reflexives, and variable use of singular and plural demonstratives (Mesthrie & Van Rooy, forthcoming; Van Rooy & Kruger, 2016).

6.3.3 Vocabulary

Transfer of indigenous vocabulary is reasonably prevalent across Outer Circle Englishes, but the contexts of use differ. When communicating about matters of local and regional relevance, such as political campaigns, community structures or activities in society, the likelihood of transferring words from other languages to convey the meaning precisely in English will be higher. Examples include the concept *satyagraha* ('devotion to truth') as a way to label the passive resistance campaign by Gandhi in the early twentieth century (first in South Africa, later in India), or the extended use of the term *ubuntu* ('humanity', but then in the communal sense of 'I am only a human through my relationship to other humans', not an individualist or rights-based concept) as a perspective in present-day South African politics. Unlike borrowing, which is done by native speakers of English for things they do not know or do not have names for, transfer by speakers of indigenous languages happens because a particular familiar concept is not adequately lexicalised in English, and therefore needs to be captured with an indigenous word. Such vocabulary transfers occur widely in Outer Circle varieties, and are used not only in conversation but also in newspaper writing and published fiction.

Direct transfer is not the only way to ensure communicative adequacy for English. Sometimes loan translations, or partial translation–partial transfer hybrid forms are used. Direct transfers from indigenous Bantu languages and Afrikaans with wider currency in South African English today include political vocabulary like *amandla* (interjection, political rallying cry) and *toyi-toyi* (verb, a fast-paced dance performed during political protest events); vocabulary for crime and violence like *tsotsi* (noun, robber, evil person) and *panga* (a kind of hand axe); traditional healers: *muthi* (traditional medicine) and *sangoma* (traditional doctor); cultural activities: *lobola* (a kind of dowry for the new bride's family); dance types such as *pantsula* and *kwaito*; or food like *braai* ('BBQ'), *boerewors* (a traditional sausage with high mince content and particular spice mix) or *pap en sous* (porridge and gravy) (Van Rooy & Terblanche, 2010). Many of these terms do not denote unusual or strange activities of the indigenous people from a settler perspective, but precisely the indigenous perspective on everyday life, using words with currency in other languages when talking about the same activities or things in English.

Some lexical elements from the pidgins have found their way into the local varieties of English that emerged in subsequent centuries, but otherwise, the pidgins have not had an enduring effect on Asian Englishes; Bolton (2002, p. 186) lists forms like *can do*, *chop*, *hong*, *piece* and *side* that are current in different registers of Hong Kong English – where the English lexical terms have different meanings and uses than they have for native speakers. The symbiosis of English and West African Pidgin English is such that it is not always sensible to draw a clear distinction between them, and thus, West African English is continuously supplied with potential vocabulary items from the local pidgin forms, which in turn may also draw on indigenous languages.

Apart from borrowed lexis, Kachru (1994, p. 524) also identifies hybrid coinages with English and indigenous morphemes. Examples include compounds like *lathi charge* 'baton charge' and *bindi mark* 'a dot-like mark put on the forehead by Hindu women', and derivations like *police walla* 'a policeman', where [-wallah] is a transferred suffix, with an English stem, or *brahmanic*, with a transferred stem and an English suffix.

Loan translations or other ways of coining new English words from existing morphemes include examples from Indian English like *clean shaven*, metonymic for religious non-conformism, *minor wife* for openly acknowledged mistress, or *mutual alliance* for 'an arrangement by which X's daughter marries Y's son and Y's daughter marries X's son' (Kachru, 1982/2015b, p. 96). Extended kinship names to specify relations not lexicalised in English also occur in Indian English, for example *cousin-brother* or *cousin-sister* (Kachru, 1994, p. 525), and in many African Englishes too.

6.4 Conclusion

Outer Circle varieties of English developed out of necessity. English speakers made territorial claims on lands inhabited by others, sometimes under the thin veneer of the legality of a treaty or a protectorate, sometimes rather more bluntly, such as the portioning of Africa by European rulers in Berlin in the late nineteenth century, where they felt themselves duly authorised to chop the continent into bits under their control.

The British needed to rule their subjects, administer laws, trade, exploit resources and manufacture things. Language was required, and therefore English was used on the basis of necessity, with a cohort of local speakers trained to provide in the need for intermediaries. The number of local speakers of English expanded with the need for more intermediaries as the British engagement with a particular place intensified, alongside the activities of missionaries to evangelise and set up schools, where many of the colonial intermediaries were trained.

At some point, the local English users began using the language for their own purposes, at which point necessity became the mother of invention. Local users started to communicate in English across local linguistic divides in some cases, about learned topics, given their English-language formal education, and also began to articulate their own conditions of exploitation and oppression as part of a wider attempt to assert their humanity in the face of colonisers who did not see them as their equals.

The twin forces of communicative need within public life and articulation of a self in the face of the colonial othering combined to give English a more permanent home in many Outer Circle countries, also after formal political independence, when control over the language passed largely to the ruling classes of the indigenous population. With rapid expansion of education and administration came rapid expansion of English-language teaching, which resulted in wider access to English, but with increasingly obvious local colour. English has become and remains valuable as a means for employment in jobs that may take people out of poverty, but at the same time, potentially acts as barrier to people who have had inadequate opportunity to master the language at some predetermined or de facto level of proficiency.

The 'local colour' has its source in indigenisation, making the language useful in a new context and slotting it into an already existing multilingual linguistic ecology. The process of second-language acquisition in the educational context, but with teachers who are from similar second-language backgrounds as the learners, strengthened the influence that other languages and learning processes had on the shaping of English in the new place. We will return to the contradictory evaluations and responses to the deviations of Outer Circle Englishes in the final chapter.

7 English without the English

'We are running after the facts.'
'And it is not open for discussion for the media. So. Point.'

These two quotes, or many other others, can be dished up for comic relief to poke fun at the English of some of the non-natives – those souls who are not among the 300 million English speakers, but whose results are, if I rephrase Bill Bryson, more mixed than others. These quotes are genuine statements, made by the Dutch football coach, Louis van Gaal, during his tenure as coach of Manchester United in the United Kingdom.[1] If one knows Dutch, one can see that they are direct translations, and one understands what Van Gaal is trying to convey. For instance, one sense of Dutch 'punt' corresponds to English 'point' but another sense of 'punt' denotes the full stop as punctuation mark, which is the first meaning Van Gaal likely had in mind.

For the entertainment of the reader, one can scrape the internet or one's personal recollections for on-the-fly translations into English made at tourist hotspots across the world, stereotypically often associated with the Far East: 'Beware of missing foot' (presumably missing one's step), 'Please do not empty your dog here' (presumably don't let your dog use this spot as a toilet). There are plenty of websites that entertain people with the bizarre English of the non-natives . . . bizarre, of course, is not my coinage, but one that I borrow from the Dutch bestseller *I Always Get My Sin: Het bizarre Engels van Nederlanders* (Rijkens, 2005). The English part of the title is a word-for-word translation of a Dutch idiom, except that the last word, 'sin', is the Dutch word with a very different meaning than the English 'sin' (the Dutch expression is better translated as 'I always have it to my liking'). The second, Dutch, part of the title is 'The bizarre English of the Dutch'.

---

1. https://www.voetbalprimeur.nl/nieuws/412947/de-tien-beste-engelse-oneliners-van-van-gaal.html

What differentiates English from earlier languages of wider communication is the scale of its geographical diffusion and the range of contexts in which it came into use beyond the presence or influence of native speakers, bizarrely, blandly, boldly or bashfully. A language of wider communication is not unique to the world; many languages have served in this role in the past, and many continue to do so at present, but as Spolsky (2004, p. 76), De Swaan (2010) and many others have observed, the spread of English is at a historically unprecedented level. A degree of political and/or military support is quite typical for the diffusion of languages beyond their native speakers, minimally a kind of power imbalance, even if rooted purely in demographic or economic power, where one party in the exchange is able to expect of the other party to conduct the conversation in its preferred language. This has been typical in colonial contact encounters, as set out in the previous chapters: English-speaking colonial representatives were able to impose the use of English on the points of contact with the colonised people (Chapter 6), and English masters were able to compel their slaves into labour but also into using English and in some cases deliberately coerced indigenous people into English by forcing them into boarding schools with English-only policies (Chapter 5). This coercion was largely a matter of convenience for the colonisers, and up to a certain point not really a policy goal, just an instance of common sense to make communication possible (for them).

After political decolonisation, many of the former British and American colonies opted to retain the use of English and in many cases became the agents of its wider diffusion within postcolonial societies. However, the various colonialisms that have been considered in Chapters 4–6 do not account for the scope of present-day use of English in full. We need to acknowledge the contribution of the Van Gaals of the world, together with the creative Asian translators of public signs, the Agnethas, Björns, Bennys and Anni-Frids who create art in English despite not coming from an English home-language background, and the non-native academics who continue to publish in English despite incurring the extra obligation to have their English checked by native speakers before submitting to some journals.

English as a world language, English as a global language, English Lingua Franca, World Language English and any other such wide-ranging, all-encompassing designations ring true because of the use of English beyond the geographical presence or political control of English speakers, past or present. This is construed metaphorically as an attack by an illness, blending health and warfare metaphors – 'English fever' in

South Korea (Park, 2009), or 'linguistic imperialism' being an aspect of 'linguistic genocide' (Phillipson, 1992). By contrast to these concerned responses, there is the triumphantalism of John Major's (1993) analysis of Britain's strength's culminating in 'And we have English, – English, the world language. We should do well with such strengths' or Bill Bryson's (1990, p. 1) charitable, if perhaps a wee bit patronising, gaze on the mixed results of them non-natives. Phillipson (1992, 2008) points to a range of interests being served by the promotion of the use of English – native speakers' interests more than others. While some disagree with aspects of Phillipson's analysis – Spolsky (2004) goes as far as labelling his argument about linguistic imperialism a conspiracy theory, which Phillipson (2007) refutes in some detail – the contest seems to be at the level of centralisation in the planning and the extent to which other causes over and above the intent of English-speaking policy makers also played a role. There isn't disagreement about the diagnosis of an imbalance that gets perpetuated, about the 'undeserved and unjustified' benefits for native speakers (De Swaan, 2010, p. 65). Yet, individuals and governments beyond the overt political control of anglophone authorities continue to make choices that serve to expand the uses and numbers of users of English, and as millions continue to use English, its value for them and those who already use it increases (De Swaan, 2010).

This chapter enquires into the reasons and consequences of the spread of English beyond the anglophone colonial empires and postcolonial continuations. The internet and present-day telecommunications connectivity introduce a whole new dimension to the position and further expansion of the use of English, but will be dealt with in the next chapter, as it came at a time when much of the position that English has come to occupy in the second half of the twentieth century was already secure.

A brief terminological digression is in order before getting to the specifics. For the Englishes beyond the colonial sphere of influence, Larry Smith used the term English as an International Auxiliary Language in his early scholarship, which he explicitly contrasted to English as a Foreign Language (Bolton & Davis, 2018). Smith's key point was that English should not be seen or taught as a foreign language, because the foreign-language approach implies that learners are taught the culture of the speakers of the target language as part of the pedagogical package. Rather, the teaching should be geared to train learners to communicate in English across different cultures, for the purposes of communication beyond just the English-speaking cultures. These early ideas of Smith matured into the notion of the Expanding Circle when Kachru (1985/2015d) made the entire model of world Englishes explicit. The shared concern of the Outer and Expanding Circles was the deculturation of English – the need to wrestle control over the uses and pragmatics of use away from native-speaker norms and make the language serviceable to all users, in a manner that does not impose the obligation to take a course in cricket to understand its international uses. Of course, if the King's English remained the sole point of reference in a traditional monocentric view of language standards, there would have been a dire need for fast-tracking the development of cricket in the United States, in order to facilitate the mastery of the cricket idioms of the standard language by his majesty's former subjects in this rogue colony. The polycentricity of English, also in the Inner Circle, is therefore a unifying strand across all three circles of world Englishes.

After the notion of an Expanding Circle was established, various other traditions continued using other terms to denote the use of English in these contexts. From certain applied linguistic corners, second language, foreign language and learner language remain current to denote the non-native Englishes, emphasising that their users continue to display errors, as measured against the standard of some native variety. Such terms represent a reductionist view of what goes on in the Expanding Circle, because proficient adult users of English are axiomatically defined as language learners, not recognising how they differ from toddlers or young teenagers who are actually engaged in learning the language in formal education. Mauranen (2017, p. 740) calls this conception of proficient adult users ill-founded.

The idea of an international language, English as an International Language, is consistent with parts of Smith's line of thought, but is a functional designation of one very prominent use of English in the Expanding Circle without providing space to make the full range of uses salient. This is exactly why Smith adapted his use of terminology, with international and all the other dimensions incorporated into the broader world Englishes frame. More recently, a specific sense of English as a lingua franca developed from the work of Seidlhofer (2001), Jenkins (2007) and Mauranen (2012), where work overlapping in spirit and scope with Smith's has brought new momentum to understanding the global use of English. There are explicit reasons why they prefer to use English Lingua Franca (ELF) rather than Expanding Circle, most notably that potential ELF uses, as they see it, cut across the circles (Seidlhofer, 2009). That is a very valid point, and to the extent that world Englishes approaches English in the three circles as completely separate, the implied criticism is valid.[2]

I will continue to refer to the Expanding Circle here, to keep the attention on the full range of contexts and uses of English, including its Lingua Franca role, but also beyond that, while acknowledging that Lingua Franca uses often involve participants from multiple circles interacting in international contact settings. The concept 'expanding' is neatly open-ended and polysemous: the use of the English language expands to ever newer settings, but the uses of the language can also expand in these settings, which seems to be a point that some of the terminological engineers tend to overlook, reading the world Englishes conceptualisation only in centre–periphery terms and therefore objecting to the potential negative value judgement of framing something as so peripheral that it is even beyond the Outer Circle – beyond the pale on steroids, the fifty-first shade of pale.

7.1 History of the global spread of English

Prior to the mid-twentieth century, the spread of English beyond the sphere of colonial occupation, settlement and conquest depended on trade and language teaching, but in ways corresponding to the languages of other important economic and colonial powers. The more active the trading partnership, the more opportunities for contact, and thus more motivation to succeed in the communication that supported the trade. Combined with this was the relative, if perceived, power of the trading partners, which influenced the language of the trade. Thus, many of the trade pidgins that developed along the African and Asian coasts had strong European roots – Portuguese and later English, rather than African or Asian ones, reflecting the maritime and military power of the dominant partners in the trading. The British economic strength of the nineteenth century, joined and superseded by American economic strength in the twentieth century, created more and more opportunities and uses for English in trade. Until the eighteenth century, for instance, there did not seem to be a clear linguistic asymmetry in British–Dutch trading across

---

2. It is beyond the scope of the present argument to deal with the reductionist interpretation of world Englishes concepts prevalent among some of its critics. I have dealt with some of these superficial readings in Van Rooy (2019), and leave it for the interested reader to explore this, alongside Seidlhofer (2009), who offers a more nuanced view of what the benefits of the ELF concept are that are underrepresented in how world Englishes typically deals with the matter. Unlike other terminological differences, in the case of ELF, I am in principle convinced that there is additional purchase in the term, and this sentiment is shared by a number of world Englishes scholars who incorporate insights from ELF research very productively in their work.

the North Sea. In the late seventeenth century, English ship-builders still relied on Dutch technology and read Dutch shipping manuals to inform their advances in constructing ships that could compete with the Dutch vessels (Frankopan, 2015, p. 268), but once the power imbalance in favour of the British became clear, English became the dominant language for Dutch–British trading and Dutch fell into disuse as contact language in this exchange pair (Edwards, 2016; Loonen, 1990).

The mid-twentieth century is a clear turning point (De Swaan, 2010). Until then, other colonial languages like French and Spanish still had reasonably wide usage too in different parts of the world on the back of their colonial expansion, with French and German having been used very extensively within Europe in language contact settings prior to the war. Russian also spread extensively during the expansion of the Russian Empire, while the aftermath of the Second World War created conditions in Eastern Europe and the People's Republic of China for further learning and use of Russian. Yet, the conditions 'conspired' to favour English, because whatever intentional planning there was, as outlined by Phillipson (1992), similar initiatives were undertaken by the French, and the Soviet Union certainly did its centrally planned best to promote Russian – yet these languages have not attained the global role of English.

One should not be blind to the basic military reason; with the allied forces winning the Second World War, and English speakers ending up leading the recovery, English came to be seen in a very favourable light. This was followed by the post-war reconstruction, such as the Marshall plan in Europe but also the US-led reconstruction phase in post-war Japan and its role in the Korean War shortly afterwards. US military personnel were stationed in that part of the world, many of whom decided after their military service to become teachers – see Baratta (2021) for one such insider account, or generations earlier, the influence that Larry Smith's experience as a teacher in Thailand, as part of the Peace Corps, had on his understanding of the role of English (Bolton & Davis, 2018). A significant presence of American soldiers is still maintained in various places across the world, including Korea, where there is even a programme for Korean soldiers to work alongside the American soldiers for extended periods of time (Rüdiger, 2019). The winners spoke English, and those engaged in post-war support for recovery did their job in English, which gave English an early advantage that it has not relinquished. This expansion came on top of its already assured position in North America, Australasia, and some of the economic and demographic strongholds in Africa (e.g. Nigeria, South Africa, Kenya) and Asia (e.g. India, Pakistan, Singapore) due to colonial expansion.

Trade in the post-war period became increasingly interconnected, diffused in the age of globalisation (Friedman, 2005), which in turn expanded the number of communicative contacts required to keep the organisation of manufacturing, distribution and sales going. This came to be exploited very carefully by the economies and marketing of the very strong English economies from the mid-twentieth century.

The export products stretched beyond tradable goods to entertainment, where the availability of English-language music, films and television programmes led to their permanent presence across the world – Phillipson (1992, p. 59) emphasises the critical contribution of these cultural products to the spread of English. Musical icons like Elvis Presley and The Beatles did their bit for the profiling of the language in the first decades after the war, selling large numbers of records in English-speaking countries, but also beyond – and they were of course not the only icons of English-language music in the 1950s and 1960s. By the 1970s, non-English-speaking entertainers using English got in on the act too: the commercial success of ABBA after their decision to make music in English rather than Swedish was certainly due to language more than a sudden jump in the artistic quality, and they became as commercially successful, also in anglophone countries, as the top anglophone artists of their generation. Film entertainment likewise created international stars out of English-speaking actors, even if they were dubbed or subtitled in countries who had the money and technology to do so. And others wanted to join: there are more Arnold Schwarzeneggers, Juliette Binoches and Gérard Depardieus making movies in English than English actors plying their trade in German or French. Bill Bryson admits to his hard time ordering beer in German . . .

There is a certain snowball effect: the English speakers started the post-war reconstruction period on the front foot, with the war having had very little effect on the day-to-day economic activity and infrastructure in America and Canada, also Australia and New Zealand, while Britain suffered comparatively less damage than many parts of (continental) Europe and Asia. Ever since the entertainment market was secured, it has turned out very hard for others to break through on the scale of English-language entertainment, with Bollywood and Nollywood doing their bit to keep things going too in recent decades – the names already say a lot.

Beyond economy and entertainment, international academic exchange became the next virtual territory that the English language conquered. Publications recorded in the 'benchmark' international databases are in English in approximately 80 per cent (Van Weijen, 2012) to 90 per cent (Curry & Lillis, 2022) of all cases, with an ongoing rise in the volume of articles published in English by researchers located in non-anglophone countries. Of course, as Curry and Lillis (2022) point out, these numbers typically overestimate the proportion of English, since the inclusion rules for the major international databases of scholarly publication usually stipulate that publications in languages other than English need to have English titles and/or abstracts to be included in the database, excluding some journals from around the world. Yet, the overall trend is quite clear. International academic research publication has become synonymous with the English language – hence the 'quirk-y' concern of one of Edwards's (2010) interviewees that 'many editors of international journals are not necessarily native speakers themselves' (p. 22). International academic conferences likewise conduct their affairs mostly in English (Phillipson, 2008). Such international academic exchanges form a very prominent strand of research across the English Lingua Franca approach (Mauranen, 2012).

The position of English is secured not only by academic publishing and research communication. The internationalisation of higher education further contributes to the spread of English, in two ways. Because of the perceived prestige and value of the qualifications and the opportunity for development of their English language, some students from non-anglophone countries opt, where financially possible, to study in anglophone countries, with Australia having benefited from Asian students in recent decades, alongside the traditional share of North American and British universities. Where money is tight, there is a smaller stream of Asian students opting for the Outer Circle context as well (Coetzee-Van Rooy, 2008), and even parts of the Expanding Circle are getting in on the act as some European universities offer courses and degree programmes in English too. The majority of institutions in Scandinavia and the rest of northwest Europe offer such programmes, with some universities in countries like Denmark and the Netherlands offering up to a third of all their programmes in English (Wächter & Maiworm, 2014). Such extension of English in education also reaches into the secondary and, in a smaller number of cases, the primary schools. In the Netherlands today, more than a thousand secondary schools offer the option of bilingual education for several years (usually three) where half the subjects are taught in English and the other half in Dutch, a socially desirable opportunity for parents and pupils alike (Edwards, 2016).

In the arena of international politics, the spread of English received substantial impetus from its use in multinational organisations such as the EU and ASEAN (Kirkpatrick, 2007, pp. 155–170), as well as the regional organisations of Sub-Saharan Africa. Whereas the precursors to the European Union used French and German more, English came to the party after the entrance of the United Kingdom in 1973 (and seems to remain in the union despite the decision of the United Kingdom to leave it). Often, the smaller European nations preferred the use of English over German and French. An even stronger case arose in ASEAN, where English has been the main working language since its inception in 1967. ECOWAS, EAC and SADC in Africa likewise make use of English more than French, Swahili or other languages, so much so that Rwanda, historically a French-using country, has switched to English to enable better collaboration with its East African regional trade and development partners. Given the practices within the multilateral organisations, bilateral contact among member states or across these various regions also provides space for the use of English more than other languages, with interpreting used in large meetings, but not always at the level of working committees and where diplomats and administrators get together to work on the detail.

7.2 Social factors

7.2.1 Contact

Contact with speakers of English used to be quite limited for the Expanding Circle. Only trade and education served as regular contact points with speakers of English. Although native-speaker teachers or university lecturers were present to various degrees, the teachers were mainly from the local speech community rather than native speakers.

As globalisation led to increased mobility of people, contact between residents of Expanding Circle countries and native speakers increased, if still with a focus on trade contact. The gradually increasing sites of contact remained transient, though. With increased use of English as a lingua franca, the contact with non-native English users from other countries then became a fixture of the contact settings within which English continued to be used. Native-speaker contact became but one part of the international contacts in the overall experience of those Expanding Circle users who used English for such lingua franca purposes. Contact is thus with other speakers of English, without the requirement that those speakers be native speakers.

Mediated contact, for example through films, books and music, provides a further opportunity to receive English-language input, alongside face-to-face contact in international encounters. Most recently, as is explored in more depth in Chapter 8, the internet has brought about a rapid expansion of contact opportunities, by removing the requirement to travel physically to get in contact with other speakers of English.

7.2.2 Use

English is used for an expanding range of reasons in the Expanding Circle. It does not function only as a foreign language that is learnt for the purpose of communication with native speakers, as part of a curriculum of learning about the culture of these foreign people, reading their literature, understanding their communicative strategies. This is sometimes called *Landeskunde* – German for knowledge of the country. However, such a rather traditional conceptualisation of English still permeates regulatory discourse, for instance in the way departments of English are named in continental Europe: English Language and Culture, British and American Studies, Anglistics, and so on, matched by similar departments for other foreign languages – Italian Language and Culture in Denmark, 'Scandinavistics' in Switzerland, Arabic Language and Civilisation in France, and so on.

The contemporary uses of English follow its historical route of expansion, much like in the Outer Circle, as the previous chapter shows. The oldest use, which remains very important, is the use in trade. International trade contact, expanded to the global scale of interconnectedness today, is most likely mediated through English. To the extent that English speakers participate in such interactions, trade contact may resemble other foreign-language uses, but English is often used in trade contact by people who are not speakers of English as a native language. Most of the trade between continental Europe and the Far East is mediated in English, while the use of typical foreign-language German, French or Italian by Asians, or Chinese, Japanese or Korean by Europeans is a minority option – not non-existent, just considerably less prevalent.

The use of English to do business goes further than just trade contact. Contemporary global manufacturing and multinational companies conduct a considerable part of their international business but also within-company liaising in English, such that multinational company offices in many continental European cities make extensive use of English alongside other languages, and particularly use English extensively for record-keeping purposes, to the extent that meetings held in other languages are often recorded afterwards in minutes written in English. The influence of English extends to the adoption of English job titles in some countries; at the time of writing, my online Dutch-language newspaper offers its readership a choice of the following vacancies in the Netherlands:[3] *Consultant Recruitment Marketing, Manager Datastandaarden, Manager Ontwikkeling en Architectuur, Strategisch HR-Adviseur/Businesspartner,*

---

3. https://www.nrc.nl/index/carriere/ (date of access 7 July 2022).

Businesscontroller F&C Team TLC and several more; good luck making sense of these job titles if you do not know English, but also if you do not understand enough Dutch to know that there are no spacing errors: compounds are usually written as one word in Dutch.

Trade extends quite easily into tourism, another commercial activity involving contact between people. While travellers often do take the trouble of learning some phrases in the language of the country they travel to, more often they rely on English irrespective of whether English is a language of the destination (Schneider, 2016). Passengers on commercial airlines and cruise ships have a reasonable expectation of service in English, alongside other languages perhaps, but English has become a backbone or default in these contexts. English restaurant menus are also available to tourists in many non-anglophone countries, even if the serving staff do not all speak English extensively. Admittedly, depending on context, more languages might be available, since a menu is a relatively small piece to translate and is reused extensively, making the investment to add, say, a German or French menu alongside the English one a common option in tourist destinations within Europe; some tourist meccas in Europe even offer the option of a Mandarin Chinese menu. Jaworski and Thurlow (2010) rightly point out that other languages are often used to enhance the experience, to exoticise for instance through profiling unusual or very long names, or using local languages to address tourists, but all of these additional linguistic resources are embedded in a frame that usually involves an English backbone.

In conjunction with trade and tourism, English is used very extensively in advertising worldwide. Advertising aimed at local audiences does of course make primary or extensive use of local languages, but English is used alongside, blended into advertisements or in parallel to advertisements in other languages (Bhatia, 2019). English-language slogans for products, together with such attention grabbers as 'world's number one . . .' on billboards or in newspaper advertisements, are found alongside advertisements entirely in English in newspapers in non-English-speaking countries, especially but not limited to job and holiday advertisements. However, as Li (2019) shows, this is not mere imposition of English on a local advertisement. There is often creative tension in the way English and other languages interact in the construction of advertisements, in which English is not reduced to a simplex signifier of some exotic quality, or globalisation and the hegemony of English.

English is the principal language of international scientific communication, and is thus used extensively in academic publishing and for academic conferences. This use of English extends into the domain of popular writing, such that English magazines, especially in technological domains, and popular non-fiction are also available in many places, even though translation of English popular books into other languages is very common in places where the market size justifies this.[4] English does not reign supreme in the popular dissemination of knowledge worldwide, but it is certainly more prominent than any other additional language. Edwards (2016, p. 61) notices, for instance, that on the website of a Dutch-language newspaper in the Netherlands, the weekly longreads offered to the readership include several English-language stories, which receive no comment or apology for being in English, again making English-language journalism available for use to a keen reading public.

The language of science role extends to the language of higher education, where English is very widely used in higher education across the world, not only in the prescribed book market but also as the language of instruction in universities in non-anglophone countries, as noted in the historical exposition earlier in this chapter. As something of an elite phenomenon, English private schools are gaining traction in some parts of the world, where parents see them as an opportunity to strengthen their children's mastery of the language. Such schools range from those that cater for an international or expat community, some of which are even reasonably affordable for international families in cities across the world, to private schools that target the local population but offer them an English immersion opportunity. A key observation here is that an 'international school', be that in continental Europe or the affluent countries of the Far East, or even middle-income countries, is often an English-medium school but caters for a wide range of nationalities and linguistic backgrounds.

English is one of a few languages of international diplomacy and politics. Through very competent and fast translation and interpreting services, major multinational political organisations are able to make more languages than English widely usable, for example at the United Nations and within the European Union. Yet, speakers of many languages still choose to address these meetings in English and not the languages of the countries they represent, perhaps trusting their own English enough that they want to address 'the world' directly and not through translation, or at least not through relay translation. The adoption of English as the sole or main working language of international organisations noted above consolidates this role.

---

4. By way of illustration, Chomsky's scholarly work in generative linguistics is not so widely translated, but his political writing, where he acts as a public intellectual rather than a disciplinary expert, is widely available in some other languages, as the Wikipedia entries on Chomsky in German, French and Dutch very easily show.

The use of the English language in the entertainment domain is extensive, and, as noted in the historical sketch earlier in this chapter, entertainment is a key driver of the worldwide expansion of English. In some ways, the entry threshold is relatively low – opera music is still revered by some today, even if they do not understand Italian, German, French or other languages in which the famous eighteenth- or nineteenth-century operas are performed. This applies even more strongly to contemporary English-language music. The extensive role of English is very visible, for instance, in the annual Eurovision song contest, where English-language lyrics are favoured in years when there are not language restrictions, and since the final abolition of the language restriction in 1999, more than half of all winning songs have had English lyrics. And of course, the act voted best Eurovision winner of all time was ABBA, who won with 'Waterloo', an English-language song, in 1974, the first year after the requirement to sing in the national language was relaxed. English is thus widely used for music, not only for consuming it but also for producing it. After the success of ABBA, several European artists also became prominent makers of English-language music, while several very successful artists like Julio Iglesias and Celine Dion enhanced the commercial success of their careers with English records alongside the Spanish and French for which they initially became global stars, respectively.

The production of films and television in English is largely still the province of English speakers from the Inner and Outer Circles, though. Although Bollywood mainly produces films in the languages of India, with Hindi very dominant, there are several English-language films annually too, some of which are commercially very successful and widely screened across the world. Nollywood produces many films in Nigerian languages alongside English, but English is much more dominant in Nollywood productions compared with Bollywood, as is the regional focus and incorporation of Ghanaian actors and productions. English-language films produced in Japan or even continental Europe are not a common occurrence, if not unattested. Consumption of film and television worldwide in English is extensive, though, despite (and in part because of) the availability of subtitling and dubbing. Given the market for English-language entertainment worldwide, it becomes possible to sell such films and television series at lower cost than producing them originally in other languages, conferring a competitive advantage on English-language entertainment, and threatening the viability of producing material in other languages through 'dumping' (De Swaan, 2010, p. 63).

An offshoot of the internationalisation of the workplace in a selection of cosmopolitan cities across the world is the coming into existence of larger expat communities in cities like Amsterdam and Berlin, but also cities in the Outer Circle like Johannesburg, Lagos and Singapore, where people use English to socialise. The use of English thus extends, in these international contact sites, into the personal domain. The same use of English is also found in Inner Circle contexts, where expat groups – be they international student residences (Meierkord, 2012) or middle-class professionals – make extensive use of English, in ways not specific to the country but owing to the fact of being groups of people who share the status of international guests in another country and use English amongst themselves beyond the public domain.

7.2.3 Acquisition

The acquisition of English in the Expanding Circle is strongly dependent on education. Beside trade contact with English, education was central to the spread of English beyond the British Empire. In many parts of Europe, German and French had a significant share of the foreign-language offering in school education in the emerging formal education systems of Europe during the eighteenth and nineteenth centuries. Since the end of the Second World War, the share of other languages has been shrinking, and in almost all systems, English is now the (prescribed or preferred) first additional language, after a period in the Cold War era when Russian played an important role in Eastern Europe (e.g. Schröder, 2018, on the German-speaking part of Central Europe; Wilhelm, 2018, on the Netherlands). In China, after the choice of Russian as an additional language from the middle of the twentieth century, and the strong anti-English sentiment during the years of the Cultural Revolution, English has become established as the first additional language in the education system again since the 1980s (Bolton, 2003, p. 236). South America installed English as a foreign language in the school curriculum only towards the end of the twentieth century, but even there, it has become the preferred first additional language (e.g. Rajagopalan, 2003, on Brazil; Nielsen, 2003, on Argentina).

English continues to be construed as a 'foreign language' in government policies in much of the Expanding Circle, which is reflected in a decision to introduce it at a later stage, often only in secondary education. However, a trend since the late twentieth century, and more so in the northwest of Europe than elsewhere, has been to introduce English to learners at a younger age. In addition, and going beyond the foreign-language curriculum, the acquisition of English is enhanced by out-of-classroom exposure on a scale not matched by typical foreign languages – entertainment for younger learners (computer games, music, television, film), access via the internet, and real-life use by adults honing their skills. Many of the accelerated opportunities are tied with the internet, and will receive attention in the next chapter.

7.2.4 Attitudes

The varied uses raise important questions about attitudes towards English, particularly in the face of the rather more traditionalist approach to foreign-language teaching that remains dominant in most Expanding Circle educational policies. The bottom line here is that attitudes are ambivalent and contradictory. There is a strong instrumental drive, where people use English because it is expedient, in a self-reinforcing cycle, where the more English is used, the more it becomes useful and desirable to use and hence more people learn to use it, which in turn makes it more useful (De Swaan, 2010). In such a cycle, attitudes are favourable in an instrumental sense – people use English because it is so useful and aspire to use it well, since the better you are able to use it, the more valuable it becomes. It is generally used in ways that require little identity work, and might be perceived as a great equaliser, which is exactly the role that it plays in political contexts such as the European Union (even more so with the United Kingdom out of it) or ASEAN.

The matter is complicated by a construal of English as a foreign language, and reinforced by an assumption of native-speaker control, the need for being in constant touch with the native speaker, as Sir Randolph Quirk reminded the audience of the Japanese Association of Language Teaching in 1988:

> We must not forget that many Japanese teachers, Malaysian teachers, Indian teachers have done postgraduate training in Britain and the United States, eager to absorb what they felt were the latest ideas in English teaching. Where better, after all, to get the latest ideas on this than in the leading English-speaking countries? (p. 21)

Thus, in contrast to the instrumentalist attitude, English is also perceived as foreign by some, placing the non-native users on the back foot – a difficult language that isn't used correctly. This attitude is reinforced by an education system and an applied linguistics industry that promote native-speaker norms and teaching material grounded in the native-speaker culture. Where countries in the Outer Circle have the option to valorise their local variety of English (which they may or may not do), such an option hardly seems available to those learning to use English in the Expanding Circle, and hence the use of the term 'Learner Englishes' persists in many academic circles to refer to the Englishes of adults in Expanding Circle contexts, despite such adults not being in formal language training programmes any more. Even a country like the Netherlands, characterised by widespread use and strong overall English-language proficiency across the entire population (exceeding the average proficiency in many Outer Circle countries, and exceeding the base of English speakers too), remains a country where the exonormative attitude to grammar (Edwards, 2016) and pronunciation (Van den Doel & Quené, 2013) remains dominant. In some cases, such as Korea or Japan, where societal proficiency is not very high, English serves as a 'skill' (Edwards & Seargeant, 2020, p. 343), or marker of elite class membership, with test scores based on standardised native varieties playing a role in selection for jobs – with the clear sense that English has to be as native-like as possible (even if not with high proficiency).

A recurrent trope in much writing and native-speaker public opinion is the poor English of the Other, supplying the humour that Bryson uses on the rest of the first page of his book to draw the reader into his no doubt fascinating account of the mother tongue, or supplying the opportunity for the language entrepreneurs to develop their English-language teaching resources, train the teachers, or advertise their editorial services for aspiring academic writers who were born on the wrong side of the native-speaker railway tracks. The imbalance and native-speaker control are obvious from the high status that British and American tests enjoy, also for access to universities in non-English-speaking contexts, not to mention the strong market for English-language learning material produced in and by native speakers from the Inner Circle countries, most especially Britain and the United States.

7.3 Linguistic features

7.3.1 Pronunciation

Expanding Circle Englishes are characterised, like Outer Circle Englishes, by transfer from the native languages of the speakers. The educational provision, with similar reliance on local teachers, typically serves to reinforce such patterns of transfer. Mauranen (2017, pp. 738–739) refers to the similects: similar patterns coming into being because different individuals each create their approximation of English, in interaction with the same other language(s) that provide cross-linguistic influences, rather than societal transmission. In consequence, her prediction is that long-term change will be quite limited, because speakers of the same similect don't need to use English with one another, but mostly rely on their other shared language(s).

Jenkins (2017, p. 555) identifies typical transfer features like Korean speakers substituting /f/ by [p], for example in *family* and *wife*, or consonant cluster reduction by Chinese speakers, rendering 'product' as *podac*. However, she makes the crucial point that these features are variable, and speakers are often able to accommodate in the direction of native forms in contexts where intelligibility plays a more important role, while showing transfer features in higher concentrations in contexts where social rather than informational concerns dominate. Rüdiger (2019) identifies a range of characteristic morphosyntactic features in the spoken English of Koreans – in comparison with British and American native-speaker corpora, as is quite typical for such variety-description research. A number of these are potentially due to transfer from Korean, but many potential features are relatively infrequent. While reduction of redundant plural markers is quite widespread, for instance, the placement of prepositions after the noun phrase ('postpositions') is extremely rare. Many features that Rüdiger identifies, such as variability in article use, fewer pronouns and fewer copular verbs, can be attributed in part to transfer and in part to simplification typical of non-native speakers, but are similar to other Expanding Circle varieties, such as European English (Mollin, 2006).

Intelligibility is a key concern in research on Expanding Circle pronunciation. Much of the linguistic research has been conducted in Inner Circle countries, particularly in the United States, among foreign students living there temporarily. However, some valuable information can be obtained despite that contextual limitation. A surprising finding from earlier research was that non-native participants surveyed in the United States showed similar favourable biases towards native speakers and unfavourable biases towards non-native speakers, including speakers with whom they share a native language (Munro et al., 2006). This is based in part on the use of accent as a cue to identify the nativeness of a speaker in the absence of visual cues, but also extends to identical voices projected to be different speakers using visual cues to prime the identification of someone as being from a particular group (Yang et al., 2017), suggesting that it concerns the evocation of stereotypes, rather than just simply being a matter of intelligibility of comprehensibility (Fuertes et al., 2002).

Major et al. (2005) found that non-native listeners have an overall lower comprehension score than native listeners, but they also found that non-native listeners score lower on the understanding (intelligibility) of ethnic African American English and 'international' (Australian and Indian) varieties than standard and Southern regional American English, whereas native speakers generally understood the different native accents and even the Indian English equally well. Intelligibility is also lower for listening to non-native speaker English than when listening to native-speaker English (Major et al., 2002), although non-native listeners tend to score better than native listeners when listening to another non-native speaker of English in the study of Fuse et al. (2018), unlike the finding of Major et al. (2002, 2005).

In some contexts of evaluation, the degree of perceived accentedness is a mediating variable, such that perceived heavier accents are evaluated more negatively than perceived milder accents (Lev-Ari & Kaysar, 2010), or that there is a correlation between perceived intelligibility/comprehensibility and subjective attitudinal ratings (Fuse et al., 2018).

An alternative perspective comes from world Englishes inspired research into intelligibility, especially the work of Larry Smith. Smith and Rafiqzad (1979) collected intelligibility evaluations from 1,386 listeners across eleven Asian countries. They listened to performances of prepared reading representing a classroom lesson, from nine different countries. One of these was a native American English speaker, and the other eight speakers were from Hong Kong, India, Japan, Korea, Malaysia, Nepal, the Philippines and Sri Lanka. The results were unexpected. The American English speaker was not the most intelligible. Speakers from Sri Lanka and India, followed by Japan and Malaysia, were judged most intelligible, while the native speaker was close to the bottom, with the Hong Kong speaker judged least intelligible.

The speakers were selected by local fieldworkers to represent the local educated form of English, but at the same time, were restricted in terms of extent of contact with native speakers in education and in adult life. The listeners were all educated individuals representing a range of professions, but living in their country of origin. The authors do note that in a subsequent retest of the material in the USA, with both native-speaker and Asian listener-judges, the native speaker scored much higher, but this did not happen with the almost 1,400 judges who lived in Asia and had minimal contact with native speakers. There is thus a very fundamental methodological difference between Smith and Rafiqzad's study and the typical more recent study (apart from the fact that the number of participants in Smith and Rafiqzad's study is also much higher than any subsequent study): they tested listeners who were not exposed extensively to American or other forms of native-speaker English, whereas the bulk of subsequent work was done in the USA with bilingual English L2 users recruited from people living there permanently or for a longer period of time (e.g. as full-time postgraduate students).

This raises an interesting question about the difference between Smith and Rafiqzad's findings and subsequent research. Does it matter a lot that Smith and Rafiqzad's study was conducted among individuals with limited exposure to native speakers? Has the world changed so much in the forty years since then that such individuals are hardly to be found today – that people all over the world are now exposed very extensively to native speakers because of telecommunications technology (entertainment, electronic news media, the internet)? Potential supporting evidence for such a proposition comes from the studies of Major et al. (2002) and Yang et al. (2017), who sampled their non-native listener-judges from their countries of residence and not from the USA or Canada, where most other studies got their participants from. What Yang et al. (2017) show is that even when the same speaker (with a mild Chinese accent) reads passages but, in the evaluation task, is paired with a picture of a Chinese or Western female, evaluations are different, and the Western picture is evaluated more favourably and judged to be more comprehensible. Thus, a sense of prestige informs these judgements, where the expectation is that an English-speaking instructor should be a native speaker rather than an L2-speaker from the local environment, and a non-native speaker is deemed to be less credible than a native speaker (Lev-Ari & Keysar, 2010).

7.3.2 Grammar

Transfer and learning phenomena play an important role in the grammatical features of Expanding Circle Englishes as much as in Outer Circle varieties (Edwards, 2010; Edwards & Laporte, 2015; Gilquin, 2015; Gilquin & Granger, 2011; Laporte, 2012). Idiomatic restrictions in native varieties at the interface of grammar and vocabulary, such as which nouns conventionally take an article (*at the office, in a spot of bother*) and which ones don't (*at school, at work, in town*), or which verbs are complemented by an infinitive clause (*continue to eat*) and which ones by a participial clause (*stop eating*) provide a further area where differences are easily observed, as is the case with the Outer Circle Englishes. A selection of typical deviant features in the English of many Dutch speakers – a pretty proficient Expanding Circle context – identified by Edwards (2010) includes using the present tense and simple aspect more widely where native speakers will use marked options (*I work at the university since 1990*), using adjectival forms in adverb function (*international renowned economist*), finite complement clauses where native varieties opt for non-finites (*This bilingual list is an initiative to achieve that terminology is translated unambiguously*), or prepositional differences (*participate on*).

Such differences have given rise to a rich literature identifying these 'common errors', such as Barker's (2010) *An A–Z of Common English Errors for Japanese Learners*. These user features, some of which persist also with the more mature users, are real, of course, and display only partial systematicity, but are usually detected in educational contexts and are particularly noticeable to the concerned listener.

Differences remain between Outer and Expanding Circle varieties (Götz & Schilk, 2011; Gries & Deshors, 2015; Van Rooy, 2006), especially to the extent that creative extension and new uses of constructions become established in the Outer Circle varieties, and serve as a springboard for further extension. Where Expanding Circle varieties often show a higher frequency of prototypical instances of an English construction, the safe choices, Outer Circle varieties show more extensions that go beyond transfer. It is usually a matter of degree, rather than some absolute difference, which Van Rooy (2011) explains as the effect of nativisation in combination with the greater degree of acceptance that such innovations enjoy in the Outer Circle, in terms of which deviant/ innovative uses gain acceptance more easily and serve as a springboard for further extension.

An important dimension of Expanding Circle usage, particularly in Lingua Franca contexts, is that the need to communicate overrides the limitations on grammatical (and lexical) restrictions. This has given rise to more frequent novel word coinages, using regular English derivation and compounding, but producing novel outcomes. Examples include *intentiously, undoubtly, militarian* in the register of everyday language, and in more technical communicative settings, creations like *governation, translationeses, conceptionalising, parallelly* (Mauranen, 2017, p. 746). Similar coinage strategies are also used in the Outer Circle, however (Van Rooy & Terblanche, 2010), where they usually do not gain stability and acceptance. This is not an issue, though, as Mauranen (2017) notes that in academic Lingua Franca communication in the Expanding Circle, strategies to make the communication succeed are more important and more characteristic than adhering to conventionalised, native-like Englishes.

7.3.3 Vocabulary

Vocabulary innovations, other than in-the-moment creations or lexical transfer to fill a communicative gap, are not very prominent in Expanding Circle communication. In general, speakers aim to be understood, given the purposes of communication, and hence select from their own available vocabulary what they expect to be most accessible to their audience (Meierkord, 2012). The consequence of this strategy is that the more frequent, everyday vocabulary carries more of the communicative load than in native-speaker communication (Mauranen, 2017, pp. 744–745).

At the same time, in their intent to communicate, speakers often draw on successful examples from their other languages and try to recreate these in English, leading to loan transfers of idioms, or slight adjustments of English idioms. Such usage may also serve an identity-marking function, where speakers infuse English with conceptualisations that they find more telling than those available in English (Jenkins, 2017, pp. 553–554). These choices are not in principle different from what speakers in the Outer Circle do to extend the communicative potential of English, but are decidedly less frequent in the Expanding Circle, in large part because of the less stable and recurrent patterns of interaction, making the conventionalisation of these alternatives less likely than in more recurrent communicative contexts that occur in the Outer Circle.

7.3.4 Pragmatics and style

Expanding Circle users are as much given to transfer successful strategies from their other languages to English as Outer Circle speakers are. A straightforward concrete example is the closing salutation used in e-mail correspondence in the Netherlands, transferred from Dutch, '*I hope to have informed you sufficiently*' (Edwards, 2010, p. 20), which is a direct translation of a typical Dutch conclusion like '*Ik hoop u hiermee voldoende te hebben geïnformeerd*' (gloss: I hope you hereby sufficiently to have informed). Like many such formulae, one shouldn't take it too literally – the 'most humble and obedient servants' of the eighteenth- and nineteenth-century English letters were not always all that humble or given to servitude as their letter endings suggested. Yet, within the context of a letter of information, the ending makes sense, at least to Dutch speakers, and signals the conclusion of the provision of information. To the Dutch ear, such an ending may sound more appropriate than an English alternative like 'I remain your most humble and obedient servant' or more contemporary equivalents like 'Hope this helps' or 'Let me know if you have any questions', which may well have a too informal ring to them.

Sometimes, such transfers pose a risk for mutual understanding, but this risk cuts both ways: transfers from other cultures into English Lingua Franca usage, and transfer of native-speaker usage into Lingua Franca contexts. Smith and Christopher (2001) report two illustrations of misunderstanding in relation to pragmatic transfer into English. In one case, a Japanese host of an American guest notices that there is a mistake in the flight ticket of the guest, and relays this through the expression 'that will be difficult', by which he means that the flight as recorded on the ticket is impossible. The American doesn't understand the difficulty, as his hope was for a more pointed indication of what is right or wrong. The indirect pragmatics to highlight a problem is misunderstood in this case. A further illustration is where two different Expanding Circle users, one from a Thai and the other from a Korean background, use different conventions to introduce themselves and to address the other, both drawn from their native pragmatic strategies. Both experience the other speaker as rude. Yet, by contrast, the more informal ways of addressing one another, the quick default to first-name terms from non-British Inner Circle users, may equally come across as disrespectful to interlocutors in the Far East and continental Europe alike.

The challenge cannot simply be solved by converting everybody to a set of native-speaker pragmatic norms, as such usages may continue to come across as disrespectful or too informal for some Expanding Circle users, making the use of English uncomfortable to them. Thus, effective Expanding Circle/Lingua Franca/International communication is premised on a prior awareness that pragmatic misunderstandings are likely to occur often, and thus participants need to be aware and have strategies at hand to deal with such misunderstandings.

Even below the level of pragmatic misunderstanding, Mauranen (2017) identifies persistent interpersonal strategies in Lingua Franca spoken interaction, aimed at anticipating the communicative needs of the listener. Interpersonal metadiscourse is a feature of all spoken interactions, but her data show that in Lingua Franca interactions, such metadiscourse to anticipate misunderstanding and to enhance better understanding is considerably more frequent. This ties in with the general interpretation of Lingua Franca communication as being more tied to communicative strategies than specific linguistic features.

7.4 Conclusion

English is used by people across the world, many of whom are not native speakers, nor have a history of colonisation that brought the language to their societies. To these users, in the Expanding Circle, English is not a typical foreign language, which they learn in classrooms and then use on occasion with native speakers. English is a tool for access to a wider international world, and is used with a range of speakers from other Expanding Circle contexts, but also with any other user of the language, from native-speaker or Outer Circle backgrounds. The Expanding Circle is not a mere wastebox label for those who do not fit in another circle of world Englishes, but yet another group of users who have their own stake in the English language, and for whom it serves a range of useful purposes.

The linguistic features of English that emerge in Expanding Circle contexts are in some ways similar to those of the Outer Circle, although the degree of vocabulary localisation is smaller. The degree to which conventionalisation takes place is also smaller, but not absent, and informal processes of societal codification (Baratta, 2021) continue to gain momentum. The flexible pragmatics of English as a lingua franca and the development of strategic competence to navigate a range of perpetually diverse interactive contexts are typical of the Expanding Circle, likely more so than in the other contexts where greater stability of participants creates an environment that is conducive to easier conventionalisation.

The changing world is breaking down the traditional barriers that constrained and partitioned the uses of English. Expanding Circle users in some settings come to match the Outer Circle users in what they do with the language, and gain access to a much larger pool of input features through mediated communication. Let us turn to these new opportunities for use and the implications for the users and the usage in Chapter 8.

8 New sites of contact: local and global urban migration and the internet

The second half of the twentieth century saw English expanding from being the language of the colonial empire to that of large parts of the rest of the world. Since the end of the twentieth century, the extent and density of contact of different Englishes and of English and other languages expanded further through migration and the affordances of the internet. The linguistic consequences are more hybridity, more mixing of resources, and less stability and conventionalisation in patterns of language use: fleeting innovations that come and go, with relatively few gaining a long-term foothold. Such increased hybridity forms a scale that ranges from relatively close to standard varieties to language use in which English becomes a minor component of the usage event, with a range of options in-between, and without clear-cut boundaries between where English stops and the rest begins (and vice versa, of course). Examples (1), (2) and (3), taken from Van Rooy and Kruger (2018), represent online communication and give a glimpse of what is happening.

(1) um glad um rytin' ur name down coz um not sure if maybe able to pronounce it properly (p. 91)

This utterance, a comment on an interactive online forum about television series on public television in South Africa, relies mainly on English vocabulary, but the spelling imitates pronunciation in a playful manner, especially since it is a comment about pronunciation. But of course, online forums invite more than just phonetic spelling.

(2) as 4 bernad it serves him right wateva bad thing that's happening to him..tshidi yo she wants to be a high school drop-out nogal (p. 91)
(3) LMAO, I know Cngle, and mind u lomuntu ushaye i-colgatesmile, knowing very well unezingovolo zika nogwaja (p. 93)

Rebus writing, where a digit like 4 is used to represent the preposition 'for' because of the sound, or acronyms like LMAO, are characteristic features of online communication across the world, even if writing in English is likely to be more given to this practice than writing in languages that are not widely used online, for instance isiXhosa, as Deumert and Masinyana (2008) show in their comparison of isiXhosa–English bilinguals whose creative spellings are mainly present in the English but not the isiXhosa parts of their texting.

Examples (2) and (3) show more than just online writing conventions, though. Elements that a monolingual or non-South African English reader may not understand are *yo* (a general explanation of surprise, which is widely used in South Africa, but decidedly not originating from the English language), *nogal* (from Afrikaans, meaning surprisingly), *lomuntu ushaye* (an expression used in more than one Nguni language, meaning 'this person is displaying') and *ezingovolo zika nogwaja* (also Nguni, 's/he has two big teeth of a rabbit'). You can call it code-mixing and/or -switching, you can call it translanguaging, we can have a good old fist fight as to which analysis or terminological set is right. In the world Englishes tradition, this is regarded as hybridity in the first instance, but Kachru did use the term code-mixing in his descriptions in the 1980s, at a time before the term translanguaging gained currency. I will continue to talk about code-mixing here, despite limitations that are articulated clearly by the proponents of translanguaging, for the reason that the effect of much of what is observed concerns an English baseline, into which elements from other codes are blended. These elements rely on the recognisability of the different language codes from which they are drawn for their very effect and effectiveness, as explained by Van Rooy and Kruger (2018). The code-mixing is not limited to the online environment. The extensive language contact in urban South Africa, which resulted from in-country migration to the big cities, brings about multilingualism and partial competence in several languages (Coetzee-Van Rooy, 2014), which means that hybrid utterances like those above correspond to what is done in spoken interaction, and are taken to be understood. In fact, in spoken language use in these urban settings, the hybridity may be considerably more extensive and may extend to a point where the translanguaging practices do indeed draw in-group boundaries that are intended to keep some out (Makalela, 2013, 2014), and where it does not make much sense to look for 'English', as the extent of hybridity makes the drawing of language boundaries particularly meaningless for any attempt to understand what speakers actually do. Makalela (2013) offers a detailed account of hybridity in the use of *kasi-taal*, an urban hybrid vernacular that blends resources from across the Sotho and Nguni languages of South Africa with English and Afrikaans. Example (4), from Makalela (2013, p. 120), shows how English constitutes a marginal if not unimportant part of the total repertoire of the speakers (with his translations in brackets, other language resources in italics, and Afrikaans resources additionally underlined).

(4) K: Hey bro *awungimele da*. (Wait for me there.)
L: *Eish ntwana re ka bloma kae?* (. . . my friend where should we sit)
K: *A si bloma e*cafeteria after *le*lecture, *ngifuna nje ukugawula* (Let's sit at the cafeteria after the lecture; I would like to eat)
L: Ei bro, did you get what the brother was talking about? *Iyo*, the die man *o a* bora *tjo* . . . (this man is boring . . .)

The impact of global migration and the coming of the internet as a vehicle for mass communication and entertainment were to have even further consequences for the use and users of English. These recent and ongoing changes have introduced new sources of linguistic variability and brought about new forms of contact between people. The effects are so dramatic, in the judgement of many who have been studying them, that fundamental critiques of our existing conceptual tools have been developed, including calling into question whether it even makes sense to talk about language and varieties any more. Thus, while acknowledging the contribution that Kachruvian world Englishes has made to our understanding of the diversity of uses and users of English, Seargeant and Tagg (2011) call for a post-varieties approach, and ground their critique in the sociolinguistics of globalisation (Blommaert, 2010). Their view is consistent with ideas emerging around the concept of translanguaging (Otheguy et al., 2015; Li, 2018), and particularly Makalela's (2016) concept of ubuntu translanguaging, which conceptualises the notion of translanguaging in a non-Western setting. The challenges to our understanding of world Englishes emerge not only from such conceptual developments but also from actual changes in the world and in the (use of) language.

8.1 Recent changes in the world: migration and the internet

Two recent changes in the world are identified as key drivers of current changes in language and language use practices. Migration is identified as bringing people into contact in cities where new communities of language users form, communities that do differently than those individuals would have done in their places of origin, and simultaneously do differently than the people who have been living in those cities already. In the case of the metropolitan hubs of the Global North, such migration results in what Vertovec (2007) labels 'super-diversity', a kind of multicultural diversity unlike before. These changes are not limited to the English-speaking metropoles, and are matched by similar developments elsewhere, such as the contact situation in Berlin giving rise to the development of Kiezdeutsch, or Kebabnorsk in Oslo, Straattaal in Rotterdam, or Rinkebysvenska in Stockholm, often regarded as multiethnolects by scholars studying the vernacular in highly mixed neighbourhoods of big cities. Makalela (2016) notes that urban centres in the Outer Circle are similar attractors for intra-national migration from rural areas, where equally complex language contact situations arise, compounded in the case of countries like South Africa where both intranational and international migrants converge on the big cities.

Alongside, and working in tandem with physical migration, is the rise of the participatory internet, where people are able to communicate over long distance, with no constraints of space or time zone, creating digital communities that become significant components of the linguistic experience of humans, especially those that are 'always on' (Baron, 2008) – who migrate to digital communities that are characterised by fleeting and diverse memberships, much like the super-diversity of migration to cities.

Migration is not a new phenomenon. Colonisation implied extensive migration of settlers, slaves and indentured labourers. Just over a century ago, in 1910, 41 per cent of the inhabitants of New York were foreign-born (Foner, 2014, p. 29) and an even more striking 76 per cent of the population of the city were immigrants born abroad together with their first-generation US-born children (p. 31). By contrast, after four decades of heavy immigration to New York in around 1970–2010, the percentage of foreign-born residents was 37 per cent, and the percentage of foreign-born parents with first-generation US-born children amounted to 55 per cent (p. 31). These migration numbers exceed the numbers cited by Vertovec (2007) to build the original case for super-diversity in the British city of London. The two largest groups of immigrants in the late nineteenth and early twentieth centuries to New York were Russian Jews and Italians, accounting for about 44 per cent of all immigrants from the 1880s to the 1920s. After federal legislation blocked Eastern and Southern European migrants in the early 1920s, the interwar years saw extensive in-migration of African Americans from the South, and Puerto Ricans after the Second World War, enhancing the ethnic diversity of the city (Foner, 2014).

Throughout the twentieth century, the traditional settler colonies of the British Empire continued to attract and welcome immigrants, if mainly from Europe. This was, for instance, enshrined in the White Australia policy that was officially enacted for the entire first half of the twentieth century (Britannica, 2020), while in Canada, racist prejudices and legal restrictions on non-European, actually often non-British, immigrants only gradually faded in the post-war years (Morton, 2000, p. 483).

The United States, too, has a long history of immigration policies that favoured Europeans, and Northwestern Europeans in particular, by using national quotas, such as the use of the 1890 census to limit entrance for South Europeans, and banning Asians immigrants until the second half of the twentieth century (Koven & Götzke, 2010) – in the celebrated words of a United States president from the first quarter of the twenty-first century, 'the right sort of immigrant'.

Vertovec's (2007) main point, though, is the much more fragmentary and complex nature of present-day urban communities, when compared with the migration of the post-war years in the second half of the twentieth century. If this is combined with the availability of tools for communication – low-cost voice contracts were already very important when Vertovec (2007) wrote and the full affordances of the internet were becoming apparent – then the complexity extends to much better ways to maintain contact with the place of origin, keeping the home country a salient part of the cultural and linguistic repertoires of migrants. Moreover, digital forums where migrants and home-based citizens continue to stay in touch add further opportunities, but also complexity, to the linguistic lives of the migrants (Mair, 2013b).

The concentration of research on the cities of the Global North sometimes obscures the fact that extensive migration also happens within regions, including Asia and Africa, particularly among neighbouring countries. Thus, there are more African refugees and voluntary migrants in Africa itself than beyond. Despite the extensive presence of North African migrants in Europe, which provides the trigger for certain right-wing discourses about a migration crisis, there are still more African migrants in other African countries than beyond the continent, according to United Nations data synthesised by the Africa Center for Strategic Studies (2021).[1] At the same time, India is the country of origin of the largest number of migrants across the world today, followed by Mexico and the Russian Federation, but countries like the United Kingdom and Germany are also in the top twenty countries worldwide where international migrants come from (McAuliffe & Triandafyllidou, 2022). Since 1970, according to the United Nations' *World Migration Report* (McAuliffe & Triandafyllidou, 2022), the increase in international migrants as a proportion of the global population fluctuated between a low of 2.2 per cent in 1975 and a high of 3.6 per cent in 2020, although it remained between 2.2 and 2.9 per cent from 1970 to 2005, only breaching 3 per cent by 2010, and gradually moved up to 3.6 per cent by 2020.

---

1. https://africacenter.org/spotlight/african-migration-trends-to-watch-in-2022/ (date of access 29 June 2022).

The twenty-first century has thus seen an increase, but on a global scale, the phenomenon is not new. Claims about a new phenomenon are probably overstated – one should rather consider this in the first instance to be a new item on the research agenda.

Urban migration of the kind that yields super-diversity coincides with the development of the internet and the very substantial growth in access since the start of the twenty-first century. These two developments have in common that they create new sites of contact for people who bring multiple languages, varieties, or more generally, linguistic resources within their repertoires to the contact situation, which is the foundation of Blommaert's (2010) case for a sociolinguistics of globalisation. The internet is more than a contact site, though. It also serves as a channel for access to content, and in this respect, it has been the driver of a new wave of contact with English across the world and, for the first time, in ways that are much more equivalent across contexts. The internet potentially delivers the same film, downloadable hip-hop song or music video, computer game, but also online magazine and newspaper, and English-language content generated by public figures on their social media accounts to anybody who cares to watch, listen or read, wherever they are in the world, whatever the time of the day, and irrespective of their level of command over English. As a channel of contact and a channel for delivery of content, the internet is a participatory space in which users from anywhere can share their content, and where the usual gatekeeping processes, but also the usual content and language editing processes, are not typically followed on all interactive forums, even for longer pieces like fanfiction.

The internet is accessible to more than half of the population of the entire planet at present – Statista (2022) estimates that approximately 5 billion inhabitants, representing 63 per cent of the population, had internet access in 2022, among whom 4.65 billion made use of social media, and thus interacted and not only consumed content.[2] Furthermore, approximately 62 per cent of the internet content that could be attributed to a language was in English, a figure that is striking if one considers that not a single other language accounts for close to 10 per cent of the internet content, according to W3tech (2022).[3]

One of the key game changers that the internet brings about is the possibility of transcending space. Letters were of course incredibly important to

2. https://www.statista.com/statistics/617136/digital-population-worldwide/ (date of access 29 June 2022).
3. https://w3techs.com/technologies/history_overview/content_language (date of access 29 June 2022).

emigrants from Britain and Ireland since the seventeenth century, even for a couple of generations after their relocation to a colony. Eventually, those contacts faded into history with new generations, born in the new place and forming a community there, losing touch with their third, fourth and nth cousins in the country of origin. This might yet happen in the case of descendants of present-day super-diverse migrants, but for many from the migrating generation, such ties to the place of origin still matter – staying in touch with parents, siblings and long-standing friends. The internet, interactive web forums and social media make it possible to stay in touch, with no break in continuity and no time delay as one waits for letters – which would have taken months to be exchanged between New Zealand or Australia and Britain in the nineteenth century. The idea of a diasporic community in London is not just a kind of sentimental attachment today – it is possible to stay in touch with the latest Bollywood or Nollywood films, and have instant access to the latest artistic creations from Kingston. The same is true for diasporic communities in New York, but also in Nairobi, Dubai, Amsterdam and Johannesburg. For diasporic communities today, the possibility of living in multiple worlds is more real than ever, and such multiple community memberships are bound to affect their use of language.

8.2 Contact, identity and use

8.2.1 Contact and use

The urban spaces and the internet are both sites of contact *par excellence*, where the use of English is tied directly to the contact situation. Two characteristics distinguish these two contact sites from the kinds of contact that have been considered in the previous chapters in this book: the contact is often more densely multilingual, even if English (however construed) remains the backbone of the linguistic repertoire of these contacts, and the communities that form in these contact settings are less stable and permanent, at least at present.[4]

Urban multilingual contact plays out differently depending on the broader societal context and the degree of affluence, although these broad contextual parameters are not absolute. It is useful to distinguish grassroots contact from elite contact, along the lines of Meierkord (2020). Typical grassroots settings are characterised by less affluence, a smaller role for formal education in language acquisition, and informality – the language of the street. Grassroots contexts are typically more multilingual,

---

4. There are some similarities with the dense multilingualism and impermanence of early plantation slave contact settings, though.

or at least comprise a wider range of English dialects. In elite contexts, the degree of multilingualism and multidialectalism is lower, and the newcomers tend to converge more quickly on the prestige forms, accessible through formal education, with less contestation of the norms and less hybridity or mixing.

In elite Inner Circle Contexts, the founder's effect remains strongly in place, with a dominant group, typically monolingual, defining the group norms. Any newcomers are expected to conform to a reasonable degree, and indeed do so. This is shown quantitatively in the research by Mesthrie (2010, 2017) on how elite black South Africans, who attend multiracial schools within which native speakers of settler descent form a local majority, turn out to approximate the speech habits of the dominant group over time. As fictionalised lived experience, it is illustrated by the struggles of the two indigenous protagonists in the South African novel *Coconut* (Matlwa, 2007), with characters who resemble those who participated in Mesthrie's research. These characters have to submit to the language of the monolingual social elite in order to fit in, and even then, their degree of acceptance is under constant strain, premised on conformity not only in speech and behaviour but also in social class. Their position is certainly better than that of marginalised members of society seeking access to opportunity as fictionalised in the nineteenth century by a character like *Jude the Obscure* in Hardy's late nineteenth-century novel, but even present-day Judes have a price to pay to fit in.

Such conformity is not expected at grassroots level. The multilingual and multicultural contact sites that come about as a result of urbanisation and migration offer contact settings in which the dominant, elite variety of English does not have the same attraction or immediate presence, and where individuals bring a range of varieties and languages along to the setting and use them. Such usage is characterised by hybridity, where resources are mixed more liberally and without converging on the prestige variety (Rampton, 1995). Yet, as Cheshire et al. (2011) show in their study of Multicultural London English, certain group norms and shared use of innovative forms emerge among the non-traditional/non-Anglo users of English in the neighbourhoods they study (and likewise for Kiezdeutsch, Kebabnorsk and other forms arising in complex contact settings). Speakers may remain bilingual and/or bidialectal, and do make use of elements from the full range of their linguistic repertoires, but that does not prevent similarities from emerging from the group of recent immigrants as a whole, irrespective of their linguistic backgrounds. Their patterns of contact – extensively within the migrant group and less with longer-term resident native speakers – contribute to the lack of convergence on native-speaker norms, whereas patterns of sustained contact across different immigrant backgrounds contribute to shared patterns emerging from the younger speakers. However, Quirk (1988, p. 21) already felt moved to register his concern about such urban contact forms and their effect on the acquisition of the standard variety of English, and criticised an academic journal for publishing research – in 1987 – on the appropriation of African American English by children from Spanish homes in New York. Long before it became a woke thing to do, he was worried that the airtime afforded to the research may send the wrong message to English teachers across the world, who might not, in his considered view, be wise enough to know that such findings should have no bearing on the teaching of English as a foreign language, eager as they were to learn the best ideas about language teaching from the leading English-speaking countries.

The practices in these multilingual contact settings depend on the nature of the relationship between participants. Rampton (1995) offers a very detailed analysis of interactional data to show how speakers make use of linguistic features associated with the conventional ethnolect of other participants, for example British Indians using features commonly associated with Afro-Caribbeans and vice versa, which he describes as crossing. He notes two important conditions: such usages are tolerated and accepted in the context where there is an already established close relationship within the multi-ethnic peer group; and such usages remain marked against the backdrop of the shared multi-ethnic variety that serves as the default for these interactions. In the context of the sociolinguistics of globalisation, the fluidity of such practices is emphasised from a range of angles. However, one has to keep in mind that urban multilingual contexts don't all lead to the creative hybridity of the kind Rampton describes. Meierkord (2012) finds that, in contact settings with international participants in Inner Circle cities, the tendency is to use safe choices, those that speakers anticipate will be shared and understood widely – they interact across Englishes, rather than blend the Englishes. It appears, unsurprisingly, when considering the range of contact settings, that more creativity and hybridity is characteristic of environments where there is a lot of shared understanding and rapport across individual speaker backgrounds, but more safety and choices closer to standard options prevail when there is less of such a common background.

In the Outer Circle environments, a clear differentiation between elite and grassroots settings also emerges. In elite settings, language shift to English as a native language is observed, in relatively limited numbers but nonetheless, in middle-class homes where parents are highly educated and children typically attend English-only elite schools. Such observations have been recorded for a number of African metropoles, including

Accra in Ghana (Afrifa et al., 2019) and various urban settings in South Africa, in terms of which the number of black African citizens who claim English as their home language is approaching two million (Coetzee-Van Rooy, 2012). However, the African languages continue to be used widely and are not in immediate danger; it is just that some elite families do indeed adopt English as their home language. Afrifa et al. (2019) note that this choice is even more likely when the parents speak two different languages natively, and use English as a kind of default even between themselves. This process of shift to English in the home is more advanced in Singapore, where the elite requirement is fading away and the shift becomes more widespread (Tan, 2014).

At grassroots level, the situation is quite different in the Outer Circle. Here, it is not so much a shift to English but extensive multilingual or translingual practices that emerge, in which English plays a role alongside other languages of the environment. Creative mixing of English and local languages has been known to the Outer Circle context for a long time, though, with a variety like Singlish or Singapore Colloquial English having been around for a long time, as Platt already recorded in 1975. It too has its origins in the grassroots language contact in Singapore, but traces its origins to the beginning of the independent state of Singapore at least, and has persisted despite the attempts of the government to stamp it out through a Speak Good English Campaign (Wee, 2018). The use of Singlish, within the context of Singapore, should not be confused with shift to English as a native language, although there is clearly a continuum of uses in Singapore, where speakers will adjust to setting and interlocutor. Likewise, the mixed varieties of Afrikaans and English in the Cape Flats/District Six among historically native speakers of Afrikaans have been in existence since the nineteenth century. Their practices form a continuum from vernacular-non-standard Afrikaans, through very mixed and non-standard English to a prestige variety that is similar but not identical to the standard settler variety. Its genesis was in the densely multilingual urban contact situation in Cape Town in the nineteenth century, among descendants of slaves, indigenous South Africans, biracial people, and various European and Asian immigrants of the era (McCormick, 2002).

There is a wide range of hybrid practices involving English and other language resources that emerge in present-day multilingual contact settings (Meierkord, 2012, 2020). These come about due to urbanisation within African and Asian countries, together with migrants from elsewhere in the world, such as Chinese or Indian merchants in Africa, and other Africans in South Africa in particular. A similar contact situation arises from the migration of Filipina domestic workers to Hong Kong that make English a useful code for managing the interactions. In some of these cases, the hybridity is not so much a form of identity projection or playfulness as an attempt to make communication succeed on the basis of all available linguistic resources in the non-identical language repertoires of the speakers. Apart from 'English' as a second language playing a role, Pidgin English is an important feature of the urban contact situations in West Africa, widely used in informal spaces but even among university students (Akande & Salami, 2010), while English blends into the hybrid urban forms of Swahili that develop in some East African metropoles, leading to hybrid codes such as Sheng with a stronger Swahili base, and Engsh with stronger English base (Meierkord, 2012, p. 81).

In the Expanding Circle, English is not widely used at grassroots level, but interactions across Englishes, or lingua franca uses of English in academic, business and tourist contexts occur regularly. The elite contexts are seldom characterised by much hybridity, with speakers aiming for shared understanding (Meierkord, 2012, 2020), which often involves avoidance of localised resources that other conversational participants may not know, alongside various pragmatic strategies to enhance communicative effectiveness (Björkman, 2014).

Elite use of English occurs mainly in institutionalised contexts, where the communicative goals are clear, and the instrumental motivation to get the job done, very obvious. Such contexts invite safe choices, in an attempt to minimise the risk of misunderstanding. By contrast, grassroots use takes place in informal settings, with a wider range of purposes than the mere transactional. Playfulness and creativity are characteristic of many settings, where a wide range of linguistic elements are combined.

Turning to the recent impact of the internet on the use of English, one has to distinguish between a range of uses, which bring about different kinds of contact. The internet is a democratic space in multiple ways, including that people can interact more easily, without having to gain entrance to a conversation, and hold the floor, which are harder in face-to-face contexts, especially to the extent that there are constraints on language proficiency. Thus, websurfers may engage and disengage at will; they do not have to complete conversations and do not have to respond to everything they encounter. To the extent that the internet is a delivery channel for content, contact with English can be with any form of English that is distributed, and any possible users, despite their degree of proficiency or their repertoire of varieties, can access the content. Web 2.0 brought about opportunities for interaction, and these are actively harnessed, even by live news broadcasts, where user comments are displayed on screen, or where social media accounts provide a non-stop opportunity to engage.

Yet, despite the apparent freedom, the web content is overwhelmingly in English, textual or audio-visual, which reinforces the position of English at the pinnacle of the World Language System (De Swaan, 2010), and Standard American English in turn at the pinnacle of Mair's (2013a) World System of Englishes. The entertainment and information provided on the internet do not, however, support only the more traditionally prestigious varieties. Mair (2013a, 2020) notes how certain non-standard forms, including African American Vernacular English, Jamaican Creole and Nigerian Pidgin English, also gain widespread exposure and how various other users adopt forms from these varieties, due to contact mediated by the internet and not face-to-face contact. Going beyond these overtly or covertly prestigious varieties, the web also allows for different forms of participation, such as fanfiction (Friedrich, 2020), where new communities of practice form around shared interests in particular stories, but where the usual boundaries – geographic and linguistic – do not define or restrict membership. The shared interests invite language production and exposure to a wide diversity of writing styles within such fanfiction communities.

The use of the affordances of the internet for interactive web forums, for example those used by diasporic members of communities such as the Nigerian, Indian or Jamaican communities, provide channels of contact with the 'home varieties' that speakers may identify with. English is not the only medium of potential interaction, but diasporic communities do tend to use a narrower range of the linguistic repertoire than 'home communities', which is in part also reflected on such internet forums. Research on Nigerian forums, for instance, has shown a strong role for Nigerian Pidgin, but Mair (2020) still expects that it is likely to decline over time, as second- and third-generation diasporic Nigerians do not acquire it fluently, if at all – reinforcing the question of how much of the super-diversity is likely to survive the current migrating generation of mobile speakers. Nonetheless, identity-signalling elements are important in such forums, where even if a fairly neutral English forms the backbone of the communicative repertoire, there are sufficient other elements to give it a flavour that serves the relevant identity purpose.

8.2.2 Acquisition

Internet language use, including the creative forms used by younger communicators, needs to be learnt through interaction. Online engagement is thus key to learning how to communicate effectively online, but the same is true for grassroots interaction in hybrid contact settings. These newer forms of language use are not learnt in classrooms, and require participation in the speech communities to learn. However, the entrance and engagement are not completely without support: conventional linguistic forms and meanings from English continue to provide a backbone for these communications, alongside the other resources in the linguistic repertoires of the speakers. This is true for more private interactions, like the instant messaging of native English-speaking teenagers studied by Tagliamonte (2016), where she reports relatively stable low frequencies for innovative forms across a range of studies alongside her own, for example less than 2 per cent of all tokens are actual CMC-forms. This is also true for an interactive public form in a multilingual South African setting, where conventional English forms still account for 90 per cent or more of all tokens, despite extensive hybrid and mixed linguistic choices from multiple languages and from typical CMC-forms (Van Rooy & Kruger, 2018; Piotrowska, 2022).

The effect of these new contact settings on language acquisition is extensive in another way, though, and disrupts the traditional expectations and research paradigms (Reinders & Benson, 2017). The exposure through the internet has contributed to significant new opportunities for children to learn English outside the classroom during their school years. They do not only consume and interact with online content but also play computer games where they use language more actively. Cole and Vanderplank (2016) find that Brazilian learners of English whose primary exposure is online outperform the traditional classroom learners who are otherwise direct matches for the out-of-class learners. Their participants are deliberately engaged in online learning activities, though, but incidental language learning also takes place. De Wilde et al. (2020) report that for Flanders, the Dutch-speaking part of Belgium, French (the other main language of the country) is the first foreign language introduced in primary education while formal introduction of English is delayed till secondary school, but many pupils who start secondary education have already attained considerable conversational proficiency in English and a large receptive vocabulary too. In their statistical model, the typical daily duration of access to English via computer games and social media is the strongest predictor of the attained level of proficiency prior to any formal instruction in the language.

Even when they go to school and learn English there too, Peters (2018) reports that the extent of Flemish learners' out-of-class experience had a larger effect on their vocabulary than the length of their classroom experience. This is the type of experience, given the considerable dominance of online content in English, that makes the present-day experience of learning English radically different from the learning of other languages, and also from the learning of English a generation ago.

8.2.3 Attitudes

Attitudes towards the mixed varieties in the migration and online contact settings diverge quite sharply. For users of these varieties, they form solidarity codes with strong covert prestige. For outsiders, the reactions are often quite negative and dismissive, with perpetual concerns about the effect of these varieties on the 'quality' of language use. This is seen in Quirk's (1988) concern as much as in the Speak Good English campaign of the Singapore government, aimed at dissuading the use of Singlish.

8.3 Linguistic forms

Hybridity is the key linguistic feature of these newer forms, where the pronunciation, vocabulary and grammar of multiple resources – varieties of English and resources from other languages – are combined. Interactive forums in linguistically complex settings, whose main audiences are intranational, tend to use a wider range of linguistic resources, since the audience can be assumed to have access to such material. This is evident from the analysis of South African data by Van Rooy and Kruger (2018) and Piotrowska (2022), where a backbone of general English vocabulary and grammatical patterns is expanded by non-standard English, indigenous language and online (netspeak) expressions. The contact situation involves speakers of all South African languages, with monolingual English speakers constituting an almost invisible minority.[5] The degree of mixing/translingual practice on such open forums is nowhere near the mixed-language practice observed in spoken contexts in South Africa. Some, but limited, informal language policing takes place, but speakers often show an awareness of the multiple languages they use and usually strive to maintain intelligibility for a relatively broad cross-section of the potential audience. Deviations from this norm will simply lead to being ignored, rather than being kicked off the forum.

Beyond the standard-like English backbone, Van Rooy and Kruger (2018) and Piotrowska (2022) identify features of online communication, colloquial English and transfers from indigenous languages as the key sources of hybridity. Resources typical of online communication include visual features like emojis and gifs, together with online spelling conventions, such as rebus writing, for example *b4* for *before*, *u* for *you*, abbreviations like *ppl*, *plz* or *hv*, and acronyms that have attained

---

5. Genuine monolinguals are not very many in South Africa – even native-English speakers are more likely to have some competence in other languages than most native speakers elsewhere in the world, as set out by Coetzee-Van Rooy (2021).

wordhood in their own right, like *LOL*. Features from colloquial, informal English are sourced both locally and internationally, such as exclamations and appellations like *wow* and *hey*, including the expression 'what a wow' (without some object following the word *wow*) which appears to be a South African collocation not widely attested elsewhere, or vocatives to address the online audience directly (*guys* seems to have a good run as a gender-neutral term), alongside *ppl* for people, and *admin* or indigenised to be pronounced as *atimini*. Indigenous forms often have a clear interpersonal function, such as indigenous pronouns *nna* or *wena* (1st and 2nd person singular), exclamations such as *hayibo* or *eish* that are basically not translatable into standard English, suggesting surprise and mild disapproval, *sies* (from Afrikaans, meaning something like 'shame on you'), and *shame* or *sorry* used with peculiarly South African semantics and often also indigenous spellings like *shem* or *sorrie*. Van Rooy and Kruger (2018) conclude that the identity work of the indigenous resources is quite prominent, supplementing 'English' with a local flavour that is sourced from the rest of the local linguistic ecology. At the same time, the extensive use of international online language forms suggests an embeddedness in the broader global digital culture too.

In urban contact settings, there is similar hybridity and mixing. These range from contact of the more fleeting kind, where interactions across Englishes at intranational level allow for some mixing of resources and also display convergence between speakers from different backgrounds (Meierkord, 2012), to very complex hybrid languages like *kasi-taal* (Makalela, 2014) that thrive in interactions between speakers who know one another better. Seargeant and Tagg (2011) make the crucial point that for Expanding Circle users of English, such as speakers of Thai, the hybridity of the kind just reviewed is usually limited to their online interactions, and will not be nearly as prominent in their face-to-face encounters, which is a point of difference from Inner and Outer Circle users in face-to-face settings.

Social media is yet another setting, much more interactive than other online options on average, but also often with a narrower audience (except for a few social media accounts of public figures or influencers who do reach a wider audience). Some social media uses are clearly more like private communication. Creativity and playfulness are important features of the social media use of many, involving the rich blending of elements from the linguistic repertoire of users, including elements from their offline repertoires and elements specific to online communication (Deumert, 2014), although a core of people from educated backgrounds may continue to use language in ways closer to standardised forms of English online. Social media, in conjunction with other uses of the internet, has contributed to the viral spread of social ideas and new vocabularies to capture those ideas in recent years, perhaps never so intensively as during the coronavirus pandemic, particularly in 2020 with national lockdowns in many places across the world. The lexicon of *plandemic, covidiots* and the multitude of memes went viral because of the affordances of online communication. Likewise, the impact of the Black Lives Matter resurgence in the United States and from there elsewhere in the world, as much as the backlash against the 'woke culture', the 'cancel culture' and many other vocabulary items that gained traction in the recent past, can be attributed to the internet and its role of disseminating linguistic forms to places across the world simultaneously or in a very short space of time.

8.4 Conclusion

The dual tension of local and global – the glocal – plays out forcefully online, where people are attuned to global trends, copy, appropriate and adjust them for their purposes, while also finding ways to signal originality and embeddedness in some identities. There is a clear playfulness – Deumert (2014) speaks of the carnivalesque in online communication – but similar playfulness and performativity are found in face-to-face encounters in densely multilingual environments. English shares this space with many other languages in the repertoires of its multilingual users across the world, while even monolingual native speakers participate in some of the innovations, if not to the extent of the multilingual speakers.

At the same time, one should not overlook the fact that in many encounters, the innovations are embedded in a linguistic frame provided by widely shared lexical and grammatical resources of English.[6] One should remain aware of the fact that the different quantifications of different data types and in different settings all show a general convergence of only a small proportion of innovations, unlikely to exceed 5 or 10 per cent, with the remaining forms being relatively common and widely used English forms. This is not to deny the strategic importance of the speakers' innovation, but is a word of caution against overextending the interpretation to the point where a large resource pool of shared conventions is overlooked.

---

6. Somewhat tongue in cheek, I might paraphrase the word *English* with the expression 'those bits of language often associated with speakers when they perform in what is otherwise called the named language English', or something similarly cumbersome.

Part 3
Outlook

9 Taking stock and looking ahead

English is used in very many places, for a very wide range of functions, by very different people today. This book has tracked the fortunes of the language, by travelling with the speakers and observing how their interactions shaped the language. In doing so, we have found provisional answers to two of the three puzzles introduced in Chapter 1:

- How did the position of the English language in the world today come about?
- What are the linguistic consequences of the worldwide uses of English?

The combined answers to these two questions form the basis of much of the modelling of English that has evolved: both the two major models, the concentric circles (Kachru, 1985/2015d) and the dynamic model (Schneider, 2003) including possible extensions to transnational attraction beyond the colonial sphere (Schneider, 2014), and more specialised models to account for recent developments, such as the World System of Englishes (Mair, 2013a) and the model of extra- and intraterritorial forces (Buschfeld & Kautzsch, 2017). These models and their merits and limitations are summarised competently by Buschfeld and Kautzsch (2020), and this ground need not be retraced. Rather, some key issues that emerge from our answers to the first two questions are considered in this chapter, as a basis for an answer to the third question posed in Chapter 1:

- What does the foreseeable future have in store for the English language?

The key issues that are considered, before turning to the possible futures of English, are the forces animating the spread of the language, the contestation of what counts as acceptable English, the way world Englishes fits into complex linguistic ecologies, and the ethics of how English is used.

9.1 Spreading the language

English spread because of successive historical events in which the language was not a particularly central concern – English happened to spread because of economic and military reasons. One might add the role of missionaries and mission education, but as Phillipson (2009) remarks, missionary societies 'had great difficulty in distinguishing between preaching the word of God and promoting the political and economic interests of their countries of origin. This was true of missionaries 200 years ago as it is today' (p. 29).

Only in the period since the Second World War did language become a very prominent theme, did language policy and planning become a thing. At the same time, the deliberate anglicisation policies in Ireland and South Africa in the nineteenth century, as well as the forced linguistic assimilation of indigenous minorities in the United States, Canada and Australia since the late nineteenth century already presaged the present more deliberate effort to spread the language, or invite or compel people to use the language. The outcome wasn't always great for those subjected to the great civilising mission of the English-speaking powers who somehow often managed to make a little profit on the side while manfully shouldering their white man's burden.

Colonialism was not nice or kind to people on the wrong side of the colour, class and linguistic bars. There is nothing to be said for the inhumane treatment of enslaved people, and one has to look at history in very warped ways to claim benefits of colonialism for the exploitation colonies. Infrastructure such as roads or railways were constructed to transport profitable produce, schools were built to train useful workers and intermediaries ... Whataboutism can be harnessed as a defence to argue that 'everybody else' also did it, or to point to examples of kind treatment of enslaved or marginalised people. The colonial masters did not acknowledge the equality of their colonial subjects, in some cases hardly acknowledging their humanity at all. Yet, many people whose lives were severely disrupted by their encounters with the colonial masters came to use English – because they had no alternative in the case of slaves, or because they could navigate their worlds in a dignified way only if they added some, or a lot, of English to their communicative repertoires, as many others have done.

That was in the past, and it is always convenient to draw a line and say we need to look to the future now. People are good at drawing lines, particularly ones that favour them. Thus, one can claim a country as white man's land – Australia did this overtly, and, in slightly different terms, most other British settlement colonies did this too, even if it had already been occupied by others prior to the arrival of the settlers. English spread to the rest of the colonial world in the context of control and as the passport to opportunity. The notion of 'opportunity' needs to be qualified, though, since the whole colonial imposition meant that other forms of opportunity were systematically destroyed – dispossession of land, and control over mineral and other natural resources ensured that there were very few meaningful opportunities beyond the colonial economies and the terms they enforced.

The question was posed in Chapter 6 why English was not abandoned during the decolonisation phase after the middle of the twentieth century. The answer is rather more complicated than some would concede. In Africa more than in Asia, artificial boundaries were drawn at the Berlin Conference of the late nineteenth century, unifying territories irrespective of traditional groupings of people or natural and ecological borders. The decolonising Africa did not embark on a project to undo that process, in large part because of the strife that alternatives might have provoked. This is of course not unique to the colonised world under the British Empire – relatively more peaceful boundary redrawings, such as the Danish–German border by plebiscite in 1920, are the exception rather than the rule, as shown by the more acrimonious Irish border of the early twentieth century and the ensuing 'troubles' for much of the rest of that century, or the ongoing 'special military operations' to 'renegotiate' borders of the constituent states of the former Soviet Union in the early twenty-first century. The ill-fated cessation of Biafra in Nigeria in the 1960s shows the difficulty of such undertakings in Africa too, while the establishment of Pakistan and Bangladesh was not exactly a model of peaceful conflict resolution either. Once these quite diverse groupings of people had to form states, and inherited the colonial administrative infrastructure, English became a convenient choice for most, a choice that avoided the perceived more severe difficulties of the available alternatives. The 'encouragement' and pressure of Britain and international aid organisations further entrenched the position of English (Phillipson, 1992). Even among liberation movements, which often sought affinity across national lines, English remained a useful tool for regional cooperation of likeminded anti-colonialist forces, which is why countries like Namibia and Rwanda adopted English in recent times despite not having been colonised by the British.

A factor that should not be left out of consideration is the damage that the colonial imposition inflicted on the communal psyche of the subjected people, articulated in various contexts by such thinkers as Frantz Fanon (from 'francophone' North Africa), Steve Biko (from apartheid South Africa) and Ngũgĩ wa Thiong'o (from 'anglophone' East Africa).

Colonialism was premised on a denial of the humanity of the indigenous peoples of the colonies, which invited the counter-reaction of pleading or arguing the case for one's own humanity and proclaiming it to the wider world. Thus, when Achebe or Rao wanted to tell stories of redemption, they wanted to tell those stories to their fellow citizens but also to the wider world, at which point they often chose English, as Biko and even Ngũgĩ did, or French, as Fanon did. This was again not a necessary or inevitable choice, and the clear alternative of writing in an indigenous language (and letting translation do the job of wider communication) is an option deliberately selected by Ngũgĩ (1986) later in his career, who argues that the rejection of English is a necessary step in the decolonisation of the mind. It just turns out to be that there are enough Achebes and Raos that the English language remains the beneficiary of the literary and intellectual talent of many African and Asian writers, whose choice is in part inspired by the desire to tell the world those stories and to validate those experiences that the nineteenth-century imperial authors rendered invisible. After being schooled in a Western tradition, where one is taught to regard the Western art and knowledge as the standard, one is in part bound by those terms to proclaim one's own humanity, to reclaim it. Parts of the empire want to write back with a vengeance, as Rushdie (1982) said; Caliban wants to talk back to Prospero, and Man Friday wants to tell Crusoe his story.

The end of the Second World War brought about a moment in time where those who held power, who were in a position to 'help', were English-speaking countries more than anyone else. At that moment, the strong economic position of English-speaking countries led to a decisive twist, which gave English the prime position in the post-war economic recovery as much as it retained its foothold in the decolonising empire. And while still riding that wave, the affordances of global telecommunications and the internet came along, to strengthen the position of English even further.

There is much to be critical about, and many can differ from my reading of the history – a very complex one, reduced to a few broad strokes here. Such necessary critical work has been written, and should be read alongside the work on world Englishes, from Biko to Bourdieu and from Fanon to Phillipson, and many others. There is a risk in telling a story of the spread of the English language that one indeed overlooks that apart from the countries where it is spoken natively by a majority of inhabitants, not everybody in a country such as Tanzania or Romania speaks English. Yet, as systems of education improve, a much larger proportion of younger people will continue to gain a form of access to the language and may build considerable competence in the language on the back of this opportunity, especially as out-of-classroom access options are made available by the internet and global entertainment. The worldwide use of English continues to be strengthened top-down by the combined effect of language planning (of the explicit kind that feeds into national language and education policies or transnational organisations and businesses, as well as the planning in the back rooms of economic development and development aid organisations) and bottom-up by the snowball momentum of English becoming more useful to its users to the extent that they have multiple others with whom to converse.

We may have crossed a threshold, where the past success of the spread of English, despite the selfish intentions of some key agents, has rendered the language such a valuable instrument and commodity that it has unstoppable momentum through the ongoing cycle of reinforcement: the investment in English is worthwhile for the access it grants. This is no innocent process, as the economies of scale in producing entertainment in English makes it increasingly hard for other languages to compete at the level of mass production and distribution: if you can sell the same entertainment product many times, then you can sell it so much cheaper than a product in a small language, where the investment costs are similar but the return on investment limited. This is likely to suppress the opportunities of some to express themselves creatively with the same opportunity and freedom as those who are able to and choose to do so in English.

9.2 Linguistic consequences and issues of acceptability

Linguistic features of various kinds have been identified in Chapters 4–8, and have been interpreted as characteristic of varieties of English in different settings. These features developed in the force field of such pressures as learning, indigenisation, language contact and ongoing grammatical change affecting the diversity of input forms, and subject to psycholinguistic and societal selection pressures, as explained in Chapter 3. One of the most contested issues pertaining to world Englishes is whether this step is warranted, whether there are varieties with characteristic features. This proposition is contested from two sides: there are challenges to the idea that there are features at all, and if there are, whether they add up to varieties.

The challenge of linguistic features ties in closely with the debate of error versus innovation, although it extends further than innovation into the realm of acceptability. The scepticism about whether there is a meaningful supply of 'acknowledgeable' new English features was framed explicitly by Titlestad (1996):

> An English that facilitates access to the international standard is only to a very limited extent an indigenised new English. In addition, the random errors of second-language learners at various stages of acquisition do not make a new English unless a codifiable consistency can be demonstrated. If one excludes accent, then one is hard put to identify a SAfE [South African English] apart from a body of colloquial terms. One cannot communicate at length in SAfE. (p. 168)

If framed like this, there is a clear line to be drawn between users making errors and people communicating in English, with a capital E, and in the singular, with some local flavour – South Africanisms in this case. Framing the dilemma as such is not peculiar to South Africa, but is exactly the concern raised by Quirk (1988) a decade earlier, when he worried about the detrimental effects of 'liberation linguistics' and the risk that people with good intentions would succumb to the charm of language variation. He summarised with approval the view of 'most of those with authority in education and in the media' that 'the so-called national variety of English is an attempt to justify inability to acquire what they persist in seeing as "real" English' (p. 22). One step further, he added that 'The temptation is great to accept the situation and even to justify it in euphemistically sociolinguistic terms' (p. 22).

To Quirk and Titlestad, a deviation from the international standard should not be accepted, in part because it is a potential barrier to international intelligibility, and in part because it becomes a barrier to the socio-economic opportunities of second-language learners who invest in the learning of English. Quirk (1988) puts it thus:

> It is neither liberal nor liberating to permit learners to settle for lower standards than the best, and it is a travesty of liberalism to tolerate low standards which will lock the least fortunate into the least rewarding careers. (pp. 22–23)

The opposite view is formulated by Kachru (1992, pp. 61–64), who proposes a distinction between **deviation** and **mistake**. Both deviations and mistakes are instances of language use that differ from some native-speaker norm, such as the international or standard form of English. Deviations are usages that have developed in a new context and are valid within that context. Mistakes are not systematic, and result from a learner of an Outer Circle variety not performing in terms of the (emerging) norms of the local, educated form of English. Kachru (1992) therefore assumes the acceptance of different norms for different varieties, which are derived from the usage of educated speakers of the Outer Circle variety. Bamgbose (1998) takes this matter one step further, by calling for the explicit codification of these norms – developing grammars that capture the typical usage in an Outer Circle context, to serve as a reference point for the purposes of the high-stakes examination and editing of texts.

The issue is therefore to determine what counts as an acceptable innovation and what counts as an error. Quirk really does not concern himself with extensions beyond 'the standard' at all, at least for non-native users, but Titlestad leaves some room. So let us consider how much room there is. Beeton and Dorner's *A Dictionary of English Usage in Southern Africa* (1975) offers an illuminating case, because they make their reasoning explicit. They intend to offer 'a glossary of local vocabulary and idiom, together with judgments on the desirability and efficacy of each of the words listed' (p. iv). They remark that they 'have not recommended certain South African usages where these would seem to result in what we have labelled "semantic blurring"' (p. iv). To illustrate: a typical South Africanism is the lexeme *robot* – known as 'traffic light' in other parts of the world. Beeton and Dorner (1975) advise against the use of *robot* because it results in semantic blurring. Furthermore, as to a main source of local innovation, they note that 'Afrikaans terms have usually been recommended only when **reasonable** English alternatives are not available' (p. iv, emphasis added).

All of these judgements are made in service of the greater good:

> This Dictionary could be said to represent the product of two people who wish to see English flourish in this sub-continent, who wish it to retain a universal intelligibility and acquire local colour. Our attitude, throughout, has been that standard terms should not dehydrate local adventurousness, and local assertions should not, by the same token, smother world-wide communication. (p. v)

The dilemma they pose is real – global and local, framed as tension between intelligibility and expressiveness. However, they err on the side of caution by considerable margin in their actual recommendations. There is an opposite smothering effect that they overlook; Fairman (1992, pp. 24–25) relates an example from his experience as teacher of English elsewhere in Africa that illustrates it poignantly. He notes that his students use the term *transport* to denote the 'fare' or 'cost' of public transport. This usage causes some misunderstanding for uninitiated expats, who initially misunderstand a request for 'transport' as a request for the means of transport, and elicit some rather annoyed reactions, such as 'Are they stupid enough to think I'd lend them my car when they can't even drive?' This would be a textbook case of semantic blurring, where 'international' communication is compromised in a local context.

However, Fairman concludes that, if he succeeded in 'correcting' his students' English to use the lexeme *fare* to refer to this, he and other native-speaker expats living in that space would be saved the one-off learning of the extended semantics (from their starting point) of the word *transport*, but the local users of English would risk being misunderstood in their own immediate environment. It comes down to a contest of ownership. Locals who use the 'international' form risk being mistaken for an outsider or being presumed to look down upon their interlocutors from a position of *faux* superiority. I would encounter a very similar problem if I religiously avoided the terms *robot* and *braai* in South Africa – a *barbeque* is after all a line of men waiting to have their hair cut, and should be spelled *barberqueue*, containing a sufficiently pretentious supply of silent letters and all.

The disagreement here stems in part from what one takes to be the starting point for one's attempt at understanding, and in part from what one takes to be the goal for using English. The prototypical type of 'deviation' that attracts the attention of scholars in world Englishes, dismissed as 'liberation linguistics' by Quirk (1988), is locally responsive vocabulary and discourse styles. The prototypical type of deviation that causes 'the Quirk concern', as Kachru (1991) retorted, is a grammatical error such as different tense or aspect forms and usage, and possibly the fact of variability as such (usually termed 'inconsistency' rather than 'variability' where non-natives are concerned).

It is not as if either camp is not aware of the other source of variability, it is just that the less focal data come to be interpreted within the prior frame of reference established by the more central data type on which that camp focuses. Thus, Beeton and Dorner's 'local colour' and Titlestad's 'body of colloquial terms' represent a peripheral extension to 'the staple of our communication, both spoken and written, [which] is the standard language' (Titlestad, 1996, p. 168). Kachru (1992) by contrast is happy to extend the idea of nativisation to pronunciation and grammatical features of local varieties since these also follow from the local context and occur under influence of the other languages in the context, after he has first established the existence of registers, vocabulary and code-mixing practices that are functional within a particular ecology. The debate boils down to a very basic starting axiom: is there/should there be a single supranational English that is locally responsive within relatively narrow parameters, or is there/should there be multiple Englishes that are locally responsive while retaining enough international currency for those who require the language for such a function?

The answer to this question is largely an attitudinal one, and not an educational or academic one. Schneider (2003) views this as one key development that Englishes undergo in different postcolonial contexts, the gradual acceptance of local forms, endonormativity. Kachru (1976/2015c, 1985/2015d) is also concerned with the attitudinal reorientation that is required to accept local usage that has already been established in usage prior to its recognition and possible acceptance. If one's attitude is exonormative (euphemistically called 'a concern with intelligibility'), then local usage is up against it, and will gain acceptance only if no feasible alternative can be imposed, a kind of last resort. If one's attitude is endonormative, then local usage has a better chance of acceptance. However, Kachru (1977/2015a) points to a strong sense of linguistic schizophrenia among Outer Circle users in particular, who continue to orient overtly towards an external norm, while performing in line with a local norm.

Kruger and Van Rooy (2017) propose that acceptance, at least in the Inner and Outer Circles, should be viewed as a multi-layered construct, from conventionalisation to legitimisation to codification. Usage within a society, combined with sufficient degrees of shared understanding, usually suffices to constitute conventionalisation – language change from below, without much weight attached to the degree of understanding that outsiders might share. This is, in a way, grammar in its ordinary 'descriptive' or usage-based sense: people in a particular setting use particular forms with particular meanings and functions, and their usage is understood in more or less the intended sense in that setting. Legitimisation is where a measure of approval accompanies the convention, such as not stigmatising a particular usage (conventionalised and widespread as it might be), and can be seen in what editors correct when they edit texts for publication, but also what speakers avoid using, or use less, in formal contexts. Codification is a final step, where approval is granted in dictionaries and grammars and where forms are overtly validated for use in high-stakes examinations or texts intended for widespread dissemination. Baratta (2021) argues that even in Expanding Circle contexts a process of societal codification takes place, where the society establishes its own norms through practice, without the need for official codification. This corresponds in large part to the notion of conventionalisation, but potentially also to legitimisation, in the model of Kruger and Van Rooy (2017).

Let us venture beyond the Quirk–Kachru debate to the opposite type of critique of the world Englishes framework, such as Bruthiaux (2003) or Seargeant and Tagg (2011): the concern with norms and the validation of a local norm are what is being challenged. After conceding the historical value of the world Englishes approach to validate usage beyond the Inner Circle, they nevertheless argue that even that concern has run its course and it no longer makes sense to be concerned about varieties and norms.

The arguments are in part empirical: the world has changed so that we will never have such bounded entities as varieties any more; and in part conceptual: thinking in terms of varieties and languages is to impose political boundaries on the mental grammars of individuals where such mental grammars are not bounded by political categories.

Such a critique is clear from the argument of Otheguy et al. (2015) about the psycholinguistic invalidity of the notion of a 'language', where they argue for translanguaging as a more realistic understanding of what happens in the minds of speakers. This is also consistent with Blommaert's (2010) view that speakers draw on their resources in ways that are bound not by language boundaries, but by their need to communicate effectively and express themselves – bits of languages being deployed, mobile resources used by mobile speakers.

If we take a step back and we don't get fixated on the idea of a 'variety', it remains not just useful but actually scientifically responsible to recognise that speakers use language not just to deploy resources, to have their say, but also to be understood. Such mutual understanding in language, imperfect as it might be, implies using language in ways that will optimise the chances of being understood. (This assumption is challenged, no doubt, by the languaging behaviour of some Inner Circle politicians, though, who have perfected the art of telling tales, full of sound and fury, signifying 'covfefe', but let us cast doubt aside for a moment and submit to the willing suspension of disbelief.)

Mutual understanding is achieved most easily by conventional usage – where convention is not a roundabout backdoor way to slip in aprioristic standard language under a different label, but rather something that emerges from human interaction – success breeds success, which is really how mental grammars emerge in the first place in any case, as the mind's response to repetition, as Bybee (2006) explains. Let's then not call the collection of conventions 'varieties' or 'Englishes' if that offends and reminds some readers of nineteenth-century European romantic nationalism; nevertheless, to the extent that speakers have to rely on assumptions about what others will understand, they do make mainly conventional choices. Such conventional practice leaves space for the innovative uses, the unconventional, to stand out and achieve the desired effect. The notion of conventional here is considerably more localised than the 'internationally intelligible standard' that people like Quirk or Titlestad argue for, and probably contains many more nouns and verbs than what the future King Charles was comfortable with in 1995.

Conventional language use is not a purely individual matter, not even at the level of language form and meaning. One does not store each word or grammatical pattern in one's head with a separate label for its range of contexts as if these are separate events – one's grammatical knowledge typically forms a network of related elements, where the information about the usefulness or contextual appropriateness is part of the representational network, not piecemeal individual 'bits of language'. More generally, human grammatical knowledge relies on abstraction and on pattern-seeking, without even having to subscribe to the innateness theorem, nor submitting those abstractions to some academy for approval. To ignore or dismiss the reality of systematic aspects of grammatical knowledge, which form the basis of conventional language use, is not the foundation on which to build understanding.

What does this imply for Englishes? Individuals use English because it is useful, but to be useful (instrumentally, as a means of self-expression, or any combination of these broad functions of language), it has to be understood. This can surely and obviously be achieved in the manner that Quirk and Titlestad argue for: by getting everybody to acquire and use standard English, or better still, the King's English (known as the Queen's English in the period 1952–2022). However, such an option is just a possibility, not the present reality. It makes more sense to try to understand the present reality than to wish it differently.

The present reality is that people use English and in using it, form representations of what works – imperfectly and not always in identical ways. If these mental representations work well enough to make themselves understood, the speakers will experience the entrenchment of the success recipes through repeated use, the development of grammar in the general sense of Bybee (2006). Their contexts of use will strongly influence which features will fill their feature pools from which they make their selections, and their social interactions will co-determine what will become entrenched conventions. Diversity of Englishes will thus remain a feature of the worldwide use of English precisely because of the multitude of users, the diversity of contexts of use and the functions that English is called upon to perform. At the same time, because of the opportunities to use English beyond local contexts, those users who do frequently use English in those contexts will develop conventions that transport well across contexts as opposed to those conventions that are successful and acceptable in more specific contexts only. The consequence is, unsurprisingly, a limiting of divergence in those contexts of use where contact is fleeting and familiarity among participants is low; as Meierkord (2012) argues, in interactions across Englishes, linguistic choices are safer to maximise the chances of being understood.

Englishes diverge because of their contexts of use, but converge to the extent that people communicate across multiple contexts. These two opposing forces shape the language on an ongoing basis. Much of the noise is generated around the acceptance of forms that already exist, framed in more sophisticated ways as concerns with intelligibility and the need to be in constant touch with the native speaker (but not all of them), or thinly disguised class and racial prejudice.

9.3 World Englishes in its multilingual context

The fact that English is used so widely is the main reason why there are so many sources of divergence, of new features that enter the feature pool as people continue to interact (or at least try to, as pointed out by Bill Bryson). Divergences are inevitable and unavoidable, but also sometimes appear to be underestimated radically and dismissed as 'local flavour' or devalued as 'lower standards than the best'. English is used in concert with one or more other languages outside the rarefied monolingual enclaves of the Inner Circle, dutifully protected by inherited class privilege and/or by anti-immigrant rhetoric (which is pretty rich coming from people whose forebears were undocumented immigrants themselves, who set foot on foreign soil without having paid the very expensive visa fees that many from the developing world have to pay these days to visit Inner Circle countries; humans are good at drawing a line and leaving the past where it belongs, in the past, after all).

In the past, speakers used their knowledge of other languages to help fill the feature pool from which new varieties of English emerged. These influences are less directly visible in the case of Englishes that developed in the contexts of plantation slavery, and more visible in the case of borrowings from other languages by typical native speakers, with a wide range of intermediate forms of cross-linguistic influence in all contexts. The more diverse the context, the more diverse the influences; the more concentrated the context is on just a few languages in contact, the more noticeable the mutual influence of each language on the others in the contact environment. The more vexing issue is how we should think about the multilingual ecology of English worldwide. One response is Quirk's (1988), already cited in Chapter 1, but worth repeating, as it implicitly or explicitly forms the backbone of one very typical response from the TESOL fraternity:

> No one should underestimate the problem of teaching English in such countries as India and Nigeria, where the English of the teachers themselves inevitably bears the stamp of locally acquired deviation from the standard language ('You are knowing my father, isn't it?'). The temptation is great to accept the situation and even to justify it in euphemistically sociolinguistic terms. (p. 22)

The construal of the multilingual 'situation' as a problem is not helpful – neither in social terms, nor in linguistic terms. In linguistic terms, the mutual influence of languages in a contact ecology is inevitable, as much as the blended outcome of dialect contact was inevitable in the development of the colonial Englishes investigated by Trudgill (2004), as explained in Chapter 4. People will use a word that fits a situation to the extent that they can assume that their interlocutors will understand their meaning, rather than call for native-speaker assistance in finding a word that somewhere else in the native-speaker world has currency in describing something that partially (or even fully) coincides with the meaning intended by the speaker. The same goes for grammatical and rhetorical patterns; it is inevitable that a degree of fusion takes place in the multilingual mind between patterns across languages to the extent that users notice similarities. This can be called transfer or interference, but to use these appellations presupposes an idealised view of The English Grammar as some fixed entity outside the minds of its users, and vulnerable to being besmirched by the dirty minds of multilinguals, possibly from 'shithole countries', if I may draw on modern-day presidential diction.

The goal of teaching, in such a view of language, is more to foster conformity and less to develop communication. Widdowson (1994) is quite pointed in how he exposes the fallacies in such an argument. He notes that much of what was offered as core areas for standardisation, marketed as being in service of intelligibility, actually served communal functions, identity functions, and was less pertinent to communication. The imposition of a narrow, socially exclusive native-speaker standard results in a constraint on the communicative value of English:

> It is a familiar experience to find oneself saying things in a foreign language because you can say them rather than because they express what you want to say. You feel you are going through the motions, and somebody else's motions at that. (p. 384)

He remarks that only a few native speakers customarily abide by this version of the standard. Especially in the context of international use, to try to regulate deviations has less to do with communicative effectiveness, with intelligibility, and much more to do with demarcating the boundaries of what Widdowson (1994) calls the 'self-elected members of a rather exclusive club' (p. 379).

The clearest sign of things to come, perhaps, is in the creative and deliberate play with languages that we observe in online communication. Where one might still contain the calls of Achebe and Rao for a different type of English as being applicable 'only' to literary creativity – we all know that modernists such as cummings and Pound used even more deviant language – it is harder to dismiss the widespread online creativity of millions of users as an aberration, a fringe pursuit.

This is no reason for despair, though. The fact of contact between people and the fact that communication is a two-way process function as a 'natural' converging force that interacts with the expressiveness and the resourcefulness of people who communicate. Widdowson (1994) equates standards and conventions to the extent that they develop bottom-up as the successful communicative strategies from different contexts – the inductive sense of grammatical conventions noted earlier in this chapter, or societal codification in Baretta's (2021) terms. The translanguaging critique of the construal of language as some independent object is valid in this sense: there is no English that is being damaged by its use in multilingual language repertoires. Such a view represents a monolingual mindset in which each language is a thing unto itself and speakers speak one language at a time. A monolingual person might think so, but mainly for lack of experience with language(s). This thought does not constitute a transcendental thought of pure essence, stripped of its accidentals. Rather, there are communicative strategies, grammatical patterns and vocabulary items, which are very useful in very many contexts, and these form a mental network in the mind, which we can call English if we like, but for many users, this network is part of a much bigger language repertoire and is integrated with that bigger repertoire, opening up more forms of communicative expression that speakers may find useful to achieve their diverse communicative goals.

9.4 The ethics of using and promoting English

There are several ways of arguing about world Englishes that amount to oversimplifications, but to the extent that the arguments have practical implications and people act on those, such oversimplifications are ethically dubious. These concern the way in which arguments engage with the conflicting forces of localisation, multilingualism and language learning. Beyond the ethics of academic argumentation, there is the very crucial ethical question about native-speaker privilege (and privilege for some native speakers more than others), which we cannot ignore either.

The shape of Englishes across the world results in part from localisation, is fed in part by the multilingual ecologies, but is also in part the consequence of language learning, especially by adults. In a view that takes language learning as the main reason for diverging Englishes, or at least for the divergences beyond the native-speaker user communities, the non-native user is put in a position of perpetual disadvantage. Whatever the non-native speaker does differently will be invalidated in principle.

This is precisely what journals do when they recommend, advise or require the non-natives to have their work checked by natives. It imposes an additional financial and time burden on them, over and above the message of perpetual inadequacy. The privilege of native-speaker teachers that also follows from this view, 'the need for non-native teachers to be in constant touch with the native language' (Quirk, 1988, p. 19), has material implications for the employability of natives and non-natives – favouring some people and putting the other at the back of the queue, only to be employed when there is no native available to do the job. Likewise, privilege is bestowed on the training provided by (sometimes monolingual) native speakers from the Inner Circle to the extent that Quirk's (1988) pronouncement corresponds to real-world perceptions:

> We must not forget that many Japanese teachers, Malaysian teachers, Indian teachers have done postgraduate training in Britain and the United States, eager to absorb what they felt were the latest ideas in English teaching. Where better, after all, to get the latest ideas on this than in the leading English-speaking countries? (p. 21)

Tough luck, on the one hand, for competent training programmes in Ireland or Australia (except if they too are 'leading English-speaking countries'? – somebody has to be non-leading if the very term 'leading' is to have any meaning), and even more so for India or South Africa, who are axiomatically not good enough, a fall-back position if the better option is not available. The sense of entitlement is actually quite astonishing if one thinks that these leading trainers come from societies whose own results in acquiring second languages are, if we are being charitable, rather mixed. One might expect a little more modesty and self-awareness, unless of course it was never about teaching and learning the language, but about safeguarding the continued, exclusive club membership of the fraternity of elite native speakers.

Yet, conversely, if the limitations of inadequate learning are not confronted, then indeed, some people will be denied the value of their effort to learn English. Thus, a radical emphasis on indigenisation as a cover term for all divergence, which overlooks the limits of current teaching and learning achievement, will indeed be unethical too, particularly to the extent that resources and time allocation are diverted from the learning of English, in high-stakes contexts above all. Acquiring advanced reading proficiency and mastering academic writing remain key ingredients for success in higher education, and is a more burdensome undertaking for somebody whose baseline proficiency in the language of learning and teaching is not strong enough. The clear evidence for the link between English-language proficiency and academic success should not be dismissed, despite problems with appropriate measurement of proficiency – inductive approaches with learner corpora can yield valuable information without the need to resort to imported standardised tests.

Failure to recognise the multilingual setting is just as much of a problem. In the classroom, such a monolingual approach to the teaching of English, which denies a place for other languages in the classroom (language and content subjects) and thus denies learners the use of their complete linguistic repertoire to learn – to learn English as much as to master academic content – is a potential contributing factor to inadequate learning and should be guarded against as much. In equal measure, to decry the 'inevitable stamp' of other languages, and inevitable it is, is not ethically defensible. Everybody's English betrays their background: Lord Quirk's English was rather English and bore the inevitable stamp of his background, as much as the English of New Zealand rugby players or Canadian (ice) hockey players or recent immigrants in New York, not to mention the indigenous peoples of the various Inner Circle countries, or the descendants of slaves in the Caribbean and United States. This ethical pitfall cuts more widely than just multilingual Outer and Expanding Circle contexts. The same discriminatory effects are in evidence in the Inner Circle, or against native speakers from historical language-shift backgrounds, such as Jamaican or Irish users of English, when people are discriminated against because of their accent. It is not about accent of course, it is about the social judgement (class-based, race-based, nationality-based), the so-called 'harsher but more realistic judgment of those with authority to employ or promote them' (Quirk, 1988, p. 24), in other words, about the continued maintenance of the privilege of the few – which is dispensed not only to non-native speakers but also to people seeking rental properties in the United States but who happen not to speak with the right (or is it white?) accent, as documented by Baugh (2016).

These academic arguments are already connected closely to real-world concerns, where people's employment prospects, accommodation options or quality of education are affected. Let me remind the reader of one of the quotations, already presented in Chapter 1 of this book, from an editor who completed the questionnaire in Edwards's (2010) study:

> In fact, many editors of international journals are not necessarily native speakers themselves and may not be able to judge the linguistic quality of papers. (p. 22)

The equations are clear: native = international; linguistic quality = standard English. This is no different from Bill Bryson, who also restricts the 'speakers' of English to the native speakers and reserves a bit of charity for the Others. Native speakers have an undeserved advantage, to the extent that English is a language of worldwide communication. To the extent that this advantage is leveraged against others, by denying them the editorship of 'international journals', lest they be unable to judge the linguistic quality of papers, or denying them teaching positions, it is unethical. To the extent that economies of scale are leveraged to suffocate the production of entertainment in other languages, to push American entertainment down the throat of cash-strapped consumers elsewhere in the world, who would also like to watch a bit of television at the end of a day, it is unethical. It is also unethical to reinforce the monolingual, monocultural mindset of those with inherited privilege by translating the otherness of others away through domesticating translation strategies for the English-speaking markets (or domesticating of *Harry Potter* for American audiences through editing), or suppress the exposure to others by limited, half-hearted marketing of 'commercially unviable products', by censorship decisions to 'protect the young minds from unfamiliar values' or simply not distributing 'foreign films' and translated books in affluent Inner Circle markets at all. Sure, this is simply economics, one can argue. Yeah, right. Slave labour also made perfect economic sense, much cheaper than paid labour. Just because it is economics doesn't make it just, though, nor right.

9.5 The future

There doesn't seem to be an immediate competitor for English on the horizon. One never knows, of course, and the colonisation of Mars may be a game-changer, as would access to the language of shape-shifting reptiles in control of the planet be. Barring such otherworldly interventions, English seems to have entrenched itself at the top of the World System of Languages (De Swaan, 2010), at least on planet Earth. There is a cycle of constant reinforcement: the more people use English, the more useful it becomes, and hence even more will want to learn the language, constantly enhancing its usefulness.

The same does not hold for all varieties of English. Some varieties have more currency than others, but at least here, the recent past has brought to the fore varieties beyond the metropolitan centres and created space for more varieties to occupy space in cyberspace alongside the obvious space already occupied in geographical space (Mair, 2013a, 2020). In many of these virtual and material spaces, English and other languages compete but also complement one another, and blend into hybrid forms of use that we are only beginning to understand and appreciate. Such hybridity is not universally welcomed, and is a cause of concern for educationalists and governments alike, not to mention some of those who currently hold the power to make harsh but realistic judgements. Panic about declining standards of English is a well-established rhetorical genre across the world, and serves as trickle advertising for the right kinds of language products and services. My e-mail inbox is spammed several times a week by prospective providers of language services to help me, just a poor non-native boy, get my texts published in 'international' journals. I may not need sympathy, but my English can't just come and go easily.

There is a strong likelihood that the worldwide use of English will continue to limit the use of other languages as media of wider communication. There is a growing likelihood, to take one example, that German–Dutch encounters will be conducted in English and not in German, as they would have been two generations ago, when many more Dutch pupils learnt German at school than today (of course, there never was a complementary measure of Dutch learning in German schools, so there too, one should not be blinded to the asymmetry – an asymmetry that often, if perversely, works in favour of English by serving as the neutral lingua franca in such international contact contexts). Likewise, the use of English in ASEAN is not going to foster widespread use of some form(s) of Malay or any of the other widely used languages across Southeast Asia, nor does French seem to be making a comeback, despite its erstwhile colonial foothold in the region.

There are limits to the extent of use and extent of convergence of English, though. As shown in this final chapter, but also elsewhere in the book, some communities of English users have rather ambivalent stances towards other users: happy to include them when making a case for the size of the global speech community, but not happy to acknowledge all the linguistic conventions that develop beyond their control. Tensions remain in the contradictions. This is not just a global matter. In local contexts, such as those to which Schneider's (2003) dynamic model applies, the identity reorientation and mutual acceptance of multiple strands of people in local polities seem more elusive today than when the model was proposed at the beginning of the twenty-first century. The world of the first quarter of the twenty-first century has seen an increase in polarisation between countries and within countries, with Brexit and 'America First' not really testifying to the global integrative impulse of native speakers. How the global users of English will react to the more exclusionary impulses of many native speakers remains to be seen. While Mr Joe Biden proclaimed that America is back at the table after taking over the presidency from Mr Donald Trump, many in the world are not holding their breath; they might leave again, and one has to ask if it will remain self-evident that America can vacate its seat and reclaim it at will, particularly on the presumption that the chair in question is at the 'head' of the table. English is not likely to relinquish its usability, but the degree to which people will seek alignment and hence converge will be affected.

Will English split up into multiple languages – go the way of Latin that dissolved into the Romance languages? That seems unlikely, despite the very many concerns about diversification and disintegration. In part, given widespread education across the world, standard-like input from schools exerts convergent pressure. International use adds sustained convergent pressure, and thus even in local usage, the effect of international use is felt. This is precisely what we see when we examine online language use across the world: local usage and international or widespread usage combine, and in multiple places simultaneously. The need for expressing identity is catered for at the same time as wider audiences are engaged. It does not mean that people are able to, and in fact often do, use English in ways that only the initiated local audience will understand, but most of these users have a range of styles and linguistic options in their repertoire, which they adjust to context. This is evidenced by Korean speakers who are able to differentiate [p] and [f] more when necessary for formal communication, by interactions across international Englishes that make more conservative and fewer localised choices, and by cricket lovers who suppress the use of cricket metaphors when speaking to non-cricketing outsiders despite feeling stuck in the crease . . .

English is likely to maintain its utility by remaining intelligible, but it is not likely to homogenise. It is part of the linguistic repertoires of too wide a range of peoples and cultures. Monolingual, monocultural users may find that there will be higher demands on their adaptability in the context of diverse users who may not continue to be so gullible as to grant native speakers some of the privileges they took as self-evident in international communication. That might not be a bad thing.

References

Aceto, Michael. (2020). English in the Caribbean and the Central American rim. In Daniel Schreier, Marianne Hundt & Edgar W. Schneider (Eds.), *The Cambridge handbook of world Englishes* (pp. 183–209). Cambridge University Press.

Achebe, Chinua. (1965). English and the African writer. *Transition, 18*, 27–30.

Achebe, Chinua. (2009). The education of a British-protected child. *The education of a British-protected child* (pp. 3–24). Anchor Books. (Original work published 1993)

Afeadi, Philip Atsu. (2015). Language of power: Pidgin in colonial governance of Northern Nigeria. *Legon Journal of the Humanities, 26*, 19–37.

Afrifa, Grace Ampomaa, Anderson, Jemima Asabea, & Ansah, Gladys Nyarko. (2019). The choice of English as a home language in urban Ghana. *Current Issues in Language Planning, 20*(4), 418–434. https://doi.org/10.1080/14664208.2019.1582947

Akande, Akinmade T., & Salami, L. Oladipo. (2010). Use and attitudes towards Nigerian Pidgin English among Nigerian university students. In Robert McColl Millar (Ed.), *Marginal dialects: Scotland, Ireland and beyond* (pp. 70–89). Forum for Research on the Languages of Scotland and Ireland.

Alleyne, Mervyn C., & Hall-Alleyne, Beverley. (1982). Language maintenance and language death in the Caribbean. *Caribbean Quarterly, 28*(4), 52–59.

Ashcroft, Bill, Griffiths, Gareth, & Tiffin, Helen. (1989). *The empire writes back: Theory and practice in post-colonial literatures*. Routledge.

Ballantyne, Robert Michael. (1877). *The settler and the savage*. James Nisbet & Co. Retrieved November 9, 2022, from https://archive.org/details/settlersavagetal00ball/page/n7/mode/2up

Ballantyne, Robert Michael. (1879). *Six months at the Cape*. James Nisbet & Co. Retrieved November 9, 2022, from https://archive.org/details/RM_Ballantyne_Six_Months_at_the_Cape/RM_Ballantyne_Six_Months_at_the_Cape/mode/2up

Bamgbose, Ayo. (1998). Torn between the norms: Innovations in world Englishes. *World Englishes, 17*(1), 1–14.

REFERENCES

Banjo, Ayo. (1971). Towards a definition of standard Nigerian spoken English. In *Actes du 8e Congrès de la Société linguistique de l'Afrique Occidental* (pp. 165–174). Université d'Abidjan.
Baratta, Alex. (2021). *The societal codification of Korean English*. Bloomsbury.
Barker, David. (2010). *An A–Z of common English errors for Japanese learners*. Back to Basics.
Baron, Naomi S. (2008). *Always on*. Oxford University Press.
Bauer, Laurie. (2002). *An introduction to international varieties of English*. Edinburgh University Press.
Baugh, John. (2016). Linguistic profiling and discrimination. In Ofelia Garcia, Nelson Flores & Massimiliano Spotti (Eds.), *The Oxford handbook of language and society* (pp. 349–368). Oxford University Press.
Beeton, D. R., & Dorner, Helen. (1975). *A dictionary of English usage in Southern Africa*. Oxford University Press.
Bekker, Ian. (2012). South African English as a late 19th-century extraterritorial variety. *English World-Wide*, *33*(2), 127–146.
Benor, Sarah Bunin. (2010). Ethnolinguistic repertoire: Shifting the analytic focus in language and ethnicity. *Journal of Sociolinguistics*, *14*(2), 159–183.
Bhatia, Tej K. (2019). World Englishes and global advertising. In Cecil L. Nelson, Zoya G. Proshina & Daniel R. Davis (Eds.), *Handbook of world Englishes* (2nd ed., pp. 616–634). Wiley-Blackwell.
Björkman, Beyza. (2014). An analysis of polyadic English as a lingua franca (ELF) speech: A communicative strategies framework. *Journal of Pragmatics*, *66*, 122–138.
Blommaert, Jan. (2010). *The sociolinguistics of globalisation*. Cambridge University Press.
Bolton, Kingsley. (2002). Chinese Englishes: From Canton jargon to global English. *World Englishes*, *21*(2), 181–199.
Bolton, Kingsley. (2003). *Chinese Englishes: A sociolinguistic history*. Cambridge University Press.
Bolton, Kingsley. (2013). World Englishes and international call centres. *World Englishes*, *32*(4), 495–502.
Bolton, Kingsley. (2016). Linguistic outsourcing and native-like performance in international call centres: An overview. In Kenneth Hyltenstam (Ed.), *Advanced proficiency and exceptional ability in second languages* (pp. 185–213). Mouton de Gruyter.
Bolton, Kingsley, & Davis, Daniel R. (2018). Larry Smith and world Englishes. *World Englishes*, *37*(3), 447–454.
Bosman, Herman Charles. (2013). *The complete Oom Schalk Lourens Stories*. Human & Rousseau.
Branford, Jean, & Venter, Malcolm. (2016). *Say again? The other side of South African English*. Pharos.
Britain, David. (2020). A sociolinguistic ecology of colonial Britain. In Daniel Schreier, Marianne Hundt & Edgar W. Schneider (Eds.), *The Cambridge handbook of world Englishes* (pp. 147–159). Cambridge University Press.

Britannica, The Editors of Encyclopaedia. (2020). 'White Australia policy'. *Encyclopedia Britannica*, 24 November. Retrieved June 29, 2022, from https://www.britannica.com/event/White-Australia-Policy

Britannica, The Editors of Encyclopaedia. (2022). 'R.M. Ballantyne'. *Encyclopedia Britannica*, 20 April. Retrieved May 7, 2022, from https://www.britannica.com/biography/R-M-Ballantyne

Brosnahan, Leonard F. (1958). English in Southern Nigeria. *English Studies, 39*, 97–110.

Brownell, Josiah. (2008). The hole in Rhodesia's bucket: White emigration and the end of settler rule. *Journal of Southern African Studies, 34*(3), 591–610.

Bruthiaux, Paul. (2003). Squaring the circles: Issues in modelling English worldwide. *International Journal of Applied Linguistics, 31*(2), 159–178.

Bryson, Bill. (1990). *Mother tongue*. Penguin Books.

Bryson, Bill. (1991). *Neither here nor there*. Black Swan.

Bryson, Bill. (1995). *Notes from a small island*. Doubleday.

Bryson, Bill. (2003). *A short history of nearly everything*. Doubleday.

Buschfeld, Sarah, & Kautzsch, Alexander. (2017). Towards an integrated approach to postcolonial and non-postcolonial English. *World Englishes, 36*(1), 104–126.

Buschfeld, Sarah, & Kautzsch, Alexander. (2020). Theoretical models of English as a world language. In Daniel Schreier, Marianne Hundt & Edgar W. Schneider (Eds.), *Cambridge handbook of world Englishes* (pp. 51–71). Cambridge University Press.

Bybee, Joan. (2006). From usage to grammar: The mind's response to repetition. *Language, 82*(4), 711–733.

Chambers, J. K. (2004). 'Canadian dainty': The rise and decline of Briticisms in Canada. In Raymond Hickey (Ed.), *Legacies of colonial English* (pp. 224–241). Cambridge University Press.

Cheshire, Jenny, Kerswill, Paul, Fox, Sue, & Torgersen, Eivind. (2011). Contact, the feature pool and the speech community: The emergence of Multicultural London English. *Journal of Sociolinguistics, 15*(2), 151–196.

Clarke, Sandra. (2010). *Newfoundland and Labrador English*. Edinburgh University Press.

Clyne, Michael. (2003). *Dynamics of language contact: English and immigrant languages*. Cambridge University Press.

Coetzee, Andries, & Wissing, Daan. (2007). Global and local durational properties in three varieties of South African English. *The Linguistic Review, 24*(2–3), 263–289. https://doi.org/10.1515/TLR.2007.010

Coetzee-Van Rooy, Susan. (2006). Integrativeness: Untenable for world Englishes learners? *World Englishes, 25*(3–4), 437–450.

Coetzee-Van Rooy, Susan. (2008). From the Expanding to the Outer Circle: South Koreans learning English in South Africa. *English Today, 24*(4), 3–10.

Coetzee-Van Rooy, Susan. (2012). Flourishing functional multilingualism: Evidence from language repertoires in the Vaal Triangle region. *International Journal of the Sociology of Language, 218*, 87–119.

Coetzee-Van Rooy, Susan. (2013). Afrikaans in contact with English: Endangered language or case of exceptional bilingualism? *International Journal of the Sociology of Language, 224*, 179–207.
Coetzee-Van Rooy, Susan. (2014). Explaining the ordinary magic of stable African multilingualism in the Vaal Triangle region in South Africa. *Journal of Multilingual and Multicultural Development, 35*(2), 121–138.
Coetzee-Van Rooy, Susan. (2021). Being English in multilingual South Africa. *World Englishes, 40*(1), 98–120.
Coetzee-Van Rooy, Susan, & Van Rooy, Bertus. (2005). Labels, comprehensibility and status in South African English. *World Englishes, 24*(1), 1–19.
Coetzee-Van Rooy, Susan, & Van Rooy, Bertus. (2021). The history of English language attitudes within the multilingual ecology of South Africa. In Alexander Onysko (Ed.), *Research developments in world Englishes* (pp. 121–147). Bloomsbury.
Cole, Jason, & Vanderplank, Robert. (2016). Comparing autonomous and class-based learners in Brazil: Evidence for the present-day advantages of informal, out-of-class learning. *System, 61*, 31–42.
Commonwealth of Australia. (1997). Bringing them home: Report of the National Inquiry into the Separation of Aboriginal and Torres Strait Islander Children from Their Families. Retrieved July 21, 2022, from https://humanrights.gov.au/sites/default/files/content/pdf/social_justice/bringing_them_home_report.pdf
Croft, W. (2000). *Explaining language change: An evolutionary approach*. Pearson Education.
Curry, M., & Lillis, T. (2022). Multilingualism in academic writing for publication: Putting English in its place. *Language Teaching*, 1–14. https://doi.org/10.1017/S0261444822000040
Daleszynska, Agata. (2015). The face of the local in light of the global: Analysis of variation in the use of preverbal markers in Bequia Creole. In Paula Prescod (Ed.), *Language issues in Saint Vincent and the Grenadines* (pp. 45–66). John Benjamins.
Das Gupta, Jyotirindra. (1970). *Language conflict and national development: Group politics and national language policy in India*. University of California Press.
Dasgupta, Sandipto. (2014). 'A language which is foreign to us': Continuities and anxieties in the making of the Indian constitution. *Comparative Studies of South Asia, Africa and the Middle East, 34*(2), 228–242.
Davydova, Julia. (2021). The role of sociocognitive salience in the acquisition of structured variation and linguistic diffusion: Evidence from quotative *be like*. *Language in Society, 50*, 171–196.
De Kadt, Elizabeth. (2004). Gender aspects of the use of English on a South African university campus. *World Englishes, 23*(4), 515–534.
De Kock, Leon. (1996). *Civilising barbarians: Missionary narrative and African textual response in nineteenth-century South Africa*. Witwatersrand University Press.

De Swaan, Abram. (2010). Language systems. In Nikolas Coupland (Ed.), *The handbook of language and globalization* (pp. 56–76). Wiley-Blackwell.

Deumert, Ana. (2014). *Sociolinguistics and mobile communication*. Edinburgh University Press.

Deumert, Ana, & Masinyana, Sibabalwe O. (2008). Mobile language choices – the use of English and isiXhosa in text messages (SMS): Evidence from a bilingual South African sample. *English World-Wide, 29*(2), 117–147.

De Wilde, V., Brysbaert, M., & Eyckmans, J. (2020). Learning English through out-of-school exposure. Which levels of language proficiency are attained and which types of input are important? *Bilingualism: Language and Cognition, 23*(1), 171–185. https://doi.org/10.1017/S1366728918001062

Diamond, Jared. (1997). *Guns, germs & steel: A short history of everybody for the last 13,000 years*. Vintage.

Dillard, J. L. (1992). *A history of American English*. Longman.

Dollinger, Stefan. (2008). *New-dialect formation in Canada: Evidence from the English modal auxiliaries*. John Benjamins.

Eastwood, Alexander. (2010). A fantastic failure: Displaced nationalism and the intralingual translation of Harry Potter. *The English Languages: History, Diaspora, Culture, 1*, 1–14. https://jps.library.utoronto.ca/index.php/elhdc/article/view/14365

Edwards, Alison. (2010). Dutch English: Tolerable, taboo, or about time too? *English Today, 26*(1), 19–25.

Edwards, Alison. (2016). *English in the Netherlands: Functions, forms and attitudes*. John Benjamins.

Edwards, Alison, & Laporte, Samantha. (2015). Outer and Expanding Circle Englishes: The competing roles of norm orientation and proficiency levels. *English World-Wide, 36*(2), 135–169.

Edwards, Alison, & Seargeant, Philip. (2020). Beyond English as a second or foreign language: Local uses and the cultural politics of identification. In Daniel Schreier, Marianne Hundt & Edgar W. Schneider (Eds.), *The Cambridge handbook of world Englishes* (pp. 339–359). Cambridge University Press. https://doi.org/10.1017/9781108349406.015

Fairman, Tony. (1992). Ergo lingua mihi deficit. *English Today, 29*, 23–29.

Filppula, Markku. (2008). Irish English: Morphology and syntax. In Bernd Kortmann & Clive Upton (Eds.), *Varieties of English, volume 1: The British Isles* (pp. 328–359). Mouton de Gruyter.

Fisher, John Hurt. (2001). British and American, continuity and divergence. In John Algeo (Ed.), *The Cambridge history of the English language, volume VI: English in North America* (pp. 58–85). Cambridge University Press.

Foner, Nancy. (2014). Immigration history and the remaking of New York. In Nancy Foner, Jan Rath, Jan W. Duyvendak & Rogier van Reekum (Eds.), *New York and Amsterdam: Immigration and the new urban landscape* (pp. 29–51). NYU Press.

Frankopan, Peter. (2015). *The Silk Roads: A new history of the world*. Bloomsbury.

Friedman, Thomas L. (2005). *The world is flat: A brief history of the twenty-first century*. Farrar, Straus and Giroux.
Friedrich, Patricia. (2020). When Englishes go digital. *World Englishes*, 39(1), 67–78.
Frost, Mark R., & Balasingamchow, Yu-Mei. (2009). *Singapore: A biography*. Éditions Didier Millet/National Museum of Singapore.
Fuertes, Jairo N., Potere, Jodi C., & Ramirez, Karen Y. (2002). Effects of speech accents on interpersonal evaluations: Implications for counselling practice and research. *Cultural Diversity and Ethnic Minority Psychology*, 8(4), 346–356.
Fuse, Akiko, Navichkova, Yuliya, & Alloggio, Krysteena. (2018). Perception of intelligibility and qualities of non-native accented speakers. *Journal of Communication Disorders*, 71, 37–51.
Gardner, Matt Hunt, Denis, Derek, Brook, Marisa, & Tagliamonte, Sali A. (2021). *Be like* and the Constant Rate Effect: From the bottom to the top of the S-curve. *English Language and Linguistics*, 25(2), 281–324.
Gargesh, Ravinder. (2008). Indian English: Phonology. In Rajend Mesthrie (Ed.), *Varieties of English volume 4: Africa, South and Southeast Asia* (pp. 231–243). Mouton de Gruyter.
Gilquin, Gaetanelle. (2015). At the interface of contact linguistics and second language acquisition research: New Englishes and Learner Englishes compared. *English World-Wide*, 36(1), 91–124.
Gilquin, Gaetanelle, & Granger, Sylviane. (2011). From EFL to ESL: Evidence from the International Corpus of Learner English. In Joybrato Mukherjee & Marianne Hundt (Eds.), *Exploring second-language varieties of English and Learner Englishes: Bridging a paradigm gap* (pp. 55–78). John Benjamins.
Goldswain, Jeremiah. (1946). *The chronicle of Jeremiah Goldswain, Albany settler of 1820* (Una Long, ed.). Van Riebeeck Society.
Gordon, Elizabeth, & Trudgill, Peter. (2004). English input to New Zealand. In Raymond Hickey (Ed.), *Legacies of colonial English* (pp. 440–455). Cambridge University Press.
Gordon, Elizabeth, Campbell, Lyle, Hay, Jennifer, Maclagan, Margaret, Sudbury, Andrea, & Trudgill, Peter. (2004). *New Zealand English: Its origins and evolution*. Cambridge University Press.
Gottlieb, Henrik. (2020). *Echoes of English: Anglicisms in minor speech communities – with special focus on Danish and Afrikaans*. Peter Lang.
Götz, Sandra, & Schilk, Marco. (2011). Formulaic sequences in spoken ENL, ESL and EFL: Focus on British English, Indian English and Learner English for advanced German learners. In Joybrato Mukherjee & Marianne Hundt (Eds.), *Exploring second-language varieties of English and Learner Englishes: Bridging a paradigm gap* (pp. 79–100). John Benjamins.
Greenbaum, Sidney. (1990). Standard English and the International Corpus of English. *World Englishes*, 9(1), 79–83.
Gries, Stefan Th., & Deshors, Sandra C. (2015). EFL and/vs. ESL? *International Journal of Learner Corpus Research*, 1(1), 130–159.

Hall-Lew, Lauren. (2017). English in North America. In Markku Filppula, Juhani Klemola & Devyani Sharma (Eds.), *Oxford handbook of world Englishes* (pp. 371–388). Oxford University Press.

Hamid, M. Obaidul. (2010). Globalisation, English for everyone and English teacher capacity: Language policy discourses and realities in Bangladesh. *Current Issues in Language Planning, 11*(4), 289–310.

Hawking, Stephen. (1988). *A brief history of time.* Bantam Books.

Hickey, Raymond. (2004). Development and diffusion of Irish English. In Raymond Hickey (Ed.), *Legacies of colonial English* (pp. 82–118). Cambridge University Press.

Hickey, Raymond. (2007). *Irish English: History and present-day forms.* Cambridge University Press.

Hickey, Raymond. (2008). Irish English: Phonology. In Bernd Kortmann & Clive Upton (Eds.), *Varieties of English, volume 1: The British Isles* (pp. 71–104). Mouton de Gruyter.

Hickey, Raymond. (2009). Language use and attitudes in Ireland: A preliminary evaluation of survey results. In B. Ó Catháin (Ed.), *Sochtheangeolaíocht na Gaeilge* (pp. 62–89). Léachtaí Cholm Cille, 39.

Hickey, Raymond. (2012). The English language in Ireland. *Belgisch tijdschrift voor filologie en geschiedenis, 90*(3), 881–887. https://doi.org/10.3406/rbph.2012.8266

Hickey, Raymond. (2020). The colonial and postcolonial expansion of English. In Daniel Schreier, Marianne Hundt & Edgar W. Schneider (Eds.), *The Cambridge handbook of world Englishes* (pp. 25–50). Cambridge University Press.

Hirson, Baruch. (1981). Language in control and resistance in South Africa. *African Affairs*, 80, 219–237.

Hodgson, Janet. (1997). A battle for sacred power: Christian beginnings among the Xhosa. In Richard Elphick & Rodney Davenport (Eds.), *Christianity in South Africa: A political, social and cultural history* (pp. 68–88). James Currey.

Hoffmann, Thomas. (2021). *The cognitive foundation of post-colonial Englishes.* Cambridge University Press.

Hofmann, Matthias. (2015). Mainland Canadian English in Newfoundland: The Canadian shift in urban middle-class St. John's [Unpublished PhD thesis]. Chemnitz University of Technology.

Hopwood, David. (1928). *South African English pronunciation.* Juta.

Hosali, Priya. (2005). Butler English: An account of a highly distinctive variety of English in India. *English Today, 21*(1), 34–39.

Huber, Magnus. (1999). *Ghanaian Pidgin English in its West African context.* John Benjamins.

Huber, Magnus. (2008). Ghanaian English: Phonology. In Rajend Mesthrie (Ed.), *Varieties of English volume 4: Africa, South and Southeast Asia* (pp. 67–92). Berlin: Mouton de Gruyter.

Jaworski, Adam, & Thurlow, Crispen. (2010). Language and the globalizing habitus of tourism: Toward a sociolinguistics of fleeting relationships.

In Nicholas Coupland (Ed.), *The handbook of language and globalization* (pp. 255–286). Wiley-Blackwell.

Jeffery, Chris, & Van Rooy, Bertus. (2004). Emphasizer *now* in colloquial South African English. *World Englishes, 23*(2), 269–280.

Jenkins, Jennifer. (2007). *English as a lingua franca: Attitudes and identity.* Oxford University Press.

Jenkins, Jennifer. (2017). English as a lingua franca in the Expanding Circle. In Markku Filppula, Juhani Klemola & Devyani Sharma (Eds.), *Oxford handbook of world Englishes* (pp. 549–566). Oxford University Press.

Kachru, Braj B. (1965). The *Indianness* in Indian English. *Word, 21*(3), 391–410.

Kachru, Braj B. (1986). *The Alchemy of English: The spread, functions, and models of non-native Englishes.* University of Illinois Press.

Kachru, Braj B. (1991). Liberation linguistics and the Quirk concern. *English Today, 7*(1), 3–13.

Kachru, Braj B. (1992). Models for non-native Englishes. In Braj B. Kachru (Ed.), *The other tongue: English across cultures* (2nd ed., pp. 48–74). University of Illinois Press.

Kachru, Braj B. (1994). English in South Asia. In R. W. Burchfield (Ed.), *The Cambridge history of the English language, volume V: English in Britain and overseas: Origins and development* (pp. 497–553). Cambridge University Press.

Kachru, Braj B. (2015a). Linguistic schizophrenia and language census: A note on the Indian situation. *Collected works of Braj B. Kachru: Volume 3* (Jonathan J. Webster, Ed., pp. 5–20). Bloomsbury. (Original work published 1977)

Kachru, Braj B. (2015b). Meaning in deviation: Toward understanding non-native English texts. *Collected works of Braj B. Kachru: Volume 1* (Jonathan J. Webster, Ed., pp. 85–108). Bloomsbury. (Original work published 1982)

Kachru, Braj B. (2015c). Models of English for the third world: White man's burden or language pragmatics? *Collected works of Braj B. Kachru: Volume 1* (Jonathan J. Webster, Ed., pp. 5–25). Bloomsbury. (Original work published 1976)

Kachru, Braj B. (2015d). Standards, codification, and sociolinguistic realism: The English language in the Outer Circle. *Collected works of Braj B. Kachru: Volume 3* (Jonathan J. Webster, Ed., pp. 153–176). Bloomsbury. (Original work published 1985)

Kiesling, Scott F. (2004). English input to Australia. In Raymond Hickey (Ed.), *Legacies of colonial English* (pp. 418–439). Cambridge University Press.

Kirkpatrick, Andy. (2007). *World Englishes: Implications for international communication and English language teaching.* Cambridge University Press.

Kortmann, Bernd, & Schneider, Edgar W. (Eds.). (2004). *A handbook of varieties of English: A multimedia reference tool* (2 vols). De Gruyter Mouton. https://doi.org/10.1515/9783110197181

Koven, Steven G., & Götzke, Frank. (2010). *American immigration policy: Confronting the nation's challenges.* Springer.

Kruger, Haidee, & Van Rooy, Bertus. (2017). Editorial practice and the distinction between error and conventionalised innovation in New Englishes: The progressive in Black South African English. *World Englishes*, *36*(1), 20–41. https://doi.org/10.1111/weng.12202

Kytö, Merja. (2004). The emergence of American English: Evidence from seventeenth-century records in New England. In Raymond Hickey (Ed.), *Legacies of colonial English* (pp. 121–157). Cambridge University Press.

Kytö, Merja. (2020). English in North America. In Daniel Schreier, Marianne Hundt & Edgar W. Schneider (Eds.), *Cambridge handbook of world Englishes* (pp. 160–184). Cambridge University Press.

Labov, William. (2010). *Principles of linguistic change, volume 3: Cognitive and cultural factors*. Wiley-Blackwell.

Lanham, Len W. (1967). *Teaching English in Bantu primary schools: Final report on research in Johannesburg schools*. Wits University.

Lanham, Len W. (1996). A history of English in South Africa. In Vivian de Klerk (Ed.), *Focus on South Africa* (pp. 19–34). John Benjamins.

Lanham, Len W., & MacDonald, C. A. (1979). *The standard in South African English and its social history*. Groos.

Laporte, Samantha. (2012). Mind the gap! Bridge between world Englishes and Learner Englishes in the making. *English Text Construction*, *5*(2), 264–291.

Leap, William L. (1993). *American Indian English*. University of Utah Press.

Leech, Geoffrey, Hundt, Marianne, Mair, Christian, & Smith, Nicholas. (2009). *Change in contemporary English: A grammatical study*. Cambridge University Press.

Leung, Glenda Alicia, & Deuber, Dagmar. (2014). Indo-Trinidadian speech: An investigation into a popular stereotype surrounding pitch. In Marianne Hundt & Devyani Sharma (Eds.), *English in the Indian diaspora* (pp. 9–28). John Benjamins.

Lev-Ari, Shiri, & Keysar, Boaz. (2010). Why don't we believe non-native speakers? The influence of accent on credibility. *Journal of Experimental Social Psychology*, *46*, 1093–1096.

Li, Songqing. (2019). Expanding the scope for research on global English-language advertising. *World Englishes*, *38*(3), 519–534.

Li, Wei. (2018). Translanguaging as a practical theory of language. *Applied Linguistics*, *39*(1), 9–30.

Loonen, Petrus L. M. (1990). *For to learne to buye and sell: Learning English in the Low Dutch area between 1500 and 1800*. APA-Holland University Press.

Macaulay, Thomas B. (1835). Minute by the Hon'ble T. B. Macaulay, dated the 2nd February 1835. Retrieved May 27, 2022, from http://www.columbia.edu/itc/mealac/pritchett/00generallinks/macaulay/txt_minute_education_1835.html

McAuliffe, M., & Triandafyllidou, A. (2022). Report overview: Technological, geopolitical and environmental transformations shaping our migration and mobility futures. *World Migration Report*, *2022*(1), p.e00022.

McCormick, Kay. (2002). *Language in Cape Town's District Six*. Oxford University Press.

Macdougall, Brenda. (2018). Naming and renaming: Confronting Canada's past. Retrieved May 27, 2022, from https://shekonneechie.ca/2018/08/01/naming-and-renaming-confronting-canadas-past/

McGinley, Kevin. (1987). The future of English in Zimbabwe. *World Englishes*, *6*(2), 159–164.
McWhorter, John. (2007). *Language interrupted: Signs of non-native acquisition in standard language grammars*. Oxford University Press.
Mair, Christian. (2013a). The World System of Englishes: Accounting for the transnational importance of mobile and mediated vernaculars. *English World-Wide*, *34*(3), 253–278.
Mair, Christian. (2013b). Corpus-approaches to the New English Web: Postcolonial diasporic forums in West Africa and the Caribbean. *Covenant Journal of Language Studies*, *1*(1), 17–31.
Mair, Christian. (2020). World Englishes in cyberspace. In Daniel Schreier, Marianne Hundt & Edgar W. Schneider (Eds.), *The Cambridge handbook of world Englishes* (pp. 360–383). Cambridge University Press. https://doi.org/10.1017/9781108349406.016
Major, Roy C., Fitzmaurice, Susan M., Bunta, Ferenc, & Balasubramanian, Chandrika. (2002). The effects of nonnative accents on listening comprehension: Implications for ESL assessment. *TESOL Quarterly*, *36*(2), 173–190.
Major, Roy C., Fitzmaurice, Susan M., Bunta, Ferenc, & Balasubramanian, Chandrika. (2005). Testing the effects of regional, ethnic, and international dialects of English on listening comprehension. *Language Learning*, *55*(1), 37–69.
Makalela, Leketi. (2013). Translanguaging in kasi-taal: Rethinking old language boundaries for new language planning. *Stellenbosch Papers in Linguistics Plus*, *42*, 111–125. https://doi.org/10.5842/42-0-164
Makalela, Leketi. (2014). Fluid identity construction in language contact zones: Metacognitive reflections on *Kasi-taal* language practices. *International Journal of Bilingual Education and Bilingualism*, *17*(6), 668–682.
Makalela, Leketi. (2016). Ubuntu translanguaging: An alternative framework for complex multilingual encounters. *Southern African Linguistics and Applied Language Studies*, *34*(3), 187–196.
Matlwa, Kopano. (2007). *Coconut*. Jacinda.
Matras, Yaron. (2009). *Language contact*. Cambridge University Press.
Mauranen, Anna. (2012). *Exploring ELF: Academic English shaped by non-native speakers*. Cambridge University Press.
Mauranen, Anna. (2017). Second-order language contact: English as an academic lingua franca. In Markku Filppula, Juhani Klemola & Devyani Sharma (Eds.), *Oxford handbook of world Englishes* (pp. 735–753). Oxford University Press.
Meierkord, Christiane. (2012). *Interactions across Englishes: Linguistic choices in local and international contact situations*. Cambridge University Press.
Meierkord, Christiane. (2020). The global growth of English at the grassroots. In Daniel Schreier, Marianne Hundt & Edgar W. Schneider (Eds.), *The Cambridge handbook of world Englishes* (pp. 311–338). Cambridge University Press. https://doi.org/10.1017/9781108349406.014
Mesthrie, Rajend. (1991). *Language in indenture: A sociolinguistic history of Bhojpuri–Hindi in South Africa*. Witwatersrand University Press.

Mesthrie, Rajend. (1992). *English in language shift: The history, structure and sociolinguistics of South African Indian English*. Cambridge University Press.

Mesthrie, Rajend. (1996a). Imagint excusations: Missionary English in the nineteenth century Cape Colony, South Africa. *World Englishes, 15*(2), 139–157.

Mesthrie, Rajend. (1996b). Language contact, transmission, shift: South African Indian English. In Vivian de Klerk (Ed.), *Focus on South Africa* (pp. 79–98). John Benjamins.

Mesthrie, Rajend. (1999). Fifty ways to say 'I do': Tracing the origins of unstressed *do* in Cape Flats English, South Africa. *South African Journal of Linguistics, 17*(1), 58–71.

Mesthrie, Rajend. (2002). From second language to first language: Indian South African English. In Rajend Mesthrie (Ed.), *Language in South Africa* (pp. 339–355). Cambridge University Press.

Mesthrie, Rajend. (2005). Putting back the cart before the horse: The spelling form fallacy in Second Language Acquisition Studies, with special reference to the treatment of schwa in Black South African English. *English World-Wide, 26*(2), 127–151.

Mesthrie, Rajend. (2008). Indian South African English: Phonology. In Rajend Mesthrie (Ed.), *Varieties of English volume 4: Africa, South and Southeast Asia* (pp. 188–199). Mouton de Gruyter.

Mesthrie, Rajend. (2010). Sociophonetics and social change: Deracialisation of the GOOSE vowel in South African English. *Journal of Sociolinguistics, 14*(1), 3–33.

Mesthrie, Rajend. (2014). A lesser globalisation: A sociolexical study of Indian Englishes in diaspora, with a primary focus on South Africa. In Marianne Hundt & Devyani Sharma (Eds.), *English in the Indian diaspora* (pp. 171–186). John Benjamins.

Mesthrie, Rajend. (2017). Class, gender and substrate erasure in sociolinguistic change: A sociophonetic study of schwa in deracialising South African English. *Language, 93*(2), 314–346.

Mesthrie, Rajend. (Forthcoming). Indian South African English. In *Blackwell encyclopedia of world Englishes*.

Mesthrie, Rajend, & Bhatt, Rakesh. (2008). *World Englishes*. Cambridge University Press.

Mesthrie, Rajend, & Chevalier, Alida. (2014). Sociophonetics and the Indian diaspora: The NURSE vowel and other selected features in South African Indian English. In Marianne Hundt & Devyani Sharma (Eds.), *English in the Indian diaspora* (pp. 85–104). John Benjamins.

Mesthrie, Rajend, & Van Rooy, Bertus. (Forthcoming). Black South African English. In *Cambridge history of the English language*.

Mesthrie, Rajend, & West, Paula. (1995). Towards a grammar of Proto South African English. *English World-Wide, 16*(1), 105–133.

Miller, J. (2021). Residential schools in Canada. In *The Canadian Encyclopedia*. Retrieved May 27, 2022, from https://www.thecanadianencyclopedia.ca/en/article/residential-schools

Milroy, James, & Milroy, Lesley. (1991). *Authority in language: Investigating language prescription & standardisation* (2nd ed.). Routledge.
Minow, Verena. (2010). *Variation in the grammar of Black South African English.* Peter Lang.
Mitchell, Alex, & Delbridge, Arthur. (1965). *The speech of Australian adolescents.* Angus and Robertson.
Mollin, Sandra. (2006). *Euro-English: Assessing variety status.* Gunter Narr.
Montgomery, Michael. (2004). Solving Kurath's puzzle: Establishing the antecedents of the American Midland dialect region. In Raymond Hickey (Ed.), *Legacies of colonial English* (pp. 310–325). Cambridge University Press.
Moore, Christopher. (2000). Colonization and conflict: New France and its rivals (1600–1760). In Craig Brown (Ed.), *The illustrated history of Canada* (revised ed., pp. 95–180). Key Porter Books.
Morton, Desmond. (2000). Strains of affluence (1945–1996). In Craig Brown (Ed.), *The illustrated history of Canada* (revised ed., pp. 467–570). Key Porter Books.
Mufwene, Salikoko S. (1997). The legitimate and illegitimate offspring of English. In Larry E. Smith & Michael L. Forman (Eds.), *World Englishes 2000* (pp. 182–203). University of Hawai'i Press.
Mufwene, Salikoko S. (2001). *The ecology of language evolution.* Cambridge University Press.
Mufwene, Salikoko S. (2008). *Language evolution: Contact, competition and change.* Bloomsbury Publishing.
Mufwene, Salikoko S. (2020). Population structure and the emergence of world Englishes. In Daniel Schreier, Marianne Hundt & Edgar W. Schneider (Eds.), *The Cambridge handbook of world Englishes* (pp. 99–119). Cambridge University Press.
Mühlhäusler, P. (1985). External history of Tok Pisin. In S. A. Wurm & P. Mühlhäusler (Eds.), *Handbook of Tok Pisin (New Guinea Pidgin)* (pp. 35–64). Australian National University.
Munro, Murray J., Derwing, Tracey M., & Morton, Susan L. (2006). The mutual intelligibility of L2 speech. *Studies in Second Language Acquisition, 28,* 111–131.
Ndebele, Njabulo S. (1987). The English language and social change in South Africa. *English Academy Review, 4*(1), 1–17.
Nelson, Cecil L. (2008). Intelligibility since 1969. *World Englishes, 27*(3–4), 297–308. https://doi.org/10.1111/j.1467-971X.2008.00568.x
Ngũgĩ wa Thiong'o. (1986). *Decolonising the mind: The politics of language in African literature.* James Currey.
Nielsen, Hans Frede. (1998). *The continental backgrounds of English and its insular development until 1154.* Odense University Press.
Nielsen, Paul Maersk. (2003). English in Argentina: A sociolinguistic profile. *World Englishes, 22*(2), 199–209.
Okafor, Luke Emeka, Khalid, Usman, & Burzynska, Katarzyna. (2022). The effect of migration on international tourism flows: The role of linguistic networks and common languages. *Journal of Travel Research, 61*(4), 818–836.

O'Leary, John. (1995, March 24). Prince hits out over bad English used by Americans. *The Times*, p. 2.

Otheguy, Ricardo, García, Ofelia, & Reid, Wallis. (2015). Clarifying translanguaging and deconstructing named languages: A perspective from linguistics. *Applied Linguistics Review*, 6(3), 281–307.

Park, Jin-Kyu. (2009). 'English fever' in South Korea: Its history and symptoms. *English Today*, 25(1), 50–57.

Park, Joseph Sung-Yul. (2011). The promise of English: Linguistic capital and the neoliberal worker in the South Korean job market. *International Journal of Bilingual Education and Bilingualism*, 14(4), 443–455. https://doi.org/10.1080/13670050.2011.573067

Pennycook, Alistair. (1994). *The cultural politics of English as an international language*. Longman.

Peters, Arne. (2017). Fairies, banshees, and the church: Cultural conceptualisations in Irish English. *International Journal of Language and Culture*, 4(2), 127–148. https://doi.org/10.1075/ijolc.4.2.01pet

Peters, Elke. (2018). The effect of out-of-class exposure to English language media on learners' vocabulary knowledge. *ITL-International Journal of Applied Linguistics*, 169(1), 142–168.

Phillipson, Robert. (1992). *Linguistic imperialism*. Oxford University Press.

Phillipson, Robert. (2007). Linguistic imperialism: A conspiracy, or a conspiracy of silence? *Language Policy*, 6(3–4), 377–383.

Phillipson, Robert. (2008). The linguistic imperialism of neoliberal empire. *Critical Inquiry in Language Studies*, 5(1), 1–43.

Phillipson, Robert. (2009). *Linguistic imperialism continued*. Orient BlackSwan.

Piotrowska, Carolina M. (2022). Lockdown language: Online communication in South Africa during the COVID-19 pandemic [Unpublished PhD thesis]. North-West University.

Plaatje, Solomon. (1916). *Native life in South Africa*. Ravan Press.

Platt, John T. (1975). The Singapore English speech continuum and its basilect 'Singlish' as a 'creoloid'. *Anthropological Linguistics*, 17(7), 363–374.

Polzenhagen, Frank, & Frey, Sandra. (2017). Matrimonial adverts in Indian English: Notes on the contextualisation of a type. *International Journal of Language and Culture*, 4(2), 170–196.

Pretorius, Johannes. (1953). The pronunciation of English vowels and diphthongs by matriculation pupils in Afrikaans-medium high schools in the Transvaal, excluding Pretoria and the Witwatersrand [Unpublished MA dissertation]. Potchefstroom University.

Quirk, Randolph. (1988). Language varieties and standard language. *JALT Journal*, 11(1), 14–25.

Rajagopalan, Kanavillil. (2003). The ambivalent role of English in Brazilian politics. *World Englishes*, 22(2), 91–101.

Rampton, Ben. (1995). Language crossing and the problematisation of ethnicity and socialisation. *Pragmatics*, 5(4), 485–513. https://doi.org/10.1075/prag.5.4.04ram

Rao, Raja. (1938). *Kanthapura*. George Allen & Unwin.
Raumolin-Brunberg, Helena. (2017). Sociolinguistics. In Alexander Bergs & Laurel J. Brinton (Eds.), *The history of English, volume 4: Early Modern English* (pp. 188–208). De Gruyter Mouton.
Rayburn, Alan. (2001). *Naming Canada: Stories about Canadian place names* (revised ed.). University of Toronto Press.
Reinders, Hayo, & Benson, Phil. (2017). Research agenda: Language learning beyond the classroom. *Language Teaching*, *50*(4), 561–578. https://doi.org/10.1017/S0261444817000192
Reweti, Bridget. (n.d.). Renaming Aotearoa New Zealand. Retrieved May 27, 2022, from https://www.bl.uk/the-voyages-of-captain-james-cook/articles/renaming-aotearoa-new-zealand
Rijkens, Maarten H. (2005). *I always get my sin: Het bizarre Engels van Nederlanders*. Prometheus.
Rüdiger, Sofia. (2019). *Morpho-syntactic patterns in spoken Korean English*. John Benjamins.
Rushdie, Salman. (1982). The empire writes back with a vengeance. *London Times*, July 3.
Schmied, Josef. (1991). *English in Africa*. Longman.
Schmied, Josef. (2008). East African English (Kenya, Uganda, Tanzania): Morphology and syntax. In Rajend Mesthrie (Ed.), *Varieties of English volume 4: Africa, South and Southeast Asia* (pp. 451–471). Mouton de Gruyter.
Schmied, Josef. (2017). East African English. In Markku Filppula, Juhani Klemola & Devyani Sharma (Eds.), *Oxford handbook of world Englishes* (pp. 472–490). Oxford University Press.
Schneider, Edgar W. (2003). The dynamics of New Englishes: From identity construction to dialect birth. *Language*, *79*(2), 233–281.
Schneider, Edgar W. (2007). *Postcolonial English: Varieties around the world*. Cambridge University Press.
Schneider, Edgar W. (2011). *English around the world: An introduction*. Cambridge University Press.
Schneider, Edgar W. (2014). New reflections on the evolutionary dynamics of world Englishes. *World Englishes*, *33*(1), 9–32.
Schneider, Edgar W. (2016). Grassroots Englishes in tourism interactions. *English Today*, *32*(3), 2–10.
Schröder, Konrad. (2018). Eight hundred years of modern language learning and teaching in the German-speaking countries of Central Europe: A social history. *The Language Learning Journal*, *46*(1), 28–39. https://doi.org/10.1080/09571736.2017.1382054
Seargeant, Philip, & Tagg, Caroline. (2011). English on the internet and a 'post-varieties' approach to language. *World Englishes*, *30*(4), 496–514.
Seidlhofer, Barbara. (2001). Closing a conceptual gap: The case for a description of English as a lingua franca. *International Journal of Applied Linguistics*, *11*(2), 133–158.

Seidlhofer, Barbara. (2009). Common ground and different realities: World Englishes and English as a lingua franca. *World Englishes*, *28*(2), 236–245.

Selinker, Larry. (1972). Interlanguage. *International Review of Applied Linguistics in Language Teaching*, *10*(3), 209–231.

Sharma, Devyani. (2009). Typological diversity in new Englishes. *English World-Wide*, *30*(2), 170–195.

Sharma, Devyani. (2012). Second-language varieties: English in India. In Alex Bergs & Laurel Brinton (Eds.), *English historical linguistics, volume 2* (pp. 2077–2091). Mouton de Gruyter.

Siebers, Lucia. (2007). Morphosyntax in Black South African English: A sociolinguistic analysis of Xhosa English [Unpublished PhD thesis]. University of Duisberg-Essen.

Siebers, Lucia. (2010). An abundant harvest to the philologer? Jeremiah Goldswain, Thomas Shone and nineteenth-century South African English. In Raymond Hickey (Ed.), *Varieties of English in writing: The written word as linguistic evidence* (pp. 263–294). John Benjamins.

Silva, Penny. (1996). Lexicography for South African English. In Vivian de Klerk (Ed.), *Focus on South Africa* (pp. 191–210). John Benjamins.

Smith, Larry E., & Christopher, Elizabeth. (2001). 'Why can't they understand me when I speak English so clearly?' In Edwin Thumboo (Ed.), *The three circles of English: Language specialists talk about the English language* (pp. 91–100). UniPress.

Smith, Larry E., & Rafiqzad, Khalilullah. (1979). English for cross-cultural communication: The question of intelligibility. *TESOL Quarterly*, *13*(3), 371–380.

Spencer, Brenda. (2011). International sporting events in South Africa, identity re-alignment, and Schneider's EVENT X. *African Identities*, *9*(3), 267–278.

Spolsky, Bernard. (2004). *Language policy*. Cambridge University Press.

Sridhar, Kamal K., & Sridhar, S. N. (1986). Bridging the paradigm gap: Second language acquisition theory and indigenized varieties of English. *World Englishes*, *5*(1), 3–14.

Stahle, David W., Cleaveland, Malcolm K., Blanton, Dennis B., Therrell, Matthew D., & Gay, David A. (1998). The lost colony and Jamestown droughts. *Science*, *280*(5363), 564–567. https://doi.org/10.1126/science.280.5363.564

Steyn, J. C. (1980). *Tuiste in eie taal*. [At home in one's own language.] Tafelberg.

Swift, J. (1712). A proposal for correcting, improving and ascertaining the English Tongue; In A Letter To the Most Honourable Robert Earl of Oxford and Mortimer, Lord High Treasurer of Great Britain. Printed for Benj. Tooke, at the Middle-Temple-Gate, Fleetstreet (2nd ed.). Retrieved May 19, 2022, from https://link.gale.com/apps/doc/CW0109997793/ECCO?u=amst&sid=bookmark-ECCO&xid=c186bc3f&pg=1

Tagliamonte, Sali A. (2016). So sick or so cool? The language of youth on the internet. *Language in Society*, *45*, 1–32.

Tan, Ying Ying. (2014). English as a 'mother tongue' in Singapore. *World Englishes*, *33*(3), 319–339.

Tembe, Juliet. (2006). Teacher training and the English language in Uganda. *TESOL Quarterly, 40*(4), 857–860.
Titlestad, Peter. (1996). English, the constitution and South Africa's language future. In Vivian de Klerk (Ed.), *Focus on South Africa* (pp. 163–173). John Benjamins.
Trudgill, Peter. (2004). *New-dialect formation: The inevitability of colonial Englishes*. Edinburgh University Press.
Van den Doel, Rias, & Quené, Hugo. (2013). The endonormative standards of European English: Emerging or elusive? *English World-Wide, 34*(1), 77–98.
Van Rooy, Bertus. (2002). Stress placement in Tswana-English: The makings of a coherent system. *World Englishes, 21*(1), 145–160.
Van Rooy, Bertus. (2006). The extension of the progressive aspect in Black South African English. *World Englishes, 25*(1), 37–64.
Van Rooy, Bertus. (2008). Black South African English: Phonology. In Rajend Mesthrie (Ed.), *Varieties of English volume 4: Africa, South and Southeast Asia* (pp. 177–187). Mouton de Gruyter.
Van Rooy, Bertus. (2010). Societal and linguistic perspectives on variability in world Englishes. *World Englishes, 31*(1), 3–20.
Van Rooy, Bertus. (2011). A principled distinction between error and conventionalised innovation in African Englishes. In Joybrato Mukherjee & Marianne Hundt (Eds.), *Exploring second-language varieties of English and Learner Englishes: Bridging a paradigm gap* (pp. 191–209). Benjamins.
Van Rooy, Bertus. (2019). Reconsidering Kachru's work on Englishes in their multilingual ecologies. *World Englishes, 38*(1/2), 280–293. https://doi.org/10.1111/weng.12402
Van Rooy, Bertus. (2020). Present-day Afrikaans in contact with English. In Raymond Hickey (Ed.), *English in multilingual South Africa: The linguistics of contact and change* (pp. 241–264). Cambridge University Press.
Van Rooy, Bertus. (2021). Grammatical change in South African Englishes. *World Englishes 40*(1), 24–37. https://doi.org/10.1111/weng.12470
Van Rooy, Bertus, & Kruger, Haidee. (2016). The innovative progressive aspect of Black South African English: The role of language proficiency and normative processes. *International Journal of Learner Corpus Research, 2*(2), 205–228. https://doi.org/10.1075/ijlcr.2.2.04van
Van Rooy, Bertus, & Kruger, Haidee. (2018). Hybridity, globalisation and models of Englishes. In Sandra C. Deshors (Ed.), *Modeling world Englishes: Assessing the interplay of emancipation and globalization of ESL varieties* (pp. 77–108). John Benjamins. https://doi.org/10.1075/veaw.g61.04van
Van Rooy, Bertus, & Piotrowska, Caroline. (2015). The development of an extended time period meaning of the progressive in Black South African English. In Peter Collins (Ed.), *Grammatical change in English world-wide* (pp. 465–483). John Benjamins.
Van Rooy, Bertus, & Terblanche, Lize. (2010). Complexity in word-formation processes in new varieties of South African English. *Southern African Linguistics and Applied Language Studies, 28*(4), 357–374.

Van Rooy, Bertus, & Van Huyssteen, Gerhard. (2000). The vowels of BSAE: Current knowledge and future prospects. *South African Journal of Linguistics*, Supplement 38, 15–33.

Van Weijen, Daphne. (2012). The language of (future) scientific communication. *Research Trends*, 1(31). Retrieved July 24, 2022, from https://www.researchtrends.com/researchtrends/vol1/iss31/3

Van Zyl, A. J. M. (2016). The native speaker debate: The case of the Afrikaans-English teachers' identity in Thailand [Unpublished MA dissertation]. North-West University.

Velupillai, Viveka. (2015). *Pidgins, creoles & mixed languages: An introduction*. John Benjamins.

Vertovec, Steven. (2007). Super-diversity and its implications. *Ethnic and Racial Studies*, 30(6), 1024–1054. https://doi.org/10.1080/01419870701599465

Wächter, Bernd, & Maiworm, Friedhelm (Eds.). (2014). *English-taught programmes in European higher education: The state of play in 2014*. Lemmens.

Walker, James, Gaffney, Vincent, Fitch, Simon, Muru, Merle, Fraser, Andrew, Bates, Martin, & Bates, Richard. (2020). A great wave: The Storegga tsunami and the end of Doggerland? *Antiquity*, 94(378), 1409–1425. https://doi.org/10.15184/aqy.2020.49

Watermeyer, Susan. (1996). Afrikaans English. In Vivian de Klerk (Ed.), *Focus on South Africa* (pp. 99–124). John Benjamins.

Wee, Lionel. (2018). *The Singlish controversy: Language, culture and identity in a globalizing world*. Cambridge University Press.

Wee, Lionel. (2020). English in Southeast Asia. In Daniel Schreier, Marianne Hundt & Edgar W. Schneider (Eds.), *The Cambridge handbook of world Englishes* (pp. 263–281). Cambridge University Press.

Wells, John C. (1982). *Accents of English, volume 1: An introduction*. Cambridge University Press.

Widdowson, H. G. (1994). The ownership of English. *TESOL Quarterly*, 28(2), 377–389.

Wilhelm, Frans. (2018). Foreign language teaching and learning in the Netherlands 1500–2000: An overview. *The Language Learning Journal*, 46(1), 17–27. https://doi.org/10.1080/09571736.2017.1382053

Wolf, Hans-Georg, & Polzenhagen, Frank. (2009). *World Englishes: A cognitive sociolinguistic approach*. Mouton de Gruyter.

World Tourism Organization. (2019). Global and regional tourism performance. Retrieved May 27, 2022, from https://www.unwto.org/tourism-data/global-and-regional-tourism-performance

Yang, Minmin, Mao, Haoran, & Zheng, Yifan. (2017). 心理趋同感知在中国二语学习者听力习得中的效应研究 [Perceived-homophily effect on ESL learners' listening acquisition in China]. *Foreign Language Education*, 38(4), 67–82.

Zipp, Lena. (2014). Indo-Fijian English: Linguistic diaspora or endonormative stabilization? In Marianne Hundt & Devyani Sharma (Eds.), *English in the Indian diaspora* (pp. 187–214). John Benjamins.

Index

ABBA, 145, 150, 156
academic, 6, 11, 19, 32, 35–6, 83, 145, 150–1, 154, 177, 199–200
accent, 59, 84, 111, 126, 160–2, 200
accent neutralisation, 84, 126
acceptability, 6, 7, 21, 42, 51–2, 64–5, 71, 88, 163, 175, 189–96
advertising, 38, 41, 50–1, 154
Afrikaans
  language, 28, 45–6, 47, 49, 61, 63–4, 81, 83, 94, 136, 141, 168, 176, 181, 191
  people, 28, 46, 53, 81, 94, 136–7
American native, 13, 98
ancestral language, 9, 48, 73, 80, 98, 105, 109, 111, 112, 114
Arabic, 23, 37, 82–3, 122
assimilation
  absorption, 28, 72, 75, 77, 98, 101, 105
  forced, 30, 102, 108, 186
  gradual, 28, 73, 75, 80, 98
  incomplete integration, 28, 30, 47, 75, 80, 98, 102, 107
attitude
  towards language(s), 40–1, 131–2, 158
  towards linguistic variants, 58, 64–5
  towards people, 13, 16, 23–5, 65, 79
  towards varieties of English, 41–2, 80, 86–9, 109–10, 132–3, 158–9, 180, 192–3
  see also normativity: endonormativity, normativity: exonormativity, stigmatisation
Australia, 8, 12–13, 14, 15–16, 20, 27, 28, 45–6, 64, 71, 72, 73, 76, 77, 78–9, 80, 81, 82, 87, 90, 93–4, 102, 106, 108, 126, 150, 151, 170, 186
Australian aboriginal, 72, 98

Bangladesh, 34, 125, 130, 187
basilect, basilectalisation, 29, 105, 112, 129
bilingualism, 28, 53, 56, 63–4, 81, 103, 106, 115, 128, 129, 132, 151, 161, 168, 174; *see also* multilingualism
Ballantyne, R. M., 24–5
Barbados, 14, 82, 100, 109
Barbier, A., 132–3
baseball, 70, 83
Belgium, 179
Biko, S., 187–8
boarding school, 30, 102, 106, 108, 126, 145
Botswana, 36
British Empire, 7, 17–18, 24, 34, 38, 69, 81, 100, 107, 131, 170, 187; *see also* United Kingdom

221

Bryson, B., 3, 5, 6, 7, 24–5, 39, 41, 65, 69–70, 117–18, 144, 150, 159, 196, 200

call centre, 84, 125–6
Cameroon, 124
Canada, 8, 12, 13, 20, 27, 28, 45, 64, 71, 72, 73, 74–5, 78–9, 80–1, 82, 94, 96, 102, 108, 126, 150, 170, 186
cancel culture, 84, 182
Charles, Prince of Wales/King, 5, 14, 42, 43, 70, 194
China, 10, 11, 12, 16, 32, 118, 119–20, 149, 157, 162
Chinese, 37, 120, 153, 154
code-mixing, code-switching, 63, 168, 192
codification, 64, 166, 190–1, 193, 198
colonisation, 8, 10–18, 170
　of Africa, 8, 14, 16, 17, 18, 118–19, 120–1, 122–3, 142, 187
　of Asia, 8, 16–17, 18
　of Australia, 8, 12–13, 14, 15–16, 27, 28, 72, 76, 78–9, 81, 101–2, 106, 186
　of Britain, 9
　of Canada, 12, 74–5, 186
　of Caribbean, 10, 11, 14–15, 29, 98, 99–101
　of East Africa, 17
　of Ghana, 119, 123
　of India, 10, 11–12, 16–17, 23–4, 118–19, 120, 121–2, 130
　of Ireland, 8, 9, 72–3, 102–3, 186
　of Kenya, 12–13, 120
　of New Zealand, 8, 12, 13, 14, 60, 72, 76, 78–9, 81, 82, 90–1, 95
　of Nigeria, 20, 121, 123
　of North America, 10, 12, 14, 27, 73–4, 106
　of the Philippines, 20, 123, 124
　of Sierra Leone, 11, 119
　of Singapore, 12, 23, 120
　of South Africa, 8, 13, 14, 17, 18, 24, 28, 53, 76–7, 78–9, 80–1, 121, 123, 186
　of South China, 10, 11–12, 16, 118–20
　of Sri Lanka, 122
　of the United States of America, 12, 73–4, 186
　of West Africa, 10, 11, 13, 17, 119, 121
　of Zambia, 12
　of Zimbabwe, 12–13, 120
colonisation types, 10
　exploitation, 8, 10, 15, 16–18, 30–1, 54, 120–3, 126–7, 186
　plantation, 8, 10, 11, 14–16, 52, 73, 99–101, 104–6
　settlement, 8, 10, 12–14, 17, 20, 25, 26, 30, 51, 72–7, 103, 106, 120
　trade, 10, 11–12, 17, 118–20
concentric circle model of world Englishes, 20, 88, 146–7, 185
　expanding circle, 20, 54, 127, 146–8, 151, 152, 153, 157, 158–9, 159–65, 165–6, 177, 181, 193
　inner circle, 20, 43, 51, 54, 69, 83, 88, 90, 91, 108, 156, 174, 175, 193, 196, 200
　outer circle, 20, 43, 54, 94, 117–18, 123, 125, 127–33, 133–41, 141–3, 147, 151, 156, 175, 176–7, 190–1, 193
conventionalisation, 45, 49, 165–6, 167, 193, 194–5, 198, 202
convict, 12–13, 14, 76, 78
Couzier, T., 107
cricket, 69, 71, 83, 86, 93, 107, 111, 147, 203
cross-linguistic influence, 31, 136, 159, 196–7

decolonisation, 118, 145, 187–8; *see also* postcolonialism

INDEX

deculturation, 147
Denmark, 36, 151, 187
deviation, 5–6, 54, 65, 180, 190, 192, 196, 197
dialect contact, 25–7, 62, 75, 78–80, 85, 90–3, 167, 172, 178
diaspora, 120, 173, 178
diplomacy, 152, 155
diversification, 44, 51, 52, 65–6, 79, 85n, 111, 189, 195, 196, 203
Dutch, 24–5, 28, 34n, 45–6, 73, 81, 94, 121, 144, 148–9, 151, 153–4, 155, 202
dynamic model of postcolonial Englishes, 21, 64, 80, 88, 138, 185, 202

East India Company, 16–17, 23
education
  colonial, 17, 23–4, 30–1, 54, 108, 120, 121–3, 126, 127, 129–30, 186
  elite, 34, 59, 74, 122–3, 126–7, 129–30, 133, 135, 155, 174, 175
  foreign-language, 32, 157, 179
  higher, 107, 124–5, 129, 151, 155, 199
  missionary, 10, 17, 30–1, 53, 119, 121–3, 126, 127, 129, 133, 142, 186
  post-independence, 18, 54, 127, 129–31, 142
  pre-school, 35
  school, 11, 30–1, 32, 39, 40, 41, 47, 54, 74, 83, 102, 106, 109, 120, 121–3, 124–5, 126–7, 129–31, 133, 135, 151, 157, 174, 179, 188, 203
  see also boarding school
e-mail, 33, 164, 202; *see also* mobile communication
England, 26, 69, 74, 75, 76, 77, 78, 87
English (as) Foreign Language, 18–19, 20, 121, 146–7, 153, 157, 158
English (as) International Language, 18–19, 35, 83, 86, 146–8
English (as) Lingua Franca, 18–19, 20, 61, 127, 145, 147–8, 151, 152, 163, 164–5, 166, 177, 202
English varieties
  African American Vernacular English, 42, 74, 109–10, 113, 160, 175, 178
  African English, 50
  Afrikaans South African English, 28, 46–7, 61, 63–4, 136–7
  American English, 27, 28, 42, 44–5, 64, 71, 80, 84, 85–6, 88, 89, 90, 161, 178
  Asian English, 114, 117, 141, 161–2
  Australian English, 27, 28, 42, 44–6, 46, 72, 76, 78, 85–6, 87, 89, 93, 94, 160
  Bequia Creole, 113
  Black South African English, 58, 59, 133–5, 137–8, 140, 174
  Boxwallah English, 38, 130
  British English, 42, 63, 64, 71, 84, 89
  Butler English, 31, 38, 119, 130
  Canadian English, 27, 28, 46, 72, 74–5, 88, 89, 93, 94
  Cape Flats English, 53, 176
  Caribbean English, 10, 29, 98, 103, 107, 109, 110, 111, 113, 114
  Cockney, 76, 78, 87, 89
  creole, 10, 20, 29, 99, 100, 106, 110, 112, 113, 119
  East African English, 138–9, 191
  English in Belgium, 179
  English in China, 10, 11, 12, 16, 32, 119–20, 157, 160, 162
  English in Germany, 7, 62
  English in Japan, 149, 158, 159, 162–3, 164
  English in Korea, 35, 36, 145–6, 149, 159, 160, 165

English varieties (*cont.*)
  English in the Netherlands, 6–7, 21, 31–2, 144, 148–9, 151, 153–4, 155, 159, 162, 164
  English in Thailand, 38, 149, 165, 181
  Hong Kong English, 141, 161
  Indian English, 38, 47, 50, 54, 62, 132, 142, 160
  Indian South African English, 58, 109, 110, 111, 112, 114
  Irish English, 27, 110, 111, 112, 115
  Jamaican Creole, 178
  Jamaican English, 42, 109–10
  Krio, 11, 119, 120
  Kriol, 106
  New Zealand English, 44, 46, 60, 72, 76, 79, 82, 87, 88, 90–3, 94, 95, 103
  Nigerian English, 42, 49–50, 128
  Nigerian Pidgin English, 178
  North American English, 77, 89, 90
  pidgin, 10, 11–12, 15, 38–9, 99, 100, 106, 110, 118–20, 128, 141, 148, 177
  South African English, 28, 45–46, 47, 49, 53, 58, 60, 61, 63–4, 76–7, 78, 87, 89, 93, 94, 132–133, 141, 167–9, 180–1, 189–90, 191
  Southern American English, 74, 160
  Southern hemisphere English, 77, 79, 89, 92–3
  Tok Pisin, 16
  Ulster Scots, 9, 72, 73, 77, 111
  West African English, 135, 141
  West African Pidgin English, 11, 119, 120, 141, 177
entrenchment, 61, 62, 108, 195
error *see* learner error
ethnic dialect, ethnolect, 30, 80, 102, 103, 107, 109, 110, 135n, 160, 175
expat, 155, 156–7, 191–2

Fanon, F., 187–8
Farquhar, W., 23, 121
Fiji, 101, 103, 105
Filipino, 125
foreign-language learner, 20, 32, 38, 39, 146, 147, 157–8, 162, 179; *see also* second-language learner
fossilisation, 54, 135
founder's effect/principle, 27, 28, 52, 76, 80, 82, 85, 100, 135n
France, 13, 80–1, 82–3
French, 3, 18, 28, 31–2, 36, 39, 82–3, 93, 124, 149, 150, 151–2, 153, 154, 156, 157, 179, 188, 202

German, 3, 7, 32, 105, 149, 150, 151–2, 153, 154, 156, 157, 202
Germany, 7, 20, 171, 187, 202
Ghana, 32, 119, 123, 130, 156, 176
globalisation, 8, 32, 118, 125–6, 150, 152, 174
GloWbE (Global Web-based Corpus of English), 58, 71n
grammar
  adverb, 63, 136–7, 140, 162
  after perfect, 112
  article, 160, 162
  aspect marker, 110, 113–14, 137
  auxiliary omission, 140
  can be able to, 4
  causative, 139
  compound, 45, 141, 154, 163
  dative of advantage, 53
  derivation, 38, 141, 163
  emphasiser *now*, 63–4
  extended progressive, 4, 137–8
  modal auxiliary, 4, 6, 64
  preposition, 138–9, 160, 162, 167
  pronoun, 49, 53, 63, 114, 140, 160, 181

quotative *be like*, 62
reanalysis, 48, 56, 138–9
reduplication, 57–8
transfer, 48, 49, 112, 136–8, 162–3
unstressed *do*, 53
verb complementation, 138, 139, 162
word order, 112, 113, 136–7, 160
Guyana, 101

Hindi, 37, 38, 101, 103, 105, 124, 156
Hindi-Bhojpuri, 101, 105
Holding, M., 107
homogeneity (of variety), 9, 21, 27, 72, 75, 76, 79, 85n, 87, 90, 110, 119, 203
Hong Kong, 12, 176–7
hybridity (linguistic), 167–9, 174, 175, 177, 180–2, 201

ICE (International Corpus of English), 63, 139
identity, 28, 64, 80, 88, 89, 113, 120, 132, 135, 164, 177, 178, 181, 197, 203
identity reorientation, 21, 64, 87, 88, 202
illness, 27, 99, 101
indenture, 11, 14–16, 29, 81, 98–9, 100–1, 104–6, 108
India, 8, 10, 12, 16–17, 20, 23–4, 32, 34, 36, 38, 50, 84, 101, 118–19, 120, 121–2, 124, 126, 128, 130, 149, 156, 171, 178
Indian Removal Act of 1830 (USA), 88
indigenisation, 21, 128, 143, 189, 199; *see also* nativisation
indigenous elite, 129, 142
indigenous language, 25, 28, 30–1, 34, 40, 44–5, 47, 50, 81–2, 83, 93–6, 101–3, 105, 106–7, 121–2, 124–5, 126, 127, 129, 132, 133–4, 138, 140–1, 180–1, 188
indigenous people, 10, 12, 13, 15, 17–18, 21, 24, 27–8, 30–1, 53, 72, 81–2, 88–9, 98–9, 101–3, 104, 106–7, 108, 109, 115, 118, 121–2, 126–7, 128, 131, 141, 145, 176, 186, 188, 200
innovation, 50, 51, 55, 58, 61, 64–5, 66, 85n, 112, 136, 138, 163, 167, 182, 189–91
input, 9, 15, 26–7, 29, 30, 46, 48, 51–7, 58, 59–60, 62, 73, 76, 77, 78–80, 85, 86, 91–3, 98, 104–6, 108, 110–15, 116, 129, 130, 133–4, 138, 152, 189, 203; *see also* variants, variability
instrumental value of English, 41, 43–4, 131–2, 158, 177, 189, 195
integration *see* assimilation
intelligibility, 51, 91, 134–5, 160–1, 164, 177, 180, 190–1, 193, 194, 197, 203
interactions across Englishes, 32, 61, 177, 181, 195, 203
interlanguage, 54
intermediary, 10, 11, 17–18, 28, 81–2, 102, 106, 118, 121, 122, 126, 127–8, 131, 142, 186
internet, 32–3, 36, 85n, 125, 131, 146, 152, 157–8, 167, 169, 170, 171, 172–3, 177–8, 178–9, 181–2, 188–9
Ireland, 9, 10, 14, 27, 73, 77, 102, 106, 172–3, 186
Northern Ireland, 8, 12, 45, 72, 102
Republic of Ireland, 38, 45, 102, 115, 199
Irish
language, 49, 73, 83, 102–3, 105, 106, 111, 112, 115
people, 9, 37, 73, 88–9, 97, 98–9, 101, 102–3, 104, 106, 109, 115, 200

Jamaica, 14, 100, 101, 103, 109, 110
Japan, 20, 82–3, 149, 156, 159
Japanese, 82–3, 153

Kachru, B. B., 19–20, 21, 41, 42, 50, 64, 88, 118, 122, 128, 131, 132, 147, 168, 185, 190, 192, 193
Kenya, 12, 13, 20, 120, 124, 149
Kiswahili, 121, 124
koine, 14–15, 101
Korea, 35, 36, 145–6, 149, 159
Korean, 153

Landeskunde, 71, 153
language change, 25, 26, 43–66, 75, 80, 86–96, 97, 109, 110–15, 116, 133–42, 159–65, 169, 189, 193
language contact, 12, 15, 25, 27–8, 29–31, 32, 44, 46, 53, 56–7, 58, 63–4, 80–2, 83, 84, 93–4, 96, 100, 103–7, 108, 110–15, 126–9, 131, 133–5, 152, 167–9, 170, 173–8, 180–1, 196–8
language shift, 8, 9, 10–11, 12, 15, 20, 27, 28, 30, 34, 37–8, 52–3, 72, 73, 80, 98–116, 132, 136n, 175–6, 200
language-shift Englishes, 20, 37–8, 72–3, 98–116, 200
Learner English(es), 39, 140, 147, 158, 200
learner error, 19, 43, 48, 54, 140, 147, 162, 189–92
legitimisation, 193
liberation (from colonisation), 94, 124–5, 130, 187
liberation linguistics, 190, 192
linguistic imperialism, 7, 146
localisation, 20, 51, 55–7, 165, 194, 198, 203; *see also* indigenisation

Macaulay, T. B., 23–4, 128, 135
Macaulay Minute, 23–4, 122
Major, J., 69–71, 86, 146

Malay, 23, 31, 34, 121, 202
Malaysia, 34, 124, 125
Mandarin *see* Chinese
Māori
 language, 83, 95, 103, 108
 people, 72, 98, 103, 108
Mauritius, 101, 103
Meierkord, C., 32, 61, 173, 175, 177, 181, 195
metaphor
 cultural, 50, 56, 69–71, 86, 203
 for language, 43–4, 51, 145–6
 illness, 145–6
Mexico, 20, 39, 171
migration, 9, 11, 12, 26, 27, 74, 75, 76, 79, 83, 99, 167, 168, 169–72, 174, 176–7
 emigration, 13, 26, 91, 172–3
 immigration, 27, 72, 73, 74, 76, 78–9, 83, 98, 101, 105, 170–1, 174, 176, 196, 200
military, 13, 16, 17, 27, 30, 101–2, 145, 148, 149, 186; *see also* warfare
mistake *see* deviation
mobile communication, 33, 131; *see also* e-mail, texting
Mufwene, S. S., 10, 20, 21, 27, 29, 38, 51, 80, 82, 100, 104–5, 106, 108, 113
multilingualism, 4, 33–4, 38, 57, 62–3, 83, 113, 129, 133, 135, 168, 173–7, 182, 196–8, 200; *see also* bilingualism
multinational organisations, 19, 151–2, 155
 Association of Southeast Asian Nations (ASEAN), 19, 36, 151–2, 158, 202
 East African Community (EAC), 152
 Economic Community of West African States (ECOWAS), 152
 European Union (EU), 19, 69–70, 151–2, 155, 158

Southern African Development
  Community (SADC), 152
United Nations, 155

Namibia, 124, 187
native speaker, 6–7, 8, 12, 19, 22, 27,
  28, 33, 34, 37, 38, 41, 42, 44,
  45, 47, 48, 49, 59, 61, 62, 63–4,
  71–2, 80, 82–9, 98–9, 105, 106,
  108, 112, 135, 141, 146, 152,
  158, 159, 160–2, 174, 180n,
  182, 191–2, 196, 197, 198–201,
  202
nativisation, 21, 56, 131, 138, 163,
  192; *see also* indigenisation
Netherlands, 6–7, 13, 31–2, 144,
  148–9, 151, 153–4, 155, 157,
  159, 202
new-dialect formation, 62, 75, 90–3
Newfoundland, 72, 75, 77, 78
New Zealand, 8, 12, 13, 14, 20, 44,
  45, 52, 60, 64, 71, 72, 76, 77,
  78–9, 80, 81, 82, 87, 88, 90–3,
  94, 95, 102, 103, 150, 200
Ngũgĩ wa Thiong'o, 4, 187–8
Nigeria, 20, 32, 121, 123, 128–9,
  130, 149, 156, 178, 187
non-native speaker, 7, 18, 22, 41, 44,
  45, 47, 48, 52, 53–4, 59, 61, 62,
  63–4, 112, 117, 133, 136, 141,
  145, 152, 160–2, 165, 191–2,
  198–201
non-standard language, 22, 34–5,
  41–2, 108, 109–10, 116, 126,
  176, 178, 180–1, 189–96
normativity
  complaints, 4, 43, 130
  editing, 6–7, 138, 172, 191, 193,
    196, 200
  endonormativity, 21, 64, 80, 86,
    88, 132, 192–3
  exonormativity, 21, 79, 80, 86, 87,
    107, 109, 159, 193
  polycentricity, 147
  standardisation, 41–2, 197

see also non-standard language,
  standard language

ONZE (Origins of New Zealand
  English) corpus, 60, 90–1
othering, 39, 142, 159
out-of-classroom learning, 38, 131,
  152, 157, 179, 189
outsourcing, 32, 84, 126

Pakistan, 34, 124, 125, 149, 187
Papua New Guinea, 16
People's Republic of China (PRC) *see*
  China
Philippines, 20, 84, 123, 124, 125,
  126, 176
Phillipson, R., 7, 18, 41, 124, 146, 149
policy
  education, 36, 157, 158, 189
  English-only, 30, 102, 108, 145,
    175
  language, 34, 124, 186, 189
Portugal, 11, 13
Portuguese, 11, 18, 148
postcolonialism, 18, 34, 118, 124–5,
  131, 145, 192–3; *see also*
  decolonisation
pragmatics, 49, 83, 86, 147, 164–5,
  166, 177
prestige, 26, 41, 42, 58–9, 61, 71, 74,
  77, 79–80, 91, 109, 116, 135,
  162, 174, 176, 178
  covert prestige, 76, 79, 87, 109–10,
    113, 178, 180
pronunciation
  allophone, 46, 57, 61, 93, 111,
    133–4
  aspiration, 47, 57, 133, 134
  Canadian raising, 89
  click, 57, 133
  dental fricative, 111
  diphthong, 89, 133–4
  flapping, 46, 90
  glottal fricative, 111
  glottal stop, 89

pronunciation (*cont.*)
/h/-dropping, 59, 91, 111
/hw/-/h/ contrast, 91
lateral, 111
lax vowel, 52, 133–4
phoneme, 46–7, 61, 133–4
plosive, 47, 111, 133, 134
raised front vowel, 52, 92–93
rhotic, 46–7, 52, 57, 61, 110–11
stress pattern, 134
syllable-timing, 47, 134
transfer, 46, 111, 133–5, 159–60
unstressed syllable, 133–4
velar fricative, 47
voicing, 47, 111, 133, 134
vowel, 46, 52, 92–3, 112, 133–4
protest, 71, 128, 131
publishing language, 3, 18, 50, 145, 150–1

Quirk, R., 5–7, 71, 118, 135, 158, 175, 180, 190–1, 192, 194–5, 196, 199, 200

Raffles, S., 23, 121
reservation, 102, 106; *see also* segregation
residential school, 102, 106, 108; *see also* boarding school
Russia, 82, 149, 171, 187
Russian, 32, 82–3, 149, 157
Rwanda, 36, 152, 187

Sanskrit, 23, 177, 122
schizophrenia (linguistic), 42, 64, 132, 193
Schneider, E. W., 10, 21, 27, 42, 64, 80, 86, 87, 88, 94, 132–3, 138, 185, 192–3
Scotland, 9, 14, 72, 73, 74, 76
second-language learner, 5–6, 29, 38, 51, 54–5, 57, 107–8, 109, 130, 131–2, 133–5, 140, 143, 190–1, 200; *see also* foreign-language learner

segregation, 15, 74, 82, 105
selection (of linguistic features), 26–7, 29, 51, 52, 55, 56, 57–65, 80, 85, 91–3, 99, 107, 108, 113, 115, 134, 138, 163, 189, 195
explicitness, 110
regularity, regularisation, 55, 108, 138, 163
simplicity, simplification, 108, 110, 111, 135, 160
transparency, 48, 55
settler, 8, 9, 10, 12–15, 21, 24, 26, 27–8, 29, 34, 45, 46, 52, 56, 60, 62, 71–7, 78–80, 82, 85, 86–9, 93, 95, 100, 102, 109, 119, 121, 132, 141, 170, 174, 186–7
Sierra Leone, 11, 119
Singapore, 12, 16, 20, 23, 37, 120, 121, 124, 129, 132, 149, 157, 176, 180
Sinhala, 34
slavery, 10, 12, 14–15, 29, 30, 34, 38, 52, 74, 81–2, 96, 99–101, 103, 104–5, 108, 112, 119, 186, 196, 201
abolition, emancipation, 15, 74, 100
Atlantic slave trade, 15, 100
homestead phase, 15, 29, 52, 82, 100, 104
plantation phase, 15, 29, 52, 82, 100, 105
Smith, L. E., 20, 86, 146–7, 161–2, 164
social media, 24, 33, 36, 85n, 172–3, 179, 181–2
societal codification, 166, 193, 198; *see also* conventionalisation
sociolinguistics of globalisation, 169, 172, 175
South Africa, 12, 13, 14, 18, 24, 26, 28, 38, 43, 45–6, 53, 58, 76–7, 78–9, 80–1, 82, 87, 88–9, 93, 94–5, 96, 98, 101, 105–6, 109, 112, 114, 120, 121, 123, 132–3,

135, 136, 140–1, 149, 167–9,
170, 176, 180, 186, 190–3
Soviet Union *see* Russia
Spain, 11, 13, 71, 82–3
Spanish, 18, 37, 39, 71, 82–3, 149,
156, 175
spelling error, 57, 95, 154
Sri Lanka, 32, 34, 122
standard language, 5–6, 7, 21, 22, 33,
34–5, 41–2, 57, 58–9, 79, 87,
105, 107–8, 109–10, 111, 120,
121, 147, 159, 160, 175, 178,
189–96, 197, 200
local standard, 21, 80, 87
stigmatisation, 59–61, 76, 78, 91,
112, 138, 193
Stolen Generations, 102; *see also*
boarding school
style, 49, 50, 107, 164–5, 178, 192,
203
super-diversity, 83, 113, 169–72, 173,
178

Tanzania, 124, 188
texting, text messaging, 168
Thai, 181
Thailand, 38, 149
tourism, 11, 19, 32, 36, 39, 125–6,
129, 154, 177
trade, 10, 11, 13, 16, 31–2, 33, 35–6,
70, 100, 118–20, 129, 148–9,
150, 152, 153–4
translanguaging, 168, 169, 194,
198
translation, 3–4, 35, 49, 84, 96, 144,
155, 164, 188, 201; *see also* loan
translation
transplantation, 10, 20, 26, 33,
60, 72–7, 89, 90–3, 96, 103,
118
Treaty of Waitangi Act (New
Zealand), 95
Trinidad and Tobago, 101
Trudgill, P., 26–7, 60, 62, 76, 78,
85, 90–2, 138, 197

Trump, D., 57, 171, 194, 197, 202
Twi, 114
Twi-Asante, Maroon language, 103

Uganda, 124, 130
uniform language *see* homogeneity
United Kingdom, 32, 34, 64, 69–71,
72, 79, 96, 102, 126, 144, 152,
158, 159, 171
United States of America, 5, 12, 13,
14, 15, 19, 20, 28, 32, 34, 35, 57,
64, 65, 71, 72, 73–4, 77, 78–9,
80, 81, 85–6, 89, 96, 100, 104,
108, 110, 123, 126, 159, 160,
171, 182, 186, 200
Urdu, 34, 37, 125
use/functions of English
academic, 6, 11, 19, 32, 35–6, 83,
125, 129, 145, 150–1, 154, 159,
177, 199–200
administration, 17–18, 34, 121,
124, 128, 129, 142, 187
business, 11, 19, 34, 35, 83, 126,
153–4, 177
employment, 35, 128, 131, 142,
159, 200
entertainment, 11, 33, 36, 83, 84,
90, 107, 109–10, 129, 144, 145,
150, 152, 156, 157, 169, 172–3,
178, 189, 201
international, 11, 19, 20, 33, 35,
83, 107, 127, 129, 151–2, 153,
155, 165, 197, 203
politics and diplomacy, 19, 129,
151–2, 155
private, 33–4, 82–3, 107, 157,
179
protest, 128, 132
public, 18, 33–5, 42, 107, 124,
128, 129
tourism, 11, 19, 32, 36, 39, 125–6,
154, 177
trade, 10, 11, 31–2, 35, 118–20,
129, 148–9, 150, 152, 153
see also education

van Gaal, L., 144, 145
variants, variability, 5–6, 9, 15, 26–7, 44–65, 83, 85, 89, 91–3, 113, 114, 133–42, 159–60, 169, 190, 192; *see also* input
vocabulary, 28, 29, 41, 44–6, 50, 56, 59, 79, 85–6, 88, 89, 93–6, 114–15, 140–2, 163–4, 167, 179, 180, 182, 191, 192
  beyond the pale, 73, 97, 102, 148
  borrowing, 28, 44–5, 47, 80, 81–2, 89, 93, 94, 114, 196
  coinage, 45, 57, 93, 163
  eponymy, 45
  fauna and flora, 28, 44, 56, 82, 94
  hybrid coinage, 141
  loan translation, 45, 93, 142, 144, 164
  loanword, 28, 47, 57
  renaming, 94–6
  semantic change, 45, 191
  semantic extension, 45, 94, 137
  semantic specialisation, 45
  topography, landscape, 28, 44, 56, 81, 82, 93–4, 95

transfer, 44–5, 56, 80, 82, 114–15, 140–2, 180
woke, 85, 88, 97, 175, 182

Wales, 9
warfare, 9, 13, 16, 17, 18, 27, 34, 81, 101–2, 104, 130, 145, 148, 149, 186, 187
  Civil War (USA), 74
  Cold War, 32, 157
  Second World War, 11, 17–18, 19, 31–2, 149–50, 157, 170–1, 186, 188
world Englishes, 8, 19–22, 48, 88, 100, 118, 147–8, 148n, 161, 165, 168–9, 185, 189, 193–4, 196, 198
  criticism, 20, 21, 118, 147–8, 148n, 169, 188, 189–96
  models *see* concentric circle model of world Englishes, dynamic model of postcolonial Englishes
world language system, 4, 25, 178

Zambia, 12
Zimbabwe, 12–13, 94, 95, 120, 130

EU representative:
Easy Access System Europe
Mustamäe tee 50, 10621 Tallinn, Estonia
Gpsr.requests@easproject.com

www.ingramcontent.com/pod-product-compliance
Lightning Source LLC
Chambersburg PA
CBHW070347240426
43671CB00013BA/2433